Praises for *Buddhism ſor Aıı*

"This expertly and compassionately written book is a great guide to Buddhism, even for Buddhists, and even for a lifelong Buddhist like me."

—**TSHERING TOBGAY**, former prime minister of Bhutan

"If you want to know about Buddhist teachings, this book is a wonderful doorway! Easy to understand, heartfelt and wise, brilliant and thorough, inviting you into a path of freedom and joy."

—**JACK KORNFIELD**, author of *A Path with Heart*

"This inspiring book is one of the most valuable gifts of Dhamma one can give to anyone. Master Soryu and Meng have amazingly distilled the essence of a huge quantity of Buddhist literature in one single book! The subject matter is presented and explained in an attractively humorous and accessible way. I only wish I had had this book when I first encountered Buddhism in India. It is a must read."

—**VENERABLE BHANTE BUDDHARAKKHITA**, abbot and president of the
    Uganda Buddhist Centre, author of *Planting Dhamma Seeds*,
    and visiting professor at Columbia University

"This remarkable and brave book explores the main teachings of the Buddha, with rich detail, humor, depth, and wisdom. It will be an important lifetime resource for all who aspire to awaken. One will return to it again and again for its surprises and its joy."

—**ROSHI JOAN HALIFAX**, abbot, Upaya Zen Center

"*Buddhism for All* is a joy to read—it's a book with 'something to say' that you'll benefit from hearing, whether you're just getting acquainted with Buddhism or far along your path. Coauthors Meng and Soryu bring a fresh voice and keen sensibility to their exploration of the first cycle of the Buddha's teachings. Spirited, humorous, and serious all at once, it's a book with a generous heart that shines a clear light on the roots, persistence, and end of our suffering, and reminds us that the path to peace, joy, and awakening is in our own hands."

—**DZOGCHEN PONLOP RINPOCHE**, founder and president, Nalandabodhi and Nitartha International, and author of *Emotional Rescue* and *Wild Awakening*

"This book is beautiful and enlightening. I have never found a book that takes you by the hand so easily about the most complex elements of Buddhism. I have found the many lists and sublists that in any other Buddhist books are challenging, but Meng and Soryu made everything so natural, organic, and easy to follow. It's truly a joy to navigate them thanks to the clarity and humor."

—**ALEJANDRO G. IÑÁRRITU**, Academy Award–winning filmmaker

"Coauthored by a top-of-the-line computer guy (an early Google engineer) with a silly sense of humor and a knack for apt analogy, and a brilliant young Buddhist teacher, *Buddhism for All* is a wise and thorough discussion of Buddhism's key teachings. Carefully researched, it's a boon for the seasoned Buddhist reader, who can follow the notes (as I did) directly to original sources in translation. At the same time, astonishingly, it's a genial, plainspoken, and persuasive introduction to the how and why of Buddhist practice for the contemporary reader. You'll feel, on every page, Meng and Soryu's enthusiasm for the Dharma, and their deep wish to share it as widely as possible."

—**NORMAN FISCHER**, Zen priest, abbot, and poet; founder of the Everyday Zen Foundation; and author of *When You Greet Me I Bow*

"This book may easily be mistaken for one trying to preach Buddhism as a religion. But Buddhism is not just a religion, it is a philosophy for a way of ethical living, and science of the mind. The presentation Meng and Soryu give in *Buddhism for All* comes from a philosophical and scientific perspective rather than a religious one. I was born a Buddhist and have been engaged in Buddhist studies for all of my life, and yet the contents presented in this wonderful book helped me in many ways to look at our mind from a different angle. I say this not because I am being a biased Buddhist, but as a human brother who wishes for all sentient beings to achieve their goals in life. The goal of our life is simply called 'Happiness.' Open and read the book and find your happiness from within."

—**TELO RINPOCHE**, head lama of Kalmyk Republic and honorary
representative of His Holiness the Dalai Lama to Russia, Mongolia,
and CIS countries

"Meng and Soryu have covered a very wide area not just about Buddhism, but more important, about what it means to be a Buddhist. I find the notion of being a Buddhist without identifying with Buddhism resonating deeply with my own belief of what it means to be a Muslim—being kind and just to all around you."

—**YAACOB IBRAHIM**, former Singapore cabinet minister, current
academic, and future better person

"This is a book for our time, of deep wisdom conveyed with light touches. I have long known that Meng believes in laughter (because life is not all suffering), but here we see the source of this joyfulness as one's personal experience intertwines with sacred texts. Like vintage wine, such teachings reveal more dimensions of truth with every practitioner. Meng's Buddhism is not at all sectarian, but comes through as the answer manifesting not as mere dogma but as what Christ called the Way and the Buddha, the Dhamma: always the same yet changing us. The use of the early texts of Buddhist tradition in the following pages is both enriching and renewing, expressing what we learn as the 'miracle of instruction.' Indeed, a joy-engendering book for our time and for followers of all ways and teachings."

—**FATHER LAURENCE FREEMAN**, OSB, director of the World
Community for Christian Meditation

"This is an awesome book on Buddhism, a book written with a difference. It is crisp and refreshing like newly mowed grass in the morning. Its presentation is lighthearted and delightful, with fun and good humor. Its language will strike a chord with the computer-savvy and Google-addicted generation. It gives an excellent introduction to Buddhism, while also going in depth into Buddhist ideas and concepts without appearing academic and heavy.

I highly recommend this book to anyone who wishes to learn about Buddhism. I would also highly recommend it to people like me who have been practicing and teaching Buddhism for years."

—**DATUK SERI DR. VICTOR WEE**, founding member and former
president of Buddhist Gem Fellowship Malaysia (BGF) and honorary
secretary of the International Buddhist Confederation

"If you are looking for some spiritual joy, *Buddhism for All* is a good place to start. This is a special offering from Chade-Meng Tan and Soryu Forall, who painstakingly researched the ancient texts to supply us with the Dhamma. Written with depth and humor, intelligent and clear, one can find learning about the foundations of the Buddha's teaching a little less daunting. It's a book with so many layers and so much information it will become a favorite resource."

—**SHARON SALZBERG**, author of *Lovingkindness* and *Real Change*

"*Buddhism for All* by Chade-Meng Tan and Soryu Forall is a book about early Buddhism that you won't want to miss. It is filled with gems of early Buddhism covering the whole path, while laced with humor and humility. There are many delightful stories from the time of the Buddha and from today. Once you start, you will not want to put it down."

—**VENERABLE TENZIN CHOERAB** (Barry Kerzin, MD), founder
and president of the Altruism in Medicine Institute (AIMI) and
personal physician to His Holiness the Dalai Lama

"Few writers have attempted an introduction to Buddhism this broad and this deep. *Buddhism for All* is truly Buddhism for all. The authors' genuine wisdom, boundless compassion, and unique humor shine through on every page."

—**DAN ZIGMOND**, guiding teacher of Jikoji Zen Center and
author of *Buddha's Office*

"*Buddhism for All* is interesting, easy reading, written for our time. Well researched and documented, it reaches out and connects with the uninitiated and experienced practitioners. May the real-life stories from both East and West, Buddhist and non-Buddhist sources inspire and motivate one to walk the Noble Path and be of service to humanity. May the noble aspirations of Chade-Meng and Soryu Forall be realized."

—**VENERABLE BHANTE MAHINDA**, founder and spiritual director of the Aloka Foundation

"The Buddha is compassionate and kind enough, but expositions of Dharma, the teachings of the Buddha, are not easy to access and understand. *Buddhism for All* is easy to approach, joyful to practice, crystal clear to discern. In addition, it preserves the solid foundations of the Buddha's teachings without sacrificing their depth and subtlety. I would wholeheartedly recommend it to those with no knowledge of what the Buddha taught."

—**VENERABLE MISAN W. D. KIM SUNIM**, director of KAIST Center for Contemplative Science and developer of Heart-Smile Training

"This book is for anyone interested in learning the wisdom and compassion that is Buddhism. We are all interconnected, and there is beauty in understanding each other. Whether you are a practicing Buddhist, or someone interested in learning about Buddhism, the teachings in this book will provide tools for a life of happiness and joy."

—**DORO BUSH KOCH**, author of *My Father, My President*

"*Buddhism for All* is written in everyday language, yet verified with a myriad of notes from the Pali Canon. This gift makes it unique. The authors' emphasis on original Buddhism confirms that which is forever so intimate."

—**ZENSAN JAKUSHO** 寂照 **KWONG ROSHI**, abbot of Sonoma Mountain Zen Center

"This is a very ambitious book. In the midst of its conversational tone, cheeky asides, skillful explanations, and humor (even in the notes!), the Dharma is surprisingly deeply explored. The jocular tone belies an earnest and informed effort to detail fundamental Buddhist understandings based on the earliest texts. Bravo!"

—**GAETANO KAZUO MAIDA**, executive director of the Buddhist Film Foundation and International Buddhist Film Festival

"This meticulously researched book shows you how the practice of Buddhism helps the mind transcend its own limitations, especially in overcoming the suffering that humans feel. Meng and Soryu skillfully present profound ancient teachings in a humorous and highly readable manner."

—**RAY KURZWEIL**, bestselling author, pioneering inventor, and futurist

"An intellectually rigorous volume on the fundamental aspects of Buddhism written with lightness and humor that conveys the spiritual joy of the Dharma. Profound, engaging, and thoughtful."

—**JAMES R. DOTY**, MD, founder and director of the Stanford Center for Compassion and Altruism Research and Education and author of *Into the Magic Shop*

"For those of us untrained in Buddhism, Meng and Soryu have given us a great gift; a way to receive teachings of the Buddha 'for free'! They have borne a great cost and I am grateful for their pure intention; may it have the impact in the world to which they have committed their time and their lives."

—**SCOTT KRIENS**, cocreator of 1440

"I particularly enjoyed the lighthearted approach to some of life's deepest topics with perspectives simultaneously coming from two authors. Reading this book has greatly helped me with my own personal journey of discovery and understanding. There's no better companion to have on this trip than what lives in these pages!"

—**STEVE CHEN**, cofounder of YouTube

BUDDHISM
FOR ALL

BUDDHISM FOR ALL

The Joyful Path to Enlightenment

CHADE-MENG TAN
AND SORYU FORALL

Illustrations by Colin Goh
with guest illustrators Natalie Tsang and Angeleen Tan

BUDDHISM.NET
PUBLISHING

BUDDHISM.NET
P U B L I S H I N G

Copyright © 2023 Chade-Meng Tan

Published by Buddhism.net Publishing
Cupertino, California 95014

Website: Buddhism.net

Email: publishing@Buddhism.net

Artwork by Colin Goh unless otherwise noted. Used by permission.

*Other illustrations by Natalie Tsang and Angeleen Tan.
Used by permission.*

Printed in the United States of America

ISBN 979-8-9890136-0-9

Homage to the Buddha, the Dharma, and the Sangha.

And deep gratitude to His Holiness the 14th Dalai Lama

for giving us and this book his personal blessing.

CONTENTS

BUDDHISM
FOR ALL

You Get Two Authors for the Price of One

Meng's Story: How Buddhism Saved My Life

My name is Meng, and Buddhism saved my life.

I grew up in Singapore in a "Buddhist" family within a "Buddhist" culture. I put the word *Buddhist* in quotes because when I was growing up, the "Buddhism" I encountered was little more than idol worshipping, superstition, and elaborate funeral rites. Many of the adults around me were "Buddhists" their entire lives, and almost none of them had even the slightest idea what the core teachings of the Buddha were.

When I was in my early teens, I started searching for the meaning of life. The adults thought I was just an uncommonly smart kid doing what uncommonly smart kids did. See, my IQ was measured at 156; I learned to read at eighteen months, I taught myself computer programming at age twelve, and I won my first national programming award at fifteen. So I fit the profile. However, the real reason I was searching was because I was suffering from depression. It turned out that being smart and being very good at my craft even at a very young age did not make me happy. Actually, it was even worse than that: I was suicidal. The only thing that kept me alive was I was too cowardly to die, but I also knew it was only a matter of time before my misery exceeded my cowardice. Yeah, not good. Something had to change.

I looked everywhere for answers. I looked to science and philosophy, which were a lot of fun to learn, but did nothing to help me with my suffering. I tried to understand religion, learning about Buddhism, Taoism, Hinduism, and Christianity. The Buddhism I learned back then was Zen Buddhism, which I found mostly incomprehensible at the time with its weird, inscrutable questions (koans) such as, "The sound of two hands is clapping; what is the sound of one hand?" The most attractive of all my options was Christianity, which was glitzy and extremely well-funded and well-organized in Singapore. However, it did not provide me with the answers I sought. Worse, it required me to reject science and to have faith in things blindly, and I really, really didn't want to do that, thank you very much.

The turning point came when I was twenty-one. I was invited to a Pentecostal church. It was very different from my previous understanding of church. You see, I went to Catholic High School in Singapore, and the only reason my father sent me there was because he asked a friend who was an alumnus, and he highly recommended it. That friend later became the prime minister of Singapore. So I ended up in Catholic school, and I learned the Lord's Prayer by heart, and thought I knew what church service meant. But, oh boy, this was different.

I found that the Pentecostal church service was not boring at all, to say the least. They had energetic music, the pastor spoke like a pro, everybody "spoke in tongues," and there was a lot of crying. A *lot* of crying. I saw for myself how it worked. Every week, these people would come seeking relief from their emotional pain, hoping to flush it away. Whoa. Never mind that there were no answers here that made any sense to me. This was a place I could come to and cry every Sunday to flush out my pain for the week. I was impressed.

The week after that, I met a Tibetan Buddhist nun, Venerable Sangye Khadro. I asked her, "I went to church, I saw how they relieved their suffering. What is there in Buddhism that helps us deal with suffering?" Her answer was, "*All* of Buddhism is about dealing with suffering."

It was like suddenly somebody opened the floodgates and a million tons of water came gushing in thunderously. I immediately understood. I knew I was close to whatever I was seeking.

Coincidentally, the venerable was scheduled to give a talk in my university the following week, which I made a point to attend. In the middle of her talk, she uttered one sentence: "It is all about cultivating the mind." The moment I heard that, everything in my life made sense to me. Everything. I told myself, "From this moment on, right here, right now, I am a Buddhist." I have never looked back. It was the best decision I have ever made.

In the months that followed, I learned Buddhist meditation. It changed my life. The first truly life-changing experience for me was sitting in meditation in an alert and relaxed state, then experiencing a gentle joy enveloping my entire body and mind for about thirty minutes. I learned later that what I experienced was not magical at all. I had simply experienced the mind without its usual layer of constant agitation. Without agitation, the mind returns to its default state, and **the default state of the mind is joy**. With that, I saw clearly how Buddhism would be the solution to my misery.

I am happy to report that with that experience, I released myself from depression. I was no longer suicidal, I went on to have a successful career as an early engineer at Google, and Archbishop Desmond Tutu nominated the One Billion Acts of Peace campaign I cochair for the Nobel Peace Prize. Yeah, things kind of worked out for me. And I never had to reject science, nor force myself to blindly believe in anything that did not make any sense to me. Buddhism was the best thing that ever happened to me.

Soryu's Story: All Life Depends on It

My name is Soryu, and Buddhism can save life on earth.

Since I was a little child, I have worried about the destruction of life on this planet by human beings. My parents raised me with great skill, explaining to me the severe crises we face, from environmental destruction to dangerous new technologies to nuclear war. I was very worried. They also raised me with great love, and I offered that love to all living things. When I was four, I told my mother, "We have to stop people from killing the animals."

I was clear that people destroying all life on earth is the biggest problem in the world, and I was upset that other people didn't see it. It was hard on my parents that I was so sensitive. Once, when I was riding my bike with my father, I saw a snake in the road, and as I pointed at it to show my dad the beautiful creature, a car suddenly killed it. I rode my bike senselessly into a ditch, where for an hour I wailed, "No, no, no, no . . ."

I was lonely, sad, and angry. I wanted a mentor, someone who could tell me how to solve this problem. I looked and looked, but didn't find anyone. So at ten, when I realized the adults weren't going to do anything about this one greatest problem in the world, I decided that I needed to take charge. I worked on it day in and day out, and became even more lonely, sad, and angry.

One afternoon, after getting home from high school, I happened to find a TV magazine on the kitchen counter and opened it to an article about Buddhism. It contained a poorly written explanation of the first two noble truths: "Life is suffering because we have desires." It was like the whole world was suddenly clear, as if someone had cleaned the dirt off the windows. It was literally like that. Finally, I had found someone who understood the problem of the human heart, how truly enormous it is, and what to do about it. I learned the person who had said that, Gotama Buddha, had already died, but that there were still people alive who understood his teachings and were willing to teach. I wanted to find such a person.

My parents wanted me to go to college, though. None of the classes were useful, but there was a meditation club led by a sophomore named Sumi Loundon. I went to an evening class, confident that she could give me what I needed. I sat down with the group. She told me to follow my breath, and count it. These instructions made no sense to me. They sounded completely stupid. "That will never help," I thought. "I have real problems. Can't you see that?" But she told me to do it, and for some reason, I believed her and did it.

She rang a meditation bell, and things got very bad for me right away. The moment I followed my breath, my body tensed up. So I followed my breath. My skin started to crawl. My whole body turned to pain. I wanted to run away. Still, I followed my breath. No matter what happened, my response was always the same: follow my breath.

It was traumatic. Things were terrible after thirty seconds, and only got worse for each of the next fifteen minutes. But no matter what, I followed my breath, with full confidence in the instructions. Because I was doing the technique fully, there was no running, no hiding, no expressing of my feelings. When she rang the bell again, I was filled with the most suffering I had ever known. I looked around in terror. Everyone else was smiling and calm. I realized that there was something wrong with me, and I did what I had wanted to do the whole time, I jumped up and ran out of the room into the darkness of the night.

I eventually slowed down and continued back to my room in a daze. I couldn't understand what had happened. I was scared. I was broken. I was angry at the people in that class for being so happy and perfect. But none of this really mattered to me, somehow. My anger faded with each step and I became just confused. Then the confusion went away. There was only the scenery floating by.

And then, most of the way back to my room, I had an unusual experience. I noticed a tree. It was a strange tree. It glowed. It sparkled. It was covered with jewels, or maybe made of them. It shone in the darkness in a way that seemed impossible. More incredible, its branches spread through all of space, touching every world. Its roots spread through all of time, touching every life. It was the same size as the universe. But it was also the same size as a tree. But what was most incredible about it was that it was exactly the same as my own mind. That tree was my mind. My mind was that tree.

With no distinction between that which experiences and that which is experienced, there was no division. With no division, there was no conflict. With no conflict, there was no suffering.

It took me decades to understand what happened that day. (In fact, I'm still coming to understand it.) But now, looking back, I can say that at that moment, I knew directly, not in words or mental understanding, that *to face suffering, without holding on to it or avoiding it, ends it.* I had sat there and faced everything that arose, and then the suffering, and its source, were gone. Just gone. To realize suffering, without grasping or aversion, is the start of the path to the end of suffering.

At the time, none of these words would have been very important to me, even if someone had said them to my face. The most important realization was that by following my breath, I had purified my mind of some suffering. And because there was no division, since my mind was the same as the whole universe, I had purified the whole universe of some suffering. For the first time in my life, after years of yearning, I had done the most important thing for the world.

This was not enlightenment. Not even close. But it allowed me to believe that I could walk the path to enlightenment. The moment I believed that I could walk the path, I wanted that more than I had ever wanted anything.

By the time I got back to my room, I knew three things. First, somehow the practice that evening, which I had thought a few minutes ago was the worst thing I'd ever done, was actually the best thing I'd ever done. Second, this is exactly what the world needs. This is exactly how our problems are solved. Many other actions are needed, of course, but the mind runs all that, and if it isn't purified, none of that will work.

And third, I knew I needed to continue on. That was just a brief non-dual experience. Obviously, this is very good. It changed my life. But I had to save the world. Therefore, I needed to train on the true path. And I needed to begin as soon as possible. I told my parents I was going to leave college and go train in a Buddhist monastery and nothing could stop me.

And yet in the meantime I was still so angry. I would have great experiences and then be right back in my fury at the selfishness and stupidity of human beings. I was led by this anger. I was its slave. It brought me from monastery to monastery, teacher to teacher, burning in my chest the whole time. It whipped me eventually to Japan, where soon after my nineteenth birthday, I met Shodo Harada Roshi. Nothing much happened in our first meeting. He just sat there and said nothing of any use. He seemed utterly worthless. He was just an ordinary old man.

When I got back on the street, however, the anger that had burned in my heart for fifteen years was gone. Just gone. Completely gone!

The love that had motivated my choices when I was four had turned, bit by bit, into hate by the age of eighteen. The Roshi stole the hate from me, and it turned out I was never broken at all. The love was never broken, and it was never gone. The Roshi hadn't given me anything. He had taken my life from me. And only after it was gone could I see that the false thing I had been living for so long, the thing he took from me, was never my life at all. Only then could I begin to live my life again.

After a while, I came to see two things. First, I saw that somehow, beyond words, that ordinary old man had given me my life back. He had taken away an untrue life—untrue thoughts, delusional feelings, harmful habits—even though I deeply believed in that life and thought I couldn't do without it. How kind of him to allow me to let go of what I most believed in and felt I needed! I saw that the spiritual path is *skillfully letting go of what we believe in and feel we need.* And I saw that there are people who can help us do this hard work even though we tend to resist it. Could there be a greater gift? Therefore, I would train under him, so that I could understand what the Buddha meant when he said that suffering is caused by craving, so that I could save the world from human insanity. And second, I saw that this kind of loss is exactly what the world needs. Greed, hatred, and insanity are exactly what people need to lose. The ultimate question isn't "What can we get?" The ultimate question is "What can we lose?"

I trained under him for several years, and trained with other teachers in other traditions for several more years. It became clear to me day after day that for us to realize our true mind, and live our true life, will lead to us solving the great problems on this planet. The reverse also became clear: our efforts to solve the great problems on this planet are our expressions of compassion in action, and expressions of compassion help us realize our true mind and live our true life. Humanity can shift from being the most dangerous, destructive thing in the world to being the most peaceful, loving thing in the world.

I was fortunate to lose my life. I was fortunate to see that it was never my life anyway. I was fortunate to lose the mind that created that false life. Having received such good fortune, I hope to offer it to you also. We all need to purify our minds. All life depends on it.

Buddhism Day Sale: Buy Meng, Get Soryu Free

This is Meng again. I'm the better-looking one.

My life-changing experience with Buddhism motivated me to write this book with Soryu Forall. Soryu is one of the most impressive Buddhist teachers I have met. I know him to be wise and highly intelligent, keeping good ethical conduct, possessing a very deep practice along with an amazing wealth of knowledge that spans across multiple schools of Buddhism, and demonstrating a deeply compassionate approach to all matters. You know, the usual.

Beyond the already impressive "usual" for an admired teacher, there is one surprising quality that further distinguishes Soryu: his great ambition. Soryu is not content to spend his life enjoying spiritual bliss alone, or to just guide a handful—or a hundred, or a thousand—of his disciples to their spiritual breakthroughs. Oh no. Soryu wants to be of service to the entire world, by making Buddhism massively accessible and practicable for billions of people and, in the process, saving the planet from the worst impulses of humanity. He is also younger than me, so I often jokingly refer to him as "that blond kid from Vermont." In real life, he is a beloved friend, a brother, and an honored teacher, all conveniently rolled into one.

Books about Buddhism written by masters tend to be deep but difficult to read, while those written by non-masters tend to be approachable but insufficiently deep. By working closely together, one a master, the other a proficient non-master-level practitioner, Soryu and I hope to accomplish the best of both: we want this book to be deep enough to talk about how you can reach enlightenment, and yet fully accessible even to people with no knowledge of Buddhism at all.

So you get the best of both worlds. You get a book written by two authors for the price of one. Yay, you!

This book is written in my voice (once described by a reporter as "baritone" and "seductive," ahem).[1] We are kind of like the Penn & Teller magic act: two equal performers, but one does the talking. In addition, I invited Soryu to end each chapter with "The Abbot's Commentary." If Soryu were voicing this book, he would have placed more emphasis on virtue, compassion, and living in a way that cares for all living things, but still, his voice is deeply embedded all over in this book, and he is satisfied that all the claims made in it are correct.

We Build Upon the Solid Foundation
of the Early Buddhist Texts

In this book, you will find a large number of notes directly referencing the early Buddhist texts. The early Buddhist texts, which we will talk about in Chapter 15, consist of this huge collection of texts known to be the earliest recordings of the Buddha's teachings. It is so voluminous that not many people have actually read the whole thing. Soryu and I both have. It took him twelve months and me sixteen months of full-time study to work through all of them at an initial level of understanding. The main reason Soryu and I put in all those references is so you don't have to take our words for it, you can check the primary source for yourself to see if we are correctly representing the teachings of the Buddha. Our original intention was to hold ourselves fully accountable to the Buddha and to you, our reader, by providing an easy mechanism for you to prove us wrong. Doing that turns out to yield a happy side effect: authority. By painstakingly going through and referencing the early Buddhist texts, we find ourselves able to present the teachings with the full authority afforded to us by the primary texts, not having to rely on Soryu's authority as an abbot. We hope you find that a compelling feature of this book.

The obvious reason Soryu and I chose to base this book heavily on the early Buddhist texts is that the teachings in them are common to all major schools of Buddhism. But there is another reason, and it has to do with my frustrating early experience learning Buddhism.

When I first started learning Buddhism, what greeted me was a stark bifurcation. There were only two types of Buddhist teachings available to me, representing both extremes of the depth spectrum. On one end were the teachings on basic morality: don't lie, don't steal, be good to people, and so on. Essentially, the same things Mom tried to teach me when I was five. Also often included was a version of Buddhism so excessively watered down it had no potency left, mostly: life is suffering, so try not to crave for things, and be good to everyone. I attended numerous lectures where Buddhist teachers essentially repeated those same basic things. I was frustrated and disappointed every single time. The only other type of Buddhist teachings I had access to occupied the other extreme end of the spectrum: things that were basically incomprehensible. For example, teachings like, "there is no difference between subject and object," or "form is emptiness," or "there is no aging and death, and no end of aging and death." None of it was useful to me at the time.

Things began to change for me when I learned mindfulness meditation, which transformed me and changed my life. I then came across the early Buddhist texts and, whoa, I realized I stumbled into a large treasure house. In those texts, the Buddha takes you from the most basic stuff all the way to final enlightenment, including the steps in between. The entire path was laid out. More impressively, almost all of it was perfectly understandable. Wow. Mind you, it was understandable not because the Buddha watered anything down, but because of his amazing brilliance. Enlightenment itself is beyond description. To describe a path toward something beyond description is really hard. It takes a real genius to do it, which is why it rarely happens in history. However, to describe the path in a way that is perfectly understandable and useful to everyone is much, much harder. It takes a genius's genius to do it, and the Buddha was that super-genius. I finally had what I needed to understand Buddhism. My heart overflowed with gratitude for the Buddha.

Over the past two thousand plus years, due to a whole host of cultural, instructional, and historical reasons compounded over time, the teaching of Buddhism started trending toward the increasingly esoteric for one audience, and increasingly watered down for another audience. That is how by the time I wanted to learn Buddhism, there was this stark bifurcation staring me in my face, almost laughing at me. Fortunately, the early Buddhist texts give us everything we need to bridge this bifurcation, so that every one of us can benefit from the full spectrum of the Buddha's teachings. And that is why Soryu and I rely so heavily on the early Buddhist texts.

The Topics Are So Serious We Have to Laugh

One beautiful quality I have observed in many great Buddhist teachers is that they carry a certain lightness in their being. The Dalai Lama, for example, has a great sense of humor.[2] In public speeches, he would often tell jokes and make playful comments. Buddhist teacher Ajahn Brahm is often even funnier, having a tendency to make the audience roar in laughter. In contrast, the late Vietnamese Zen master Thich Nhat Hanh seldom joked; he carried himself with a calm, no-nonsense dignity. But even in him, that quality of lightness was so abundantly obvious, it felt as if you could always see his inner smile.

This is no accident. As you will see in this book, even during the Buddha's time, Buddhist monastics were observed to be "joyful and elated, serene and peaceful." Inner joy is a consistent theme in Buddhist practice, and inner lightness is a logical consequence of it. In some people, this lightness shows up externally as big smiles, laughter, and humor.

In writing this book, Soryu and I understand we are talking about serious and important topics such as the teachings of the Buddha, the suffering of countless living beings, and the great matter of life and death. Given the seriousness, we approached the book with the great care it deserves. For me, that means I put myself in a gentle meditative state when I write, and that meditative state is always joyful for me. Which means I wrote this entire book with the warm glow of meditative joy. That warm glow plus my sense of humor makes for a dangerous combination: I often end up writing pages drenched in lightness and punctuated with jokes and, worse, puns.

I hope the happy side effect is that we ended up with a book that is not just important to read, but also fun to read. I like to think that if something is no laughing matter, I probably did it wrong.

CHAPTER ONE

Dharma and the Features of Buddhism

What Is Dharma? Dharma Is Not Banging Your Head Against the Wall

The teachings of the Buddha can be encapsulated in a single word: **Dharma**. Dharma is one of those highly polymorphous words with annoyingly many meanings. The broadest meaning of the word *dharma* (written in lowercase) is "phenomena." In that sense, everything is a dharma because everything is a phenomenon. In Buddhism, the definition of Dharma (capitalized) that is most useful is this:

> Dharma is universal law pertaining to suffering and liberation from suffering.

"Universal law" here means the laws of cause and effect. It is akin to the laws of physics. For example, one law of physics states that force equals mass times acceleration ($F = ma$). Therefore, if I apply ten newtons of force to an object weighing one kilogram, it will accelerate by ten meters per second squared. That is universal law, the law of cause and effect.

When we talk about Dharma, we are talking about the same universal laws of cause and effect, but we restrict the domain to suffering and liberation from suffering. A silly example of Dharma is this:

- If I bang my head against the wall, I will suffer from a headache.

- Therefore, if I don't bang my head against the wall, I will not create that suffering for myself.

In that sense, Dharma is not banging your head against the wall.

In Dharma, we are specifically interested in these four subdomains of universal law:

1. The nature of suffering

2. The cause of suffering

3. The cessation of suffering

4. The methods for ending suffering

Here's how applying these four subdomains to our silly example of banging my head against the wall can relate to mindfulness practice: First, I bring mindfulness to my body and I realize there is a pain in my forehead once every few seconds. Ouch . . . ouch . . . ouch. There, *I realize the nature of suffering.* Then I observe my actions with mindfulness and discover that I'm banging my head on the wall once every few seconds. So that's why I'm getting this pain in my forehead! *I realize the cause of this suffering.* Next, I practice mindfulness to sharpen my perception and I discover that in between banging my head against the wall, there are moments where I experience no pain. *I understand the cessation of this suffering.* Finally, I mindfully stop myself from banging my head against the wall. And there, *I realize the method for ending this suffering.*

The Dharma as presented and articulated by the Buddha is known as "Buddhadharma." Hence, Buddhadharma is the version of universal law pertaining to suffering and liberation from suffering as taught by the Buddha. In Buddhism, Buddhadharma is almost always shorthanded to Dharma, and is usually thought of as "the teachings of the Buddha." Hence, in the Buddhist context (including in this book), if you see the word *Dharma*, it almost always means "Buddhadharma." Fortunately, that does not cause any confusion due to an important feature of the universal laws of cause and effect: those laws do not change regardless of who the discoverer is and how he or she articulates them.

Let's pretend that on the same day an apple fell on the head of a young man in England called Isaac Newton, another apple fell on the head of a young woman in India called Deepika Chandra. Pretend they were both inspired to do a series of experiments and both then independently discovered the law of gravity. But they described it differently: Newton described it as "attraction between bodies," while Chandra described it as "universal affinity causing bodies to resist separation." So now there are two different articulations of the law of gravity, yet the cause and effect involving gravity does not change one iota. It does not matter if it is called "Newton's Law" or "Chandra's Law," earth's gravity will still attract the same apple with the same force.

Similarly, it does not matter if it is Buddhadharma (Dharma as explained by the Buddha) or Schmodharma (Dharma as explained by some random guy called Joe Schmo), Dharma is still Dharma, the cause and effect surrounding suffering remains unchanged, and banging your head against a wall is still as painful. For that reason, within a Buddhist context, Dharma and Buddha-dharma can be used interchangeably. It is also important to note that Dharma, being universal law, is not exclusive to Buddhism. Dharma is everywhere. Wherever there is an understanding of suffering and liberation from suffering, there is Dharma.

Buddhism Is Seriously Cool with Science

The 14th Dalai Lama famously said,

> If scientific analysis were conclusively to demonstrate certain claims in Buddhism to be false, then we must accept the findings of science and abandon those claims.[1]

My initial reaction to this was an unimpressed, "Duh, of course." That may not surprise you, since you already know I'm a skeptic and a man of science. What *may* surprise you is that the Buddhist community had no adverse reaction to what the Dalai Lama said. Nobody was offended. It should be shocking for one of the paramount leaders of one of the major religions in the world to pronounce that science takes precedence over his religion. I imagine if this were to happen in some other religion, it would likely cause a huge uproar, and many of the religion's leaders and followers would be really upset. And yet, in Buddhism, such a statement feels like a non-event, almost taken for granted. The fact that it is so unremarkable is very remarkable.

That, my friends, is the first thing that fascinates me about Buddhism: its scientific spirit. The Dalai Lama even calls the core teachings of the Buddha the "Science of the Mind."[2]

Buddhism's scientific spirit did not begin with the Dalai Lama; it started with the Buddha himself. The Buddha insisted that his students accept his teachings not on blind faith, but only after careful investigation. He beautifully describes his teachings as verifiable here and now.[3] This statement is astounding coming from *any* spiritual teacher, because it makes the teacher very vulnerable. If you can prove a teacher's words true or false only after you die, then you really have no way to prove your teacher wrong for the rest of your life. In contrast, if your teacher states that his teachings are verifiable here and now, you can always try to prove him wrong today, right this minute, and that makes him very vulnerable. It takes a spiritual teacher with a lot of confidence in the teachings to put himself in that position. In fact, the Buddha didn't just say that, he repeatedly told his students to put him and his teachings to the test.[4]

Soryu had some amusing experiences in this regard. He practiced under classically trained, no-nonsense Buddhist masters in Asia. Like any good student, he would nod when he listened to them, and that would invite a challenge. They would often tell him something like, "Don't just believe this! Find out for yourself. I just taught you something and you nodded as if you understood, but have you confirmed it? If you haven't tested it then you don't know it. The only part of this training that matters is the part where you try to disprove Buddhism. So get to work! By the time you come back to see me this evening, you should know for yourself if this is true."

That really struck Soryu, because he always considered himself a Western skeptic, but it turned out in terms of skepticism, he was just a Padawan learner. Those old Asian guys put him to shame.

The true significance of this "verifiable here and now" attitude is even more striking: it moves the power in the teacher-student relationship from teacher to student. Imagine if you are a student of the Buddha, and he tells you if you do this, that will happen, and if you don't do this, that will not happen, and he tells you it is verifiable here and now. If you then follow through and find out his prediction is wrong, you know he is wrong about at least one thing. He puts you, the student, at the center of everything. You are the one who has the right to discern if he is correct, not the other way around! That is a huge amount of self-empowerment for the student. That is why learning Buddhism can feel very empowering.

Yes, Empiricism and Faith Can Play Together

Just because Buddhism is highly empirical does not mean faith has no place in Buddhism. One place faith can play a very important role is when you have not yet acquired the equipment to verify certain claims. For example, to verify some of Newton's claims regarding mechanics, I need to be equipped with a stopwatch, a measuring tape, and a piece of weight attached to a string. To verify certain claims, even claims that are verifiable here and now, I have to acquire certain equipment.

It goes further. Very often in real life, in order to make actual progress, I have to accept on faith that other people have already verified certain claims, despite not yet being equipped to verify those claims myself. For example, when I did statistics, I plugged numbers into standard statistical formulas to derive correlation coefficients and confidence intervals. The correctness of those formulas was verifiable, but I was not equipped with the mathematical skills to verify them for myself, yet I really needed to write those research papers. What to do? I accepted on faith that people mathematically more qualified than myself have already taken the trouble to verify those formulas, so I could use them to make progress in my own work.

There were three reasons I was able to have faith in those standard statistical formulas. First, I knew that if I really wanted to verify their correctness for myself, there was a path to do so. It involved me picking up certain mathematical skills, and I knew what they were, and I knew it was doable if I put in the right effort. Second, the formulas have a good track record. I have used them myself and countless others have used them for many years, and they have worked really well so far. Third, they came from a highly trusted source, in this case, from a standard college textbook recommended by my professor. For all those reasons, my faith was not blind faith, it was wisely informed faith.

In the same way, on your journey practicing Buddhism, there will be many places where you will find yourself not yet equipped to verify certain claims. For example, the ancient texts claim that when your mind first arrives at perfect calmness, you will experience energetic joy that appears to fill your whole body and mind. But you find yourself unequipped to verify that claim because you are not yet able to arrive at perfect mental calmness. What to do? Fortunately, you will find the same three reasons to have enough faith to make progress.

First, there is a path for you to acquire the equipment you need. In this case, your teacher may show you how to calm the mind by attending to the body and the breath, and how to overcome something called the five hindrances (see Chapter 7) that get in the way. Second, there is a good track record. For example, you may find other people who have already reached the same state and verified the claim for themselves; you may also find that you too have experienced the good track record for yourself: with even just a few hours of practice attending to body and breath, your mind is already much calmer and happier. And third, the claim comes from sources you trust: your teacher and, more important, ancient texts quoting the Buddha himself.

This is true also for more advanced Buddhist topics such as karma, rebirth, and nirvana, where it is much harder to collect data. But even for those, data collection is possible with a properly equipped mind. It just takes a lot more training. We will discuss all those topics in this book.

"They say they are here to measure your faith."

So no, faith and empiricism are not in conflict. In fact, they work best when they work together, and Buddhism shows us how to use each to support the other. Soryu, given his experience as a teacher, goes even further to say that doubt is the thing that makes faith work, in the same way that faith is the thing that makes doubt work. In Buddhism, we celebrate those who doubt because the result of that doubt is investigation, which means they eventually "go beyond learning" and are no longer dependent on even the Buddha for the most important teachings.

A Secular Religion? Isn't That Like a Joke?

My dear friend and teacher Norman Fischer is quite unusual. He is a Zen master (Zen being a major school of Buddhism) who received many years of rigorous training under the tutelage of classically trained Zen masters. Actually, Norman is not just any ordinary Zen master; he was a Zen abbot. Well, he was not even an ordinary Zen abbot; he was an abbot of the San Francisco Zen Center, one of the major Zen centers in the Western world. And he was, and still is, a practicing Jew. Imagine that, a classically trained Zen abbot of a major Zen center, and the entire time, he has been a practicing Jew who has never lost his Jewish identity nor his Jewish faith. Very few Buddhists I know think there is anything wrong with having a practicing Jew as a major Zen abbot.

That level of inclusiveness in any religion is mind-blowing. I have met Christians, Hindus, Muslims, and Jews who identify as practicing Buddhists while simultaneously as believers in and practitioners of their own religions. My friend and fellow Buddhist meditator Dr. Stuart Lord served as the president of Naropa University, a major Buddhist university in North America. He also held a doctor of ministry degree from the United Theological Seminary, served as a Christian chaplain, and thought of himself as both a Christian and a Buddhist. And, yes, there are atheist Buddhists too. In fact, I used to identify as one. These days, I joke that I am a full-time Buddhist and a part-time Christian. I once saw a photograph of the Dalai Lama humbly and respectfully holding a Christian cross to his forehead with his head lowered, as if in silent prayer. It was widely shared on social media (OK, fine, I was guilty of sharing it too), and I know of no Buddhist who was upset or offended. I myself was overjoyed.

It is not that Buddhism has no doctrinal differences with other religions; there certainly are obvious differences. For example, as you will find in later chapters, the Buddha disagreed that there was a creator God, or an almighty God, governing the cosmos. Of course, that also means that in Buddhism, there is no possibility of having any specific ethnic group favored as a "chosen people" by God, nor any caste system put in place by God. However, the important thing is Buddhism has no interest in turning those disagreements into conflicts. Many of us are accustomed to thinking that a disagreement regarding doctrine is automatically equivalent to a fight, but Buddhism sees it differently. The Buddha taught his disciples not to cling to any rites, rituals, or views, and certainly not to start fights over those things. Therefore, the Buddhist attitude, which you will find deeply embedded in this book, is to state clearly and firmly what the Buddha's teachings are, and to do so with open arms, inviting everybody to learn, and to just take home whatever is useful and beneficial to them.

The inclusiveness of Buddhism extends to a neutrality regarding religious beliefs, and in this sense, we may speak of it as secular. The Buddha's teachings do not require belief in nor reliance on any deities. The core teachings taught by the Buddha relate to the nature of mind and its liberation from suffering, and the core practices are mental training methods for stilling the mind, developing insight, and cultivating positive qualities such as joy and kindness. Those training methods taught by the Buddha are extremely secular. For example, as part of attentional training, the Buddha taught his students to attend to the breath. Nobody has to believe in one or more gods (nor disbelieve in gods, for that matter) to practice placing attention on the breath. In fact, the Buddha did not even require belief in mystical objects such as "energy" or "chakras" and such. The Buddha kept the set of objects for mental training to things that can be empirically understood in our daily lives, such as the body, the breath, and mental and emotional states, not anything we have to believe in (like chakras).

The degree to which Buddhism is secular, inclusive, and comfortable with science makes it, in my eyes, the most awesome religion. But how does a religion get to be this way? Isn't "secular religion" an oxymoron? Almost funny (like, "ha ha" funny)? The answer lies at the basis upon which Buddhism was founded. While every other major religion was founded based on belief in, and worship of, one or more deities, **Buddhism was founded entirely on the basis of complete liberation from suffering**. Deities are outside of oneself, so one cannot know everything about them. But whether you are suffering is known to you. There is no speculation required. The Buddha successfully pioneered the path to gaining complete freedom from suffering through deep mental cultivation, careful investigation, and gaining total understanding into the nature of suffering. He taught that path, which he simply named "the teaching and discipline" (*Dhamma-vinaya*), and that is what we know today as Buddhism. The Buddha said emphatically, "What I teach is suffering and the cessation of suffering."[5]

Buddhism is so nonreliant on deities and so discouraging of blind faith that there are even widely respected Buddhist masters, for example Dzogchen Ponlop Rinpoche, who argue that Buddhism isn't a religion at all.[6] Buddhist monk and author Ajahn Brahm says, "Buddhism is not a belief system. It is a science founded on objective observation, i.e., meditation."[7] Vietnamese Zen master Thich Nhat Hanh says:

> There is a misconception that Buddhism is a religion, and that you worship Buddha. Buddhism is a practice, like yoga. You can be a Christian and practice Buddhism. I met a Catholic priest who lives in a Buddhist monastery in France. He told me that Buddhism makes him a better Christian. I love that.[8]

Maybe that's how Buddhism gets to be the most awesome religion: by being not.

Jokes aside, the question of whether Buddhism is a religion is too nuanced for a straight yes or no answer. You will see, as early as Chapter 2 of this book, that Buddhism is not completely free of mystical elements involving gods, supernatural powers, and other mysterious stuff. You will also find that Buddhism can contain enough religious features to be legitimately thought of as a religion. However, it's important to note that the *practices* taught by the Buddha do not have to rely on anything mystical, which means you can accept or reject those mystical elements in Buddhism and the practices for ending suffering will still work for you. Whether Buddhism is a religion is a topic we will explore in some detail in Chapter 13, but for now, what I can say with certainty is that because the teachings of the Buddha are nonreliant on deities and mystical objects, and solidly grounded in empirical investigation, they are free of most trappings of religion. And that, to me, is most freaking awesome.

Buddhism Is Deeply Joyful

The Buddha was said to be "ever smiling," and his disciples to be "joyful and elated, jubilant and exultant, enjoying the spiritual life, with faculties pleased, free from anxiety, serene, and peaceful."[9]

The most amazing thing about the path taught by the Buddha is that it is joyful. You might expect a profound spiritual practice to contain nothing but pain, struggle, and sacrifice. Instead, joy is deeply embedded and prominently featured, at multiple places, on the Buddhist path. It begins with the practice of virtue, which gains us the "bliss of blamelessness" and includes the highly sustainable joy of a calm and clear mind; the peaceful joy of the present moment; the uplifting joy of kindness and compassion; the delicious joy of being free from agitation, want, and hatred; and the rapturously powerful meditative joys; and it culminates in the supreme bliss of gaining complete freedom from all suffering.

I myself am intimately familiar with the deeply joyful aspect of Buddhism because of how Buddhism saved my life. With the practice of Buddhist meditation, I went from being miserable and suicidal to becoming one who smiles aplenty. The most life-changing thing for me was the ability to experience gentle joy with absolutely nothing happening at all, which is why I spend a lot of time smiling at absolutely nothing. The change was so profound I went on to become the guy holding the job title of "Jolly Good Fellow" at Google (and, yes, like many things in my career, that job title started as a joke).

In this book, you will find how joyful the practice of Buddhism can be.

Buddhism Frees You

Buddhism is all about freedom and liberation. The final goal of Buddhist practice is total liberation from all suffering. But even before reaching that final goal, you will find yourself gaining freedom in many different ways at many different levels.

You may, for example, at some point find yourself liberated from boredom. As a Buddhist meditator, you may never suffer boredom again, because every moment of "nothing interesting happening" is an opportunity to indulge in the sweet peace and joy of meditation. Total freedom from boredom. You may later also find yourself liberated from having to feed your ego. Previously, you may find your happiness dependent on how much your ego is being fed. Your ego becomes a very cruel slave master who totally owns you. At certain points in your practice, you may find your inner happiness transcending the need to feed the ego and, right there, you have just unshackled yourself from a very cruel slave master. Freedom! The path toward enlightenment is filled with many joyous breakings of shackles, one after another.

Another dimension where you will find immense freedom is freedom of thought. You might expect a religion to force you to identify this way or that, or force you to blindly believe this or that. In Buddhism, your mind is set free. Well, more than that: the more advanced your training gets, the more you are *required* to think for yourself and to critically investigate the teachings presented to you. In other words, you are required to set your mind free.

To have a religion that is so freeing is very impressive. But even more impressive is the spread and longevity of any religion that is so deeply grounded in freedom. I mean, if a religion forces you to blindly believe in certain things and identify in certain ways and, in extreme cases, even imposes a death penalty upon people who convert to another religion and then also wages wars to spread itself, then it makes perfect sense for that religion to spread and endure for a very long time. I mean, duh.

However, if you take a religion that encourages, even requires, practitioners to think for themselves, that does not force them to blindly believe in certain things nor identify in certain ways, and does not go to war to spread itself (and, lamer still, does not even have a god in whose name you can wage war), then for that religion to spread far and wide and last for thousands of years, there must be something really, really amazing about its teachings. And Buddhism is it.

Buddhism Is Needed in the World

There is a popular quote allegedly by Albert Einstein:

> The religion of the future will be a cosmic religion. It should transcend a personal God and avoid dogmas and theology. Covering both natural and spiritual, it should be based on a religious sense arising from the experience of all things natural and spiritual and a meaningful unity. Buddhism answers this description. If there is any religion that would cope with modern scientific needs, it would be Buddhism.[10]

Nobody has shown that Einstein actually said it, but the quote is widely repeated because it is correct: that due to its unique qualities, Buddhism is uniquely suited for the scientific age.

We all experience suffering, and we all die. Sooner or later we need to confront suffering and/or death. In other words, sooner or later we all find out we have spiritual needs. The problem is people tend to think of spirituality and religion as one and the same. That becomes a real problem in the scientific age because many people perceive science as being in conflict with religion, so people think they are forced to choose one or the other. Some choose religion and decide to reject science, while others choose science and end up abandoning spirituality along with religion.

Buddhism offers a way for people to be deeply spiritual, with or without religion. That means those uncomfortable with religion can still be spiritual, and those who love religion can find, in Buddhism, a way to be spiritual and religious without ever having to reject science. Buddhism is uniquely suited to serve all people in these times.

More important, Buddhism is not just good for people, it is good for the world.

As the Buddha says, mind is the forerunner of all thoughts and actions. Mind is chief.[11] How destructive we are as a species is determined by the quality of our minds. This is especially true in the age of science and technology, where our destructive powers are greatly magnified. Our powers have become so great that we are endangering all life on earth. The more enlightened we are, the more we possess inner peace, inner joy, compassion, and wisdom, the more our minds are free from greed, hatred, and delusion, the less destructive we become as a species.

The world, and all life on earth, need us humans to be much, much less destructive. The world desperately needs us to be more enlightened. In other words, the world needs us to learn and practice what the Buddha taught.

Laugh Your Way to Enlightenment

Let us now undertake our joyful exploration of Buddhism. First we will talk about how to be free from suffering.

- In Chapter 2, we start with the story of the Buddha, the person who discovered the Dharma and founded Buddhism. Besides getting to know the founder of Buddhism, you will see some of the fascinating features of Buddhism begin to show up. For example, you will find that gods have no role whatsoever in the enlightenment of the Buddha, which explains the nontheistic nature of Buddhism. You will also find the central role of joy and investigation in the Buddha's enlightenment, again foretelling their central role in his eventual teachings.

- In Chapters 3 to 6, we will examine in detail the Buddha's core teachings, known as the Four Noble Truths. Here, the scientific nature of Buddhism really begins to show. One key insight coming from the Four Noble Truths is that suffering is subject to cause and effect, and, therefore, Buddhism is about deeply understanding the cause of suffering and, through that understanding, gaining liberation from suffering. Therefore, liberation from suffering is taken out of the realm of religion and placed squarely into the realm of careful investigation into cause and effect, which is, of course, the scientific attitude.

- In Chapters 7 to 9, we take a deep dive into three major topics: right mindfulness, right samadhi, and virtue. The secular nature of Buddhism really begins to show here. These chapters describe the core practices of Buddhism that can take you all the way to nirvana, and you will find that they have no religious elements at all. Zero. You will also find that these practices do not require identifying yourself in any prescribed way, nor adopting any particular beliefs concerning race, gender, caste, politics, or religion, and that is why Buddhism is so inclusive.

- In Chapter 10, we take an even deeper dive and explore underlying topics such as karma and dependent origination.

- In Chapter 11, we aim right for the bull's-eye with a chapter on how we can all use all that knowledge to *see nirvana directly.*

- In Chapter 12, we will present the exciting story of how one of Soryu's students arrived at the direct experience of nirvana. From that story, you will also gain a deeper understanding of liberation.

By the end of Chapter 12, you will have gained an excellent understanding of core Buddhism and the direct path to nirvana. You will also begin to see how Buddhism is joyful, secular, scientific, inclusive, and liberating.

To those of you already familiar with Buddhism who might be tempted to skip portions of Chapters 2 to 12, we say, no, do not skip any of it. Even those already familiar with Buddhism will unearth many very important gems in there. The reason is the breadth and depth with which Soryu and I approach this topic. While some may think of the Four Noble Truths as the "basic stuff" to quickly skim, Soryu and I present it in the same spirit that the Buddha had presented it in the early Buddhist texts: as one of the most important, most profound, and most transcendent teachings. You will see that Soryu and I cast a huge net over the entire breadth of the massive early Buddhist canon, combined with Soryu's familiarity with multiple schools of Buddhism, to present a teaching that is at once approachable even to those learning about Buddhism for the first time, yet deep and comprehensive enough to illuminate the path to enlightenment.

Following that, in Chapters 13 to 17, we will look at Buddhism in relation to five things:

- How Buddhism views miracles and gods, which may surprise you, answering the question of whether Buddhism is a religion or not.

- The unexpectedly intimate relationship between Buddhism and science.

- How a small, fascinating group of monks heroically preserved early Buddhism.

- How we ended up having sects in Buddhism, and how we can enjoy sects.

- How you don't have to be a Buddhist to be a Buddhist, and how inclusive Buddhism can be.

When Soryu and I encountered Buddhism, we both arrived at the same conclusion: that it can be profoundly life-changing and that it presents the true solution to all suffering. More than that, we feel it is the path to peace on earth. If large numbers of people practice Buddhism, there will be a lot more joy and less suffering in the world. The world will be far more peaceful, and the planet will be taken care of. This is it, friends! We hope Buddhism will benefit you tremendously.

The Abbot's Commentary
by Soryu Forall

Even when I was ten, I worried constantly about the suffering in the world. But other people didn't seem worried, and they told me to stop worrying so much. That's why Buddhism fascinates me. It was the one thing I encountered that didn't tell me that someone else will take care of it and it will all just be OK.

Instead it told me, yes, there's suffering. And if you do what must be done, you can resolve it. DO THAT! Do it now!

In Buddhism, there is no unseen superhero you can pray to who will swoop in and take all your suffering away. In a very real sense, Buddhism is the study of causality of suffering. You investigate what causes suffering and, consequently, how to "uncause" it. Like any investigation, the first thing you have to do is to honestly face the facts, which in this case means recognizing suffering. So if you are worried and depressed about suffering, that is due to your courage and integrity. Now, be sure to have enough courage and integrity to go beyond worry and depression. By facing the problem, find the solution.

Fortunately, honestly facing a big problem does not have to be unpleasant if there is a pleasant solution. The Buddha taught an effective path to complete liberation from suffering, and it includes increasingly refined experiences of joyful mental states. For that reason, honestly facing profound suffering turns out to be a great thing. Not only does it motivate you to reach the end goal of total liberation, but the path itself includes one experience of inner joy after another.

CHAPTER TWO

His Friends Call Him Bud

About the Buddha

The Buddha Formerly Known as Prince

Once upon a time, there was an immensely powerful being born with colossal godlike superpowers who destroyed all suffering for all time, and he lived happily ever after. That was not the story of the Buddha.

The Buddha was born a human being. It is remarkable that the Buddha was able to achieve the monumental task of gaining freedom from all suffering using only the body and mind of a mere mortal human. Even more remarkable is you and I can do the same! All we have to do is walk the path discovered by the Buddha. This is the story of how the Buddha did it, and it hints at how you and I can do it too.

This story I am about to tell is the traditional account, the one that is taught in Buddhist textbooks.[1] See, in the earliest canonical Buddhist texts, the Buddha seldom talked about himself, except as an instructional aid. That is why those texts offer few biographical details regarding the Buddha. Most of the details were filled in by later commentaries. Like all biographies that are more than two thousand years old, facts have a tendency to get mixed in with legend. Modern scholarship has cast new light on some details in the story; for example, it now appears likely that the Buddha's father was a chieftain rather than a king. These new scholarly findings are a good thing, but it does leave us with the question of what to do with the story.

The good news is that none of the new findings changes the core power of the story. For example, the power of the early part comes from seeing a privileged, pampered, young aristocrat inspired to renounce his worldly wealth in search of the highest wisdom. That is powerful whether his father was king or chieftain. The even better news is that the most important part of the story, namely the Buddha's actual path to enlightenment, was clearly documented in the earliest canonical texts. Yay! All things considered, Soryu and I decided to tell the traditional version, and as usual, where supported by the earliest canonical texts, we made sure to include references so you can check the source for yourself.

The story begins with the birth of an Indian prince by the name of Siddhattha (also commonly spelled as Siddhārtha).[2] Siddhattha was the son of King Suddhōdana and Queen Maya of the Shakya clan. He was born in Lumbini, in present-day Nepal, traditionally said to have been circa 623 BCE.

You probably did not have a famous great sage come visit you right after you were born (I certainly did not), but that was precisely what happened to Siddhattha. Soon after Siddhattha was born, the great hermit sage Asita arrived at the palace and asked to see the baby. The king gladly obliged. Asita held the baby in his arms, and he was overjoyed. A few seconds later, Asita became dismayed and started weeping. King Suddhōdana, understandably shocked, asked, "Will some misfortune befall the prince?" Asita assured the king that no misfortune will befall the prince. He further explained that his initial elation came from seeing that this prince would reach "the foremost enlightenment" and would teach an "unequaled Dharma" that will free countless sentient beings from suffering, but Asita also saw that, being already an old man, he would be dead before that unequaled Dharma would be taught, and so he would not be alive to hear it. Hence, he was "troubled, distressed, and dejected."[3]

When the baby was five days old, in keeping with local tradition, a naming ceremony was held and the prince was named Siddhattha Gotama. *Siddhattha* means "wish fulfilled" and *Gotama* was the family name (also commonly spelled as Gautama).[4] As part of the ceremony, eight distinguished Brahmin scholars were invited to read the baby's future. Seven of the scholars predicted that young Siddhattha would one day grow up either to be a great king (a "universal monarch") or a great sage. The youngest of the eight, Koṇḍañña, confidently predicted that Siddhattha would grow up to become a buddha, a fully enlightened one. Many years later, Koṇḍañña would become an early student of the Buddha and the very first to reach enlightenment.[5]

When Siddhattha was a young child, a remarkable thing happened. His father presided over the plowing festival and brought along his courtiers, his family, and their caretakers. At some point, the adults were so preoccupied that they neglectfully left the young prince unattended. Young Siddhattha, under a rose-apple tree and seeing nobody around him, sat cross-legged, focused on his breath, and spontaneously went into a state of deep meditative concentration known as the first *jhāna* (which we will discuss in Chapter 8). When the adults returned to see the young child in deep meditative concentration, they were awestruck. This was a onetime mini-miracle, Siddhattha never again went into meditative concentration until he became a full-time seeker of truth as an adult, but this incident would have a pivotal effect on his final ascent to enlightenment.

As an aristocrat, Siddhattha no doubt received a good education and train-ing in martial arts. At sixteen, he married his beautiful cousin of the same age, Princess Yasodharā. He lived a pampered, luxurious life filled with sen-sual pleasures. He had the highest-quality clothing. A white parasol was al-ways held over him so that he "might not be touched by heat or cold, dust, leaves or dew."[6] He had three palaces, one for the cold season, one for the hot season, and one for the rainy season. And yes, he had good food and on-demand entertainment by female musicians. Life was good, until the day he went out to explore.

The Four Sights, Four Signs, and Four Sighs

One glorious day, Siddhattha went into town with his charioteer Channa, and came into direct contact with the stark realities of real life outside his pampered existence. It shocked him to his core. On this trip, he saw four things that changed his life, that would later be known in Buddhism as the **Four Sights**.[7] First, he saw a decrepit old man, and he suddenly realized that he himself was subject to aging, and that everybody else was also subject to aging. Next, he saw a very sick man, and it suddenly dawned on him that he was subject to sickness, and so, too, was everybody else. The third sight must have been the most shocking of all: he saw a corpse. He realized that someday he would be just like this corpse. Someday he would die, and everybody else was also subject to death.

While the first three sights shocked and depressed him, the fourth offered him hope. The fourth sight was of an ascetic, one who had renounced the world to devote himself to finding the truth. Siddhattha must have been impressed by the calm and dignified demeanor of the ascetic, for after seeing this man, he decided that he too wanted to follow that career path. Having seen suffering, he decided that the most noble thing to do was to find the solution to all suffering. Much later (after his enlightenment), he would tell his disciples that a "noble search" was one where someone subject to birth, aging, sickness, and death seeks a solution to those things.[8] He was determined to begin his own noble search. The admission price of Siddhattha's noble search was giving up his family life and his pleasure-filled, princely existence. He was willing to pay that price.

It is remarkable that Siddhattha chose to pay the heavy price of renunciation. Being a prince, his obvious choice would have been to hire one or more holy men to teach him while continuing to live his luxurious life, as many aristocrats, princes, kings, and emperors had done all through history. Yet Siddhattha decided to go all in, renouncing all that he had, and to live the holy life. Why? Because Siddhattha made a notably astute observation: it makes no sense for one seeking the solution to birth, aging, sickness, and death to seek anything that is also subject to birth, aging, sickness, and death.[9] This is one of those insights that takes wisdom to see, but once you see it, becomes so obvious you wonder why it was not always obvious before. Siddhattha had the wisdom to see it for himself. Beyond wisdom, Siddhattha also had courage. If you are rich and powerful, it takes a lot of courage to give up everything you have in pursuit of a noble search, and Siddhattha had it in him.

Not long after Siddhattha made the decision to renounce his worldly life to become an ascetic, he received news of the birth of his son. According to popular lore, upon hearing this news, he remarked, "An impediment—*rāhu*—has been born; a fetter has arisen." Hence, the infant was accordingly named Rāhula by his grandfather, the king. Though this story is very popular, it is actually not found in the canonical texts. It is much more likely, according to modern scholars, that Rāhula was named in accordance with an eclipse of the moon rather than as an "impediment."

It is useful to understand Siddhattha's decision to renounce from the lens of compassion. Like a modern-day father who leaves his family to work in a foreign country for many years to elevate them out of poverty, Siddhattha had to take on a multiyear ascetic assignment away to elevate his family (and all sentient beings, for that matter) out of suffering. Even though Siddhattha loved his wife and newborn son, his compassion for them and for all sentient beings compelled him to leave his family to embark on his noble search for the solution to all suffering. He simply had to do it. It helped that his wife and son, being royals, would be well taken care of by the extended family in his absence. One day he made the final decision to leave in the middle of the night. On the night of his departure, he opened the door to his bedroom and took one last look at his sleeping wife and child.

And then he left quietly. He was twenty-nine years old.

The Noble Search, Without Google

After shaving his head and beard, and exchanging his princely robes for rags, Siddhattha started his life as a penniless, homeless, wandering ascetic living off the charity of strangers. Pretty soon after, he found his way to his first teacher, an ascetic of repute by the name of Alara Kalama.[10] Siddhattha turned out to be a meditation prodigy. Under the tutelage of Alara, Siddhattha quickly mastered the state of deep meditative concentration known as the "base of nothingness." Soon, Siddhattha equaled Alara, and the master could teach the student no more. Alara offered Siddhattha a place by his side to lead their community as equals. Siddhattha was touched by the offer, but he also knew that the "base of nothingness" was not the complete freedom from suffering he was looking for, so he respectfully left Alara to continue his noble search.

After Alara, Siddhattha found another teacher, an ascetic of repute by the name of Uddaka Ramaputta. *Ramaputta* means "son of Rama." Uddaka's father, Rama, had gained mastery over a state of deep meditative concentration called the "base of neither perception nor non-perception," and, yes, it is one notch deeper (and more awesome) than the "base of nothingness" Siddhattha had learned from Alara earlier. With the instructions passed on by Uddaka, Siddhattha soon mastered it. Alas, once again, in a short amount of time the student had equaled the master, and the master had no more to teach the student. Actually, it may be even worse than that. The texts hint strongly, but do not explicitly say, that Uddaka himself did not master the "base of neither perception nor non-perception," and if that was the case, Siddhattha had exceeded the master. In fact, Uddaka did not offer Siddhattha a place by his side to lead their community as equals like Alara did; instead, he asked Siddhattha to take over as sole leader of their community. Siddhattha turned down that offer for the same reason, that even the "base of neither perception nor non-perception" was not the complete freedom from suffering he was looking for. So Siddhattha gracefully left Uddaka to continue on his noble search.[11]

Siddhattha now had a major problem. You see, the "base of neither perception nor non-perception" was pretty much the deepest and most refined state of meditative concentration an ancient sage could get into, and Alara and Uddaka were basically the best meditation teachers one could have learned from at that time. Siddhattha had now equaled or surpassed them. Hence, Siddhattha now had nobody to teach him, and no clear path forward. What to do?

Siddhattha found a grove by a river near a village in a place called Uruvela where he could practice and seek the path on his own. Eventually, he attracted five followers, one of whom was Koṇḍañña (yes, the same Koṇḍañña who had earlier predicted that baby Siddhattha would one day grow up to become a buddha). The other four where Bhaddiya, Vappa, Mahānāma, and Assaji.

In ancient India during Siddhattha's time, there was a popular belief that salvation could be achieved by living a life of strict asceticism. Siddhattha tried exploring that path, and to do it better than anybody else could have done. "I will carry austerity to the utmost," he thought. "This is the way to acquire wisdom."[12] He lived a life of extreme austerity and self-mortification, torturing his own body, for six years. First, he ate very little food, like "a handful of soup" a day.[13] There was even a time when he tried eating only a single grain of rice a day. For extra humor points, he also said, "You may think the rice grain was bigger at that time, but no, it was at most the same size as now."[14] (Yes, this is actually recorded in the ancient Buddhist scriptures, I kid you not. The Buddha had a great sense of humor.)

After a while, things got pretty bad. By his own description, "Because of eating so little my limbs became like the jointed segments of vine stems or bamboo stems, . . . my ribs jutted out, my eyes sank far down in their sockets, my scalp shriveled and withered, my belly skin adhered to my backbone; thus if I touched my belly skin I encountered my backbone and if I touched my backbone I encountered my belly skin. Because of eating so little, if I defecated or urinated, I fell over on my face there. And, if I tried to ease my body by rubbing my limbs with my hands, the hair, rotted at its roots, fell from my body as I rubbed." Ouch.

He also tried "breathless meditation," which means holding his breath for long periods of time, until he had severe headaches and extreme bodily pains, presumably due to oxygen deprivation. "There were violent pains in my head, just as if a strong man were tightening a tough leather strap around my head as a headband. There was a violent burning in my body, just as if two strong men were to seize a weaker man by both arms and roast him over a pit of hot coals . . ." No, that didn't work out so well either.

Six long years of extreme austerity and self-mortification later, with absolutely nothing to show for it, Siddhattha reflected on how he should proceed. He realized that torturing one's own body does not bring about the greater wisdom that leads to the end of all suffering. As he reflected, he suddenly remembered the incident at the plowing festival when he was a young child. The adults were all distracted by the festive activities; they left him alone, and he sat, meditated, and went into the meditative state known as the "first jhāna," a state of meditative concentration filled with inner joy. As he reflected, he asked himself, "Why should I be afraid of the inner joy brought about by the first jhāna? That joy has nothing to do with sensual pleasure or unwholesome mental states, so I should not be afraid of it." This is actually a vitally important practical insight, as we shall see in Chapter 8.

In a poetic way, my friends, we can say this was the exact moment Buddhism started. It was the moment Siddhattha decided that he would turn away from self-torture, and, more important, that he would turn toward a very specific kind of joy: the wholesome spiritual joy that comes from letting go.[15] Better still, this joy is accessible to everyone—so accessible that even a young child can experience it! It would be on the foundation of this joy that Siddhattha would attain full enlightenment. You will find in this book that wholesome spiritual joy threads through the practice of Buddhism. You will also find that this joy is highly accessible even to modern people like you and me.

Siddhattha decided that the first jhāna was his right stepping stone toward his journey to full enlightenment. But to get back into meditation practice, he needed to nourish his body back to health, so he decided to accept food from donors, including a meal of milk-rice offered by a local villager, a young milkmaid called Sujata.

There is a lovely mythical story that is not supported by the canonical texts, but is widely told and appears on wall murals in many Buddhist temples. According to the story, Siddhattha was physically so emaciated at the end of his austerities that when he tried to bathe in a river, he was unable to climb back out. He started to drown. As he was drowning, Sujata saw him and pulled him out of the river, thus saving his life. Sujata was actually there to give an offering of milk-rice to a local tree god, but after she rescued him, she was so impressed with his resolve for enlightenment that she gave the offering to him instead to support his quest. Hence, according to this version, we might not even have Buddhism if not for Sujata's heroism. Everyday heroes surround us.[16]

Siddhattha's five followers saw him eating solid food and thought that he had given up on his noble search. They felt disappointed and disgusted, and they decided to abandon him. I imagine they might have felt conned. If Koṇḍañña were living in modern times, he might tell his friends sarcastically to start calling him "Conned-añña."

But Siddhattha's true path had finally begun, and nothing could stop him. He sat under a tree and began his meditation. First, he abided in the first jhāna, where his mind was concentrated, stable, calm, serene, and filled with inner joy. Next, he further refined his mind and progressed into increasingly deeper jhānas (see Chapter 8 for a detailed discussion on the jhānas) until he reached the fourth jhāna, a state of profound meditative concentration characterized by perfect equanimity and "mindfulness purified by equanimity." Using that highly refined state of mind, Siddhattha investigated deep into the nature of suffering and freedom from suffering.

That was a genius move, Siddhattha's great pioneering innovation. Other people had mastered meditative concentration too, but Siddhattha pioneered making use of it as a tool to investigate deeply into the nature of the mind in order to develop profound insights.[17] Hence, he was able to develop complete insight into the nature of suffering and liberation from suffering.

By third watch of the night, Siddhattha had gained what was called the three kinds of clear knowledge (in Pali: *vijjā*): the knowledge of his own past lives, the knowledge of how beings pass away and take rebirth in accordance with their karma, and the knowledge of the destruction of mental corruptions (in Pali: *āsava*). In doing so, he penetrated completely into the nature of suffering and had discovered complete liberation from suffering. "Ignorance was banished and true knowledge arose, darkness was banished and light arose." Siddhattha had achieved perfect enlightenment. **From this moment on, Siddhattha would be known as the Buddha, the Enlightened One**. He was thirty-five.

The word *buddha* relates to the word *budh*, which primarily means "to know, to understand." It also means "to blossom" (said of a flower) or "to awaken" (from sleep). In this context, the primary meaning pertains: the Buddha is "the One Who Has Understood."[10] In popular usage, *Buddha* is often translated as the "Enlightened One," or the "Awakened One." Siddhattha is referred to as the Buddha with a capital *B* because buddhas are so rare there is only one in the known history of the world. Uruvela, the place where the Buddha achieved perfect enlightenment, would later be known as Bodhgaya, in honor of the Buddha.

When Mara Met Siddhattha

Students of religion may find one thing very peculiar about the Buddha's enlightenment story: it does not involve any god at all. In the Bible, for example, God appeared directly in front of Abraham, and revealed Himself to Moses through a burning bush. In contrast, there was no divine revelation in Buddhism; instead, the Buddha's entire path to perfect enlightenment was one of training and investigation. Here, you begin to see the nontheistic nature of Buddhism.

There is actually a popular mythical version of the story of the Buddha's enlightenment, one that young Buddhists learn in religious education.[19] Even this mythical version is nontheistic, in the sense that no god is required for enlightenment. In this version Siddhattha sat under a fig tree that would later be known as the Bodhi Tree. He vowed not to stand up until he achieved full enlightenment, saying to himself, "May skin, indeed, and sinews, and bones wilt away, may flesh and blood in my body dry up, but till I attain to complete enlightenment this seat I will not leave!" The arch-demon Mara, the Buddhist personification of all things bad, became aware of what was happening and was determined to put a stop to it. Why did Mara bother? Because he is the Lord of Death, the Chief of Demons, the Buddhist equivalent of the Devil, so it's kind of his job to create trouble.

Mara tried to stop Siddhattha in ways that may remind you of a battle scene in Japanese anime. First, Mara gathered a huge army of scary demons surrounding Siddhattha to frighten him, but Siddhattha was unimpressed.

Mara mounted a huge war elephant the size of a small mountain, and he gave himself a thousand arms, each holding a different weapon. Siddhattha remained unimpressed.

Mara then attacked with his superpowers. Siddhattha protected himself from each attack by meditating on the practice of wisdom and compassion known as the "ten perfections."[20] Mara conjured up a powerful whirlwind, but by the time it reached Siddhattha, it barely moved the hem of his robe. Mara conjured up a mighty rainstorm, and Siddhattha's robes got a little wet. Mara attacked Siddhattha by raining rocks on him, and then swords, and then spears, and then arrows, and then fireballs, and then his magic javelin. Each time, Siddhattha transformed them into flowers. By the third or fourth round, Siddhattha probably collected enough flowers to start a flower export business.

Finally, Mara demanded his due as a major god. He declared that only a major god like himself had the right to claim the seat of enlightenment, not a mere mortal like Siddhattha. As proof, Mara asked aloud for witnesses, and every soldier in his army shouted back, "I am his witness!" Mara challenged Siddhattha, "Who is your witness?" Siddhattha gently touched the earth with his right hand, signifying, "the earth is my witness." The earth shook in agreement. With that, Siddhattha defeated Mara. Mara vanished with his army. This is the story behind the very many statues of the Buddha sitting in a meditative posture with his right hand gently touching the ground.

Siddhattha continued his meditation undistracted by Mara. By the third watch of the night, he had achieved perfect enlightenment. From that moment on, Siddhattha would be known as the Buddha.

Not long after, Mara's three daughters tried seducing the Buddha. It didn't work at all, since he had already gone beyond all sensual desire. Each of them then transformed into a hundred beautiful women of different ages to seduce the Buddha, but that didn't work either. Eventually, they gave up and went home, but at least they could say they literally tried one hundred times harder.

This mythical tale of the Buddha's enlightenment is a fun story filled with all the right special effects, but Soryu reminds us that, like most mythical stories passed down through the generations, this one also has an important instructional purpose. On the path to enlightenment, one may encounter fear, because part of the practice requires abiding in a mind of openness, self-honesty, and letting go. The closer to enlightenment, the stronger those qualities become, and the grasping mind may feel that it is losing what it understands to be safety and security: the ability to grasp and hold on. Moreover, as the mind lets go, it processes deep memories of vulnerability, facing them in visual and bodily experience. The grasping mind reacts to all that with fear. The story involving Mara and his demon army alludes to this experience. Fortunately, that fear can be overcome. In the story, Siddhattha overcame Mara's attacks with meditation on wisdom and compassion, and you will find that in real life, it is precisely those same qualities that will allow you to overcome the barrier of fear and break through into enlightenment.

In ancient Buddhists texts, the Buddha is usually introduced with his full set of epithets as the Tathāgata, the Arahant, the perfectly enlightened one, accomplished in true knowledge and conduct, well-liberated, knower of the world, unsurpassed leader of persons to be tamed, teacher of gods and humans, the Buddha, the exalted one.[21] But if a buddha were to live in modern times, I think his friends would just call him Bud.

The Buddha's Findings: The Middle Way and the Four Noble Truths

After his enlightenment, the Buddha spent seven weeks in Uruvela.[22] Some of the time was spent consolidating his teachings; specifically, the teachings on dependent origination (see Chapter 10) were formulated during the second week. Most of that time, however, was spent abiding in the state of "bliss of freedom" (in Pali: *vimutti sukha*). After seven weeks, he considered whether he should teach the Dharma or not. He was inclined toward not teaching, because teaching would be "tiresome and troublesome."[23] However, he also recognized all the suffering in the world, and saw that living beings are capable of resolving it. Consequently, he felt compelled by his infinite compassion to offer the Dharma to the world. Soryu and I, in both a lighthearted and awe-inspired way, think of him in that moment as having accepted his responsibility as a buddha.

But who to teach first? The obvious candidates were Alara Kalama and Uddaka Ramaputta, the Buddha's former teachers. Unfortunately, both of them had already passed away. Next on the list were the Buddha's five original disciples. The Buddha found out they were residing at the Deer Park at Isipatana in Benares, so he set out to Benares to meet them. It was there that the Buddha would deliver his first major discourse.

As the Buddha was approaching the Deer Park, the five ascetics saw him at a distance and made a deal with each other not to show the Buddha any respect. Why? Because in their eyes, the Buddha had "reverted to a life of abundance" (for eating solid food, for nirvana's sake!) and had given up on the noble search. So all five pretended to look cool and tried to ignore the approaching Buddha. As the Buddha got near, however, something about him deeply touched and impressed them. Without saying a word, all five ascetics spontaneously broke their agreement with each other; they "received his bowl and robe, made ready a seat, and brought water for washing his feet." After they settled down, the Buddha began his discourse.

> Monks, these two extremes should not be followed by one who has gone forth into homelessness [seeking greater wisdom]: the pursuit of sensual pleasures, which is low, vulgar, the way of worldlings, ignoble, unbeneficial; and the pursuit of self-mortification, which is painful, ignoble, unbeneficial. Avoiding either of these extremes, the Tathāgata is awakened to the Middle Way, which gives rise to vision, knowledge, peace, enlightenment, and nirvana.[24]

"The Tathāgata" is the poetic way the Buddha refers to himself in third person. It literally means either "Thus Come" or "Thus Gone." It alludes to the bold authenticity and simplicity of the "thusness" of a fully enlightened being.

For every discourse given by the Buddha, it is useful to know the context. One of the extraordinary qualities of the Buddha's teachings is that they are useful in every context. But the cherry on top is that knowing the context of the original teaching makes it even more useful. Therefore, the compilers of the texts generally recorded where and to whom each teaching was given. The context here is that the five ascetics held the then-popular belief that self-mortification brings about greater wisdom, which is why the first thing the Buddha did was to bust that myth, while also mentioning that the pursuit of sensual pleasures is equally unbeneficial for one seeking greater wisdom. Though this insight is useful even for modern people like us, it was probably more useful for those five ascetics, because, on an average weekday, you and I don't wake up in the morning thinking, "I'm going to torture my body all day today to gain greater wisdom." Still, the Buddha's teaching was henceforth known as the **Middle Way**, because it avoids overloading oneself with bodily pleasure or bodily pain.

In the rest of the discourse, the Buddha covered topics central to all of Buddhism: the nature of suffering, the cause of suffering, the cessation of suffering (nirvana), and the path to liberation from suffering. These are known as the **Four Noble Truths**.

Back in the Chapter 1, we mentioned that Dharma is universal law pertaining to suffering and freedom from suffering, and that we are specifically interested in these four subdomains of Dharma:

1. The nature of suffering

2. The causes of suffering

3. The cessation of suffering

4. The methods for ending suffering

Each of the Four Noble Truths addresses one of the four subdomains of Dharma, in the same order. We will explore each of the Four Noble Truths in the next four chapters.

The Abbot's Commentary by Soryu Forall

The story of the Buddha is primarily useful as a template to guide us in how to move forward with our own lives. It is helpful to us in the same way that knowing admirable people is helpful to us: we see them live in good ways, watch them make decisions that are virtuous and brave and inspiring, and we hope that we may do the same. The story about the Buddha may or may not be a fully accurate historical representation of a person who lived twenty-five hundred years ago, but it is definitely an accurate representation of how we should live today. As a Buddhist teacher, I don't use it so much as history, but as instruction. It tells us how real people attain enlightenment. We are real people, and we should attain enlightenment.

In essence, there are only four facts you need to know here: The Buddha was a person. You are a person. He did it. You can do it.

CHAPTER THREE

Honey, Did You Order Suffering Pre-Installed?

The First Noble Truth

Suffering an Extremely Lucky Birth

Imagine being born into an extremely lucky circumstance. Would you still have any suffering?

Hongli had one of the luckiest births in the history of the world. He was born to a family of extreme wealth and power: his grandfather was the great Emperor Kangxi of China. Young Hongli quickly became the emperor's favorite grandson. Hongli was also blessed with genetic gifts: he was highly intelligent and athletically gifted, reputed to be an outstanding fighter and hunter. But wait, it got even better. In 1735, Hongli became Emperor Qianlong of China at the lucky age of twenty-four: old enough to be an adult, but young enough to really enjoy being emperor. Better still, he became emperor at the height of China's prosperity thanks to the conscientious governance of the previous two emperors: his father and his grandfather.

Imagine being young, healthy, highly intelligent, athletic, attractive, and having absolute rule over a prosperous, powerful country representing roughly one-third of humanity and one-third of the world's GDP. But wait, it was even better than that. Emperor Qianlong had a perfect wife. Empress Fuca was known to be beautiful, kind, intelligent, talented, and virtuous. Qianlong was blessed with a genuinely loving relationship with his wife, which was rare among ancient rulers. He also had dozens of concubines, which many people may regard as lucky.

Can a man who had everything have any suffering? As it turns out, yes. Qianlong's favorite son was the one he had with his beloved empress, and he so loved this son he named him crown prince. That son died at age eight of smallpox. A few years later, the couple had another son, and again, he was so beloved that Qianlong named him crown prince. That son too died of smallpox, before he turned two. The empress was so devastated she fell into depression and died of illness just three months later. That had a devastating impact on Qianlong, and we know that because he had a great change in personality. Before the death of Empress Fuca, Qianlong was a wise, conscientious, compassionate, and highly competent emperor. Immediately after, he became murderously cruel, greedy, and increasingly corrupt and incompetent. He spent the rest of his life mostly squandering the national prosperity painstakingly built up by his father and grandfather. In 1799, Qianlong himself died at the age of eighty-seven.[1]

Even Emperor Qianlong, beneficiary of possibly the luckiest birth in the history of the world, was subject to the suffering of illness, old age, and death, both his own and of those dearest to him. So there you have it. Wish for any lucky birth, you will still suffer. Welcome, my friends, to the chapter on suffering.

Dukkha Is Suffering-Plus-Plus

The lesson from the story of Qianlong and countless others with lucky human births is clear, that no matter how lucky our birth, we are all still subject to the same suffering: aging, illness, death, separation, not getting what we want, and getting what we don't want. The great Egyptian pharaoh Ramses II, for example, another absolute ruler of great wealth, renown, and power, was known to have died suffering severe gingivitis and serious tooth decay, which means he probably suffered enormous pain in his final years.

That was how the Buddha started with his prescription for suffering: by first making a statement on suffering. The Buddha continued on with his first discourse (continuing from the previous chapter),

> Now monks, this is the truth of dukkha: birth is dukkha, aging is dukkha, illness is dukkha, death is dukkha. To be with what you do not want is dukkha. To be separated from what you want is dukkha. To not get what you want is dukkha. In brief, the five aggregates subject to grasping are dukkha.

This statement about dukkha is known in Buddhism as the **First Noble Truth**.

OK, but what is dukkha?

The most common English translation of dukkha is "**suffering**." However, dukkha is significantly broader than suffering. When we say suffering, we usually mean one or both of two things:

- The experience of physical or emotional pain

- The experience of aversion in reaction to physical or emotional pain

Note that pain does not necessarily have to be caused by the presence of stimuli; it can also be caused by the absence of stimuli. For example, if you desperately crave something or someone, their absence can be a cause of emotional pain.

While dukkha definitely includes suffering, it also includes a general sense of unsatisfactoriness and imperfection in life. Traditionally, the word *dukkha* is explained as an imperfection in the axle hole of a wheel.[2] If a carriage has a wheel with an axle hole that is improperly centered or misaligned in some way, you don't get a smooth ride. That is dukkha. It is not that the wheel is broken, it is just unsatisfactory. It is for this reason that dukkha is also often translated as "**unsatisfactoriness**." One funny story that is obviously apocryphal but helps me remember: The Buddha was walking with his attendant Ānanda along an Indian highway where horse-drawn carts were going back and forth. One particular cart had an improperly aligned wheel, so the driver was obviously not having a particularly good time. Buddha pointed to that cart and said, "See, Ānanda, that is dukkha." American Buddhist teacher Leigh Brasington half-jokingly suggested translating dukkha to "bummer."[3]

"Master, this car is dukkha."

An alternative but complementary etymology of dukkha comes from a Sanskrit word it is very closely related to: *duḥstha*. *Duḥstha* is a compound of *dus-* ("bad") and *stha* ("to stand"), so it literally means "does not stand well," or "unstable." This relates to an alternative imagery of dukkha as a potter's wheel that is unstable. If you are a potter in ancient India working on large pots with a potter's wheel that is unstable, you are not going to have a particularly good time either. Bummer.

Dukkha is not just about suffering in the present; it also considers suffering in the future. For example, if you have a great, healthy body, someday you will either get sick or get old, and you will no longer have a great body. If you have someone you love, someday either they will change (and/or you will change) and you may fall out of love, or you will be separated because either one of you will die. And if everything in your life is just absolutely perfect (you are rich, powerful, healthy, good-looking, and have the perfect family and career), someday something will change, and/or you will die. That is included in dukkha as well.

Another way to see it: dukkha is not just mere suffering; it also more broadly refers to conditions that cause both present and future suffering, and even more broadly refers to the inherent unsatisfactoriness in most of life's conditions.

That general inherent unsatisfactoriness gives rise to a wise but almost nonsensical saying popular among some Buddhist teachers: "Even sukha is dukkha." *Sukha* is often translated as "happiness," "bliss," "ease," or "pleasure."

Yes, all good things. It is the literal direct opposite of dukkha. Remember that dukkha gives you the imagery of the axle hole of a wheel not being perfectly aligned, thus giving you a rough ride. In contrast, sukha denotes perfect alignment of the axle hole, thus giving you a smooth ride. Yet some Buddhist teachers like to say "even sukha is dukkha," which when translated fully to English is even more nonsensical: "Even happiness is suffering." Huh?

The reason even sukha is dukkha is: Whatever conditions that give rise to sukha will eventually change. All sukha is impermanent. Even the most perfectly aligned wheel will eventually misalign, or wear down, or break. Hence, even sukha is unsatisfactory (dukkha), and it can at best be a temporary solution to dukkha, not the ultimate solution. If sukha were the ultimate solution to dukkha, this book might have ended right here and you might be wondering why you are paying good money for such a short book (thus breaking your sukha for the day). The true solution to dukkha lies instead in the other three noble truths, as we shall see.

For the purpose of convenience, I will generally use the word *suffering* instead of *dukkha* in the rest of this book. But know that when I do, I'm not just referring to pain; I'm usually referring to the broader sense of unsatisfactoriness as alluded to by the word *dukkha*. I will also use the word *unsatisfactoriness* instead of *suffering* in places where the context makes it necessary.

Five Aggregates

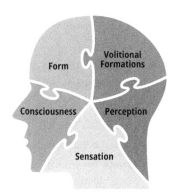

The Buddha ended his statement of the First Noble Truth with the sentence, "In brief, the five aggregates subject to grasping are suffering (dukkha)."[4]

Simply put, the five aggregates are the five physical and mental factors that, in combination, are experienced as a self. They are:

1. Form

2. Sensation or feeling

3. Perception

4. Volitional formations

5. Consciousness[5]

Form is simply the physical body.[6]

Sensation is the experience arising from the contact between sense object and sense organ, for example, when visual form contacts the eyes, or sound contacts the ears, and so on. However, *vedanā*, the word translated to "sensation," carries one other important aspect: whether a sensory experience is pleasant, unpleasant, or neither.[7] In fact, remembering that Buddhism is primarily (or solely) concerned with liberation from all suffering, this aspect is the most important among everything that comes under the umbrella of the "sensation" aggregate.

Perception is the mind picking out important characteristics of what is being sensed, and also recognizing that which had previously been perceived. You can think of this as like a computer program that recognizes cats in pictures: it figures out which parts of the picture contain cat features like cat eyes and paws, it recognizes the whole cat, and it picks out important characteristics of the cat it sees, such as "white Persian" or "wears boots and hat, carries a sword."

Volitional formations are what the mind constructs, including its reactions to what it perceives. They include thoughts and emotions, things that enable the initiation of action (e.g., intentions, planning), and the actions themselves. We once had an American friend visiting Singapore for the first time. Rehearsals for National Day celebrations were going on. Part of the celebration was having fighter jets fly low over downtown with their massive sonic booms. Our friend was in the part of downtown far enough from the rehearsals not to know it was happening, but close enough to get a full experience of sonic boom from a F-15 fighter formation flying right above.

From her perspective, she was just walking along when, out of nowhere, there was this sudden huge BOOM surrounding her. She froze, her face turned white, and she thought, "This is how I'm going to die." To her utter confusion, the Singaporeans around her stopped whatever they were doing, looked up, and cheered out loud. We had to explain it to her to calm her nerves. Those thoughts involving "this is how I'm going to die," those emotions involving fear and confusion, and then all her laughter after she figured out the comedy of what just happened—*those* are volitional formations.

Volitional formations also affect what is perceived, so yes, there is at least one feedback loop in the system. For example, if you have good feelings for somebody, all you can perceive about them are their attractive aspects, but if you come to have bad feelings for the same person, all you can perceive about them are their unattractive aspects. That last sentence is the summary of the vast majority of romantic relationships in the world. Emotions and other volitional formations always affect perception.

Finally, consciousness is "that which knows," "that which discerns," or "that which cognizes."[8] Buddhist teacher and author Ajahn Brahm beautifully depicts consciousness as "the screen upon which all these sentient experiences are played out."[9] Soryu likes to remind us that as lovely as this analogy is, it fails to relay the insight that consciousness is an active process, not a passive object. Therefore, I might say it is more like an LED screen: it appears to be only passively playing out a movie fed to it, but behind it is active processing.

But Where Do You Draw the Line?

Allow me to confess a dirty little secret: with the possible exception of form, there is no consensus among Buddhist teachers on the precise definition of each aggregate. The definitions given in the ancient texts do not allow us to draw precise boundaries between aggregates. Hence, Buddhist teachers all have definitions of the five aggregates that are similar but do not overlap 100 percent.

For example, most teachers I know place thinking squarely in the "volitional formations" bucket, but one puts most of it in the "perception" bucket.

Teachers disagree on whether recognizing the features of an object happens at the level of perception, or consciousness, or both. The definitions of the five aggregates I present in the section above is my own curated collection of what I have learned from a variety of teachers and books. Hence, do not be too alarmed if you find a Buddhist teacher agreeing with only 84 percent of how I define the aggregates; that teacher probably knows the same dirty little secret I just shared with you, so we're good.

It turns out that precise boundaries between the mental aggregates cannot actually be drawn. Sāriputta, the Buddha's wisest disciple, made this point when he stated that, "Sensation, perception, and consciousness are conjoined. It is impossible to separate each of these states from the others in order to describe the difference between them."[10]

There is so much codependence and there are so many feedback loops between the mental aggregates that it is probably impossible to draw clear lines between them. There is a fascinating example that you can immediately verify for yourself. Try this: Bring attention to your scalp. Notice tingly sensations in your scalp? Notice those feelings were not there when you were not paying attention? Why? According to neuroscience, we have brain circuits that usually inhibit those tingly sensations, and when we pay attention to the scalp, those circuits are temporarily turned off, which is why you suddenly feel those sensations. This is an example of conscious attention influencing sensation. We usually think of sensation as raw data to be further processed by perception and consciousness, but even sensation itself is subject to feedback loops. There are feedback loops everywhere.

Trying to draw clear boundaries between mental aggregates is like trying to draw precise boundaries between seas. For example, the Coral Sea and the Tasman Sea, located right next to each other, are positionally distinct enough that you can label them separately on a map, but you also cannot draw an exact line and say everything this side of the line is the Coral Sea, and everything that side is the Tasman Sea. Well, you can draw an artificial line in your head, but there are really no natural boundaries between the seas, because at the end of the day, it's really just one huge continuous body of water. It is the same with the mental aggregates: they are distinct enough that we can roughly label them, but also intertwined enough that there are really no real precise boundaries discernible between them.

"Arrr—draw a line on the water, savvy?"

In any case, the precise definitions for the aggregates do not really matter. Always remember the first principle: that Buddhism is primarily (or solely) concerned with liberation from all suffering. Suffering relates to the grasping to the five aggregates, and where the exact boundaries of each aggregate lie does not change the nature of the grasping. Hence, we really only need to focus on the aspects of the five aggregates that relate to suffering and liberation from suffering, and those the Buddha clarified precisely and emphatically.

Like Grabbing Hold of Water

The Buddha taught that the five aggregates subject to grasping are suffering. What does that mean? One way to think of it is like trying to grab hold of water with your hands to drink it. No matter how hard you try grabbing it, you cannot hold it; it will flow away. That desperation to grab hold of water is the grasping, and the suffering.

In the same way, we want our experiences to be a certain way. We want our own form (body) to be a certain way: attractive, healthy, and fit and all. We want to have certain sensations. We want to perceive certain things. We want to have certain emotions, or some particular ways to see ourselves. We want to live in eternal bliss. In addition to the wanting, there is the not wanting: we do not want certain bodily configurations, or certain sensations, or to perceive certain things. Unfortunately, we do not have full sovereignty over the five aggregates; we cannot always make them into what we want. In that sense, the five aggregates are unreliable.

That desperation of wanting, and not wanting, *that* is the grasping. To grasp onto something unreliable is suffering.

There is a solution. In the case of holding water, the solution begins with developing an understanding into the nature of water, the nature of grabbing, and the nature of hands. With that insight, you will find that grabbing it does no good for you at all. You abandon grabbing. Instead, you find a solution based on your insight that goes beyond grabbing, which is to cup your hands. That way, you can hold and drink the water skillfully.

"Which one of us is going to tell him?"

In the same way, the solution to suffering begins with developing an understanding into the nature of suffering, the nature of grasping, and the nature of the mind. With that insight, you will find that grasping does no good for you at all. You abandon grasping. Instead, you will find a more skillful way to relate to the aggregates that goes beyond grasping.

Life Is Not All Suffering, and That Is a Problem

It is common among Buddhists to erroneously claim that the First Noble Truth proclaims, "Life is suffering." That mistake is understandable; I catch myself doing it frequently too.

There are two problems with that claim. First, according to the canonical texts, the Buddha never actually said that. What he said instead was, "the five aggregates subject to grasping are suffering."

Second, saying "life is suffering" gives the impression that life is exclusively painful, but it is not. There is indeed a lot of pleasure in life, and that can become a problem, because it blinds us to suffering and traps us in situations of inevitable future suffering.

This topic came up in a conversation between the Buddha and a man called Mahāli. Mahāli asked why "beings are defiled [with suffering]," and the Buddha answered, "If, Mahāli, the five aggregates were exclusively suffering, beings would not become enamored with them. But because the five aggregates are pleasurable, immersed in pleasure, steeped in pleasure, beings become enamored with them. By being enamored with them, they are captivated by them, and by being captivated they are defiled."[11]

In other words, if life were exclusively painful, beings would know to seek a solution. If life were exclusively pleasure (and never any suffering) for all of eternity, that is obviously not a problem. The problem is that suffering is mixed with enough pleasure to enamor us, causing us to be blind to the suffering, and trapping us here in situations where future suffering is inevitable. That is the problem.

In a separate discourse, Sāriputta, the Buddha's wisest disciple, illustrated this point with a rather startling parable.[12] There was a murderer who wanted to rob from a rich man, but that rich man was protected by bodyguards. What to do? The murderer decided to become a perfect servant for the rich man. He would "rise up before him, retire after him, do whatever he wants, be agreeable in conduct and endearing in speech." Eventually, the rich man would come to regard him as a bosom friend. Once he gained the complete trust of the rich man, he would cut him down with a knife when he found him alone, and rob him.

The entire time the murderer was the rich man's servant, the rich man did not see the murderer as what he really was; he thought he was a bosom friend and perfect servant, because he was good in many obvious ways. In the same way, Sāriputta said, because the five aggregates give us pleasure, we become enamored and do not see the five aggregates as they really are: causes of suffering.

The solution is wisdom. With wisdom, we see the nature of suffering as it is, and then use that insight as a propellant out of suffering. The Buddha continued with his conversation with Mahāli, "But because the five aggregates bring suffering, [wise] beings experience disenchantment toward them. Experiencing disenchantment, they become liberated from lust, and through liberation from lust they are purified [from suffering]. This, Mahāli, is a cause and condition for the purification of beings."

Turns Out You Didn't Have to Order the Self-Destruct Option

Imagine living in a weird world where cars come with a self-destruct button that you can order as an add-on. It's a big red button right beside the cupholders that says, "Self-Destruct, DO NOT PRESS." If you press the button, the car blows up, with you in it. Of course you don't want to buy that. Duh.

Your power in this situation is that you do not actually have to buy the self-destruct add-on. Or, if you end up buying a secondhand car with this add-on, you can have it taken off, since it's only an add-on, and all add-ons can be uninstalled. This is the same power we have over our suffering: it turns out we can choose not to order it. And when we do actually have it, it turns out to be an add-on that can be uninstalled.

Guest artist: Natalie Tsang

In this chapter, we talked about the various types and causes of suffering in life. When you are knee-deep into such a discussion, it is easy to mistakenly consider suffering to be deeply embedded in the system of our experience when, in fact, it is actually an add-on. If you understand the system well enough, and you're equipped with the right tools (e.g., the right screwdriver and all), you can remove any add-on. Buddhism is about helping you understand the mind and suffering well enough, and giving you the right tools, to allow you to uninstall suffering. In the rest of this book, you will acquire the understanding and the right tools.

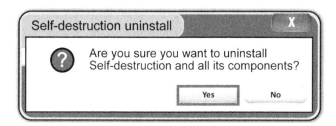

But even before learning to uninstall the self-destruct feature in your car, there is an essential first step: facing the fact that it is actually there. Imagine you bought yourself one of those cars with the self-destruct add-on. Why? Because it is 20 percent off (just for the add-on, not for the whole car!), and it is really hard to resist 20 percent off, I know. Trust me, I know. But you have buyer's remorse very soon after that, especially considering how you're going to have to explain to your spouse why you paid extra for a self-destruct button. What to do? Well, you can always pretend it is not there, and put duct tape over it to hide it from your spouse or something. Unfortunately, pretending it is not there will not solve the problem. Every time you put your large drink in the cupholder, you could miss and accidentally trigger self-destruction regardless of whether you pretend it is not there. The only real solution is to uninstall it, and there is no way to begin without first facing the fact that it is there.

In the same way, in uninstalling suffering, there is an essential first step: facing the fact that it is there. Soryu has a powerful way of articulating it, so I'm just going to quote him:

> The path begins with a willingness to face our problems.
>
> This is so hard, and so unusual, that the Buddha made it the First Noble Truth. He could have chosen anything as the starting point of his teaching. He could have begun with the goal, nirvana. Or he could have started by telling people how his teachings would help them get what they want. But he started by asking people to face their problems.
>
> If, whatever problem arises throughout the day, you are willing to face it, and wish to understand it, you understand the transformative power of the First Noble Truth. To face suffering begins to transform suffering into happiness.

As the Buddha says, our suffering is the direct result of our grasping to the five aggregates. Things are impermanent, yes, but the suffering does not come from things being impermanent; it comes from our desperate grasping to the hope that some things are permanent. All five aggregates everywhere are unreliable, yes, but again, our suffering does not come from things being unreliable; it comes from our grasping to things despite them being unreliable. In contrast, not having to grasp to the five aggregates gives us perfect freedom, total security, and the highest happiness. We will explore these topics in detail in the coming chapters.

The Abbot's Commentary by Soryu Forall

I tell people that the world isn't trustworthy, that if you depend on anything external, you will find that it is unreliable and unfulfilling, and if you grasp to it, you will get hurt. I tell people that their inner world isn't trustworthy either, that whether you depend on intelligent thoughts or powerful emotions, you will find that they are unreliable and unfulfilling, and if you grasp to them, you will get hurt. They often think I'm pessimistic, maybe even mean. In reality, this is optimistic, because I'm telling people that when they stop grasping, they find freedom from suffering. They find a true happiness that doesn't depend on anything. It's not just optimistic, it's uplifting.

It also says something wonderful about you personally. If suffering is not inherent, you are not inherently flawed. You are not fundamentally broken. Suffering is not necessary. Suffering is not you.

Since it's not you, you can do something about it. What is to be done about suffering? It is to be resolved. See this clearly, and it will change your life. Every time suffering arises, you will feel exhilarated, because you know what to do now: resolve it! And you'll feel confident, because you know that it can be resolved. You can always do that which must be done. Buddhism offers the instructions on how to do it.

CHAPTER FOUR

Suffering Is All About Cause and Effect

The Second Noble Truth

How to Stop a Bomb

It was the final climatic scene of the movie. A huge bomb was about to blow up an entire building. The clock was in its final countdown. All attempts by the hero to disarm the bomb had failed. They were mere seconds away from the explosion. What to do?

Being the jester in the audience, I shouted, "Pull the plug!" I was just joking, of course. My friends chuckled. In the final seconds, the hero decided to run, and he tripped over a wire. It turned out that the bomb's timer was connected to the power socket, and by tripping over the wire the hero accidentally pulled the plug and stopped the countdown. Everybody was saved! The cinema audience roared into laughter. Yes, that was the infamous final bomb scene of the comedy movie *The Naked Gun 2½: The Smell of Fear*.

It may seem absurd that such a huge problem in the movie could have such a simple solution, which is why it was so funny. What if there is an analogue of it in real life? In our actual lives, we face this overwhelming and enormous problem of suffering. Imagine that, through the Buddha's sheer brilliance, he discovered an actionable cause, and that by taking actions on that one cause, *you* can solve that huge problem of suffering. That is what this chapter is about.

Where Suffering Stops Being About Religion and Starts Being About Cause and Effect

In his first discourse, the Buddha explained the causes of suffering. Here, he only identified one cause: craving. This statement, that the cause of suffering is craving, is the **Second Noble Truth**. Within this simple statement is a major life-changing insight and a genius move.

The life-changing insight is that **suffering has causes**. Suffering is neither inherent nor arbitrary. Instead, it is subject to the universal laws of cause and effect, just like everything else in the natural world. If suffering were not subject to the laws of cause and effect, then there's really not much we can do about it. However, if it is indeed subject to cause and effect, then all you have to do is find and then eliminate the causes of suffering.

Of the long list of causes, the Buddha strung it to one necessary cause: *taṇhā*, which literally means "thirst," but is often translated as "**craving**."[1]

That is the Buddha's genius move: he found *one* necessary condition for *all* suffering. Imagine that you are able to identify a complete list of, say, 127 causes of suffering. Then, people who want to eliminate suffering have to deal with 127 different things. Then, imagine that instead of doing that, you find a single necessary condition for all suffering. A "necessary condition" is a condition that needs to exist for something to happen. For example, to have a fire, you need oxygen and fuel, so oxygen and fuel are each a necessary condition for the fire. To extinguish the fire, you need only to take away either *one* of the necessary conditions: the oxygen or the fuel. In the same way, if there is a necessary condition for suffering, then take that away and suffering goes away. And the Buddha identified that condition: craving.

But wait, there's more. If your goal is to end suffering, then finding a necessary condition for suffering is not good enough; that condition also needs to be **actionable**. That means whatever the necessary condition for suffering that you find, there must be actions that can be taken to eliminate it. Otherwise, it's just a complete waste of everybody's time. This challenge is so difficult it takes a genius to solve, and the Buddha was that genius.

Earlier, in Chapter 1, we talked about Dharma being "universal law pertaining to suffering and liberation from suffering." In that context, Soryu and I both think the Second Noble Truth is the linchpin of the Four Noble Truths. By clearly stating that "the cause of suffering is craving," the Buddha takes liberation from suffering out of the exclusive domain of religion and mysticism and puts it squarely into the folder labeled "natural laws of cause and effect." This is why understanding cause and effect is central to Buddhism, and is in turn why Buddhism has such a strong secular and scientific attitude. Furthermore, it enables the construction of universal and secular solutions to suffering, which is contained in the Fourth Noble Truth (which we will talk about later, in Chapter 6).

As usual, the Buddha had a humorous way to illustrate the point regarding cause and effect. He said that if a man wanted milk but instead of pulling on the cow's udder he pulled on the cow's horns, he would get no milk.[2] Why? Because of the natural laws of cause and effect with regard to procuring milk. In the same way, the path to liberation from suffering begins with understanding the natural laws of cause and effect with regard to suffering, and then taking suitable action in accordance with those laws.

Guest artist: Natalie Tsang

In the first discourse, the Buddha went into a little more detail and identified three specific types of craving. They are:

1. Craving for sensual pleasure

2. Craving for existence

3. Craving for nonexistence[3]

Craving for Sensual Pleasure

"Craving for sensual pleasure" is actually significantly broader than what a typical modern reader may have in mind. Yes, "craving for sensual pleasure" includes the grasping for things that are pleasant to the five senses ("I want, I want, I want!"), but it also includes the flip side, which is aversion to things that are unpleasant to the five senses ("I don't want, I don't want, I don't want!"). In addition, Buddhist psychology classifies the thinking and attending aspects of mind, *mano*, as a sense base. In the same way that the eye senses sights and the ear senses sounds, mano senses thoughts. Hence, the pleasant (or unpleasant) feelings associated with thoughts count as objects of sensual pleasure as well. This includes pleasant or unpleasant thoughts relating to ego, such as "I am superior" or "I am inferior," or pleasant or unpleasant thoughts relating to other people, such as "I love him," "I hate him," "he loves me," or "he hates me."

In short, the domain for "craving for sensual pleasure" includes the grasping and aversion to all pleasant and unpleasant experiences relating to all objects sensed by the six sense bases, including thoughts.

The Buddha gave a rather stark simile to illustrate the suffering caused by craving for sensual pleasure. He compared it to a leper "with sores and blisters on his limbs, being devoured by worms, scratching the scabs off the openings of his wounds with his nails, cauterizing his body over a burning charcoal pit."[4] The leper in this story then went to see a skillful doctor, who cured him of leprosy. After that, he realized that while he was afflicted with leprosy, he felt good when he scratched and burned his skin, but now that he was cured, he realized that to not have leprosy, and to not have a desire to scratch or burn his skin, felt even better, much better. In the same way, someone afflicted with the craving for sensual pleasure feels compelled to gratify that craving, and when he does, he feels good, but once he is cured of that craving, he finds that not having a craving for sensual pleasure feels even better, much better.

As a result of craving for sensual pleasure, we want to have pleasant experiences from the five senses (pleasant sights, sounds, smells, tastes, and touch). We also want to have pleasant thoughts: thinking of ourselves as competent, living a meaningful life, and being loved and admired. If we don't have any of those things, we suffer. If we have the inverse of one of those things—for example, we experience unpleasant smells or tastes, or have unpleasant relationships—we suffer. Even if we have everything pleasant that we want, we have to work hard and make sacrifices to maintain them, and so we suffer. We are afraid to lose what we have, and so we suffer. And even if we keep all our pleasant things, we eventually habituate to them, so we need increasingly stronger pleasant stimuli just to keep the same amount of happiness. And at the end of the day, no matter how perfect our lives, things will change. Every single person we hold dear will die. We will die. We suffer.

Hence, craving for sensual pleasure is guaranteed to cause suffering now, or in the future, or both.

It is important to note that the suffering is not caused by the sensual pleasure per se, but the craving for it. That's why this component of the cause of suffering is not *kama* ("sensual pleasure"), but *kama-taṇhā* ("craving for sensual pleasure"). In day-to-day life, this craving shows up most often in the mistaken but widely held belief that happiness can only come from sensual pleasure. In other words, we can be happy *only* if we experience pleasant sights, smells, sounds, tastes, and touch, and pleasant thoughts arising from having a fluffed ego and desirable relationships, and if we avoid the reverse. The key word is *only*, and that *only* compels us to grasp on desperately to all pleasant things in our lives, and that grasping causes suffering. An antidote for this is experiencing states of bliss that do not depend on having any pleasant sensation or thought, which we will discuss in Chapter 8.

You may be wondering: OK, if the suffering is caused by the craving for sensual pleasure, and not the sensual pleasure per se, then is it possible to experience sensual pleasure without any craving and, therefore, without any suffering? The answer is yes.

Moggallāna, one of the Buddha's two top disciples, gave a discourse where he described what it is like to have sensory experience without suffering. This was during the first night the monks occupied a newly built hall, so Moggallāna skillfully used the building itself as a teaching aid. He called having sensory experience without suffering being "uncorrupted by the senses." He said to the monks, "And how, friends, is one uncorrupted? Take a monk who sees a sight with the eye. If it's pleasant he doesn't hold on to it, and if it's unpleasant he doesn't dislike it. He dwells with mindfulness of the body established and a measureless mind. And he truly understands liberation of mind and liberation by wisdom, where those arisen bad, unskillful qualities cease without remainder."[5]

He repeated the same thing for all the other five senses, and then compared such a mind to a well-constructed building that is designed to be fire-resistant. "Suppose, friends, there is a peaked house or hall built of thickly packed clay and freshly plastered. If a man approaches from any direction with a blazing grass torch, the fire fails to gain access to it, fails to get a hold on it. In the same way, when a monk dwells thus, even if Mara [personifying suffering] approaches him through any of the senses, Mara fails to gain access to him, fails to get a hold on him."

The bad news is to get to *zero* suffering with regard to sensory experience, you need *zero* grasping and aversion, which means *zero* craving, and it could take quite a while to get to zero. The good news is it can occur in degrees, which means that the less you experience pleasantness with grasping and unpleasantness with aversion, the less suffering you experience. The effect can be quite dramatic. Some of the students in my Search Inside Yourself (SIY) course find that with only a few hours of meditation practice, they develop enough of a reduction in grasping and aversion that they gain a meaningful upgrade in their ability to deal with suffering, and that changes their lives.[6]

Craving for Existence and Nonexistence

On the day-to-day level

The last two cravings, craving for existence and craving for nonexistence, can be easily understood on a day-to-day level. Craving for existence means a desperate wanting to stay alive. It shows up commonly as the fear of death. Craving for nonexistence is the opposite, and shows up as suicidal intentions, when life seems so unpleasant you want to die. Both cravings cause suffering. In a very sad way, these two are not mutually exclusive. I know that because when I was suicidal, I suffered from both, simultaneously, all the time.

On the level of meditative experience

These two cravings show up on another level: in meditative experience. What most people are not aware of is that the mind constantly reconstructs a subjective sense of selfness in reaction to sense stimuli and to thoughts. When the mind is sufficiently calm in meditation, there are times and circumstances where the mind is *so* calm it does not construct that subjective sense of selfness, so the sense of selfness fades away. For less experienced meditators, the common reaction to this experience is fear and sometimes panic. The mind clings to the existence of this sense of selfness, and so when it seems to be disappearing, the mind is alarmed. This is craving for existence in action. There are, however, more experienced meditators with the opposite problem. These meditators become accustomed to the fading away of the subjective sense of selfness; they find that when it happens, the mind experiences serenity and joy. And then, when the sense of selfness reappears, it is as if somebody disengaged the mute button on a radio and it suddenly went from silent to full volume—it feels loud and jarring. They get annoyed and wish the sense of selfness to disappear again. That is the craving for nonexistence at this level.

On the cosmological level

Yet another level where these two cravings show up relates to the Buddhist worldview. In talking about the Buddhist worldview, we start venturing into the mystical side of Buddhism. Earlier I mentioned that Buddhism is not free from having a mystical side, and if you want a full, in-depth understanding of Buddhism, you cannot avoid learning about this mystical side. However, I also mentioned that one of many genius moves by the Buddha is that the practices he formulated are so secular and universal they are effective whether or not you buy into the mystical side of things. In any case, I hope your exploration into this side of Buddhism will be as much fun for you as it was for me.

First, it turns out that, yes, there is a concept of heaven and hell in Buddhism. Actually, Buddhism is probably "greedier" than your average religion, because in the Buddhist cosmology, there is not just one heaven but twenty-six realms of heaven, each more refined than the previous one.[7] Thankfully, there is only one hell realm, but I imagine it must be very crowded, because, hey, it is hell.[8]

The most important feature of Buddhist cosmology, in contrast to that from other religions, is the *universality of impermanence*. In Buddhism, all life spans are finite, including those of the gods. On earth, all humans have finite life spans. Some people are good; they create good karma for themselves (karma is a topic we will explore in some detail in Chapter 10), and after they die, they get reborn in the heavens as gods. Others are reborn either as animals, hell-beings, or ghosts, or are recycled back to earth as human beings. Whatever they are reborn as, they will have finite life spans. Even those who are reborn as gods in the heavens have finite life spans; some thousands or millions of years after birth, they die just like everyone else, and they get reborn based on their karma just like everyone else. It reminds me of a Buddhist joke: all gods are immortal, until they die.

In fact, even the realms themselves are impermanent. In Buddhism, there is the concept of the "world cycle," which is the time it takes for a universe to come into being, to expand, and then to contract and disappear.[9] So even universes have life cycles, and the human universe and all those heavenly realms are in different stages of that life cycle. Hence, it is not just the gods, but even heavens and universes, that are impermanent.

It is because of impermanence that a rebirth in heaven is not considered an ultimate solution to suffering for Buddhists. You may go to heaven; you may even bliss out there for a very long time, perhaps thousands of years, perhaps millions of years. And then what? Back to square one. After the Buddha was newly enlightened, he thought of teaching the Dharma to his former teachers, Alara and Uddaka. However, they had both already passed away. In fact, due to their deep practices and impeccable karma, both were reborn in the highest and most refined heavenly realms. According to popular lore, the Buddha felt sad for them because they would both be there for "only" eighty-four thousand world cycles.[10] That is a duration of eighty-four thousand times the full life span of a universe, spent in a state of supremely refined bliss in the highest of heavens. And nope, even that is not good enough for a Buddhist. Told you we're greedy.

In fact, it is said that even gods can experience real suffering. This especially happens near the end of their life spans, when they know they are dying. Their radiance begins to fade, and other gods start avoiding them. So they suffer an existential crisis, panic arising from impending death and loneliness all at once. It's good to be a god, but it really sucks to die as one.

Given this cosmological worldview, there is an important concept in Buddhism called **samsara**. The word *samsara* literally means "wandering on."[11] It signifies the repetitive cycle of birth, aging, death, and rebirth, including in the heavenly realms, the hell realm, and all the other realms that contain humans, animals, and ghosts. Uninstructed, unenlightened beings just wander aimlessly in these realms from one lifetime to another to another, all the time experiencing suffering. Hence, samsara is usually described with terms such as "suffering-laden cycle of life, death, and rebirth, without beginning or end" or, simply, "endless cycle of suffering."[12]

Once I was at a large carpark at a retreat center. It was totally full. There was a large overflow parking lot that was mostly empty, but there was no proper signage to point drivers to it, so nobody knew it existed, hence the cars just kept literally circling the main carpark endlessly in a futile search for parking. And I told my wife, "See, that is samsara, endless cycle of suffering."

Guest artist: Natalie Tsang

In the context of samsara, the craving for existence is the thirst, desire, compulsion to exist, either with a form or without a form, and, in doing so, to stay indefinitely within samsara, and hence to suffer endlessly. You might think, if that is the case, then the solution is to wish not to exist, and by not existing, break out of samsara. But no, that wish to not exist is the craving for nonexistence, which is also a cause of suffering.

I find it illumining that the Buddha lists the craving for nonexistence as one of the three cravings, because some people mistakenly think that Buddhism is a form of nihilism, and some mistakenly think the purpose of practicing Buddhism is to end up not existing. In listing the craving for nonexistence as one of the three cravings, the Buddha busts both myths at once. In fact, the Buddha flatly denies that he teaches the annihilation of self.[13]

It also illuminates one other point. You see, existing and nonexisting are opposites, so to have craving for both in the same list appears to put opposites on the same "list of things that are true"; it makes no sense. However, note that the commonality between the two is the word *craving*. That illuminates the point that neither existing nor nonexisting is a cause of suffering per se; it is the craving for either or both that causes suffering. It is all about the craving. In one discourse, the Buddha describes craving for existing as "holding back" and craving for nonexisting as "overreaching."[14] To fully understand the Buddha's teachings is to neither hold back nor overreach.

So I guess the Buddhist answer to the age-old Shakespearean question, "To be or not to be?" is, "No, thank you."

Not Mine, Not I, Not My Self

There is a particularly powerful form of grasping that relates to all three forms of craving, and also relates to the "five aggregates subject to grasping" from the last chapter. It is grasping to the five aggregates as "this is mine," or "this is me," or "this is my soul." For example, we identify this body as mine. Mine! Or these thoughts and emotions as me. Me! Or this consciousness as my soul. My soul! In other words, we grasp onto selfness. We like to think that selfness is something that is rock solid, that we can rely on, that we have ownership of and sovereignty over. That is suffering, because selfness can offer us none of those things.

In the famous Discourse on a Lump of Foam, the Buddha compares bodily form to a lump of foam floating on the river: it appears substantial at first, but when properly inspected, one would find it to be "void, hollow, insubstantial."[15] In the same way, all the other aggregates appear to be substantial but, when carefully inspected, are shown to be void, hollow, and insubstantial. Sensation is compared to water bubbles: they look real, but they form and disappear very quickly. Perception is compared to a mirage: it looks real, but is nothing more than a projection.

The analogy for volitional formations is extra-interesting to me because it involved something I did not know: that a banana tree does not actually have a trunk. In fact, a banana tree is not even a tree; it is a giant herbaceous plant with large leaves that roll up tightly one over another in a way that makes them resemble a trunk. A man who needs heartwood for construction might cut down a banana tree, but he will soon find that there is no useful heartwood there at all, merely a roll of giant leaves. Similarly, thoughts and emotions may seem real, but when investigated closely, they turn out merely to be creations of mind: insubstantial and often not particularly useful.

Finally, and this is one of Soryu's favorite analogies, the Buddha compared consciousness to a magician's illusion. Everything a magician does looks so real. It looks like he really made a ball disappear and then reappear somewhere else. It looks like he really cut a woman in two and then put her back together. But these are all just deceptive illusions. Similarly, consciousness appears substantial, but when it's investigated, nothing is found that has any substance.

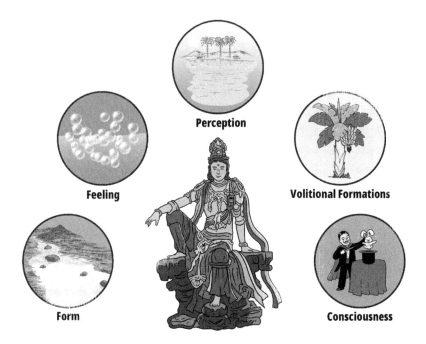

Every aggregate, when closely investigated, is shown to be void, hollow, and insubstantial. Buddhist teacher Shinzen Young has a very nice description of selfness: "The experience of self is a process, and there is no thing in that process that is a self." Due to its insubstantiality, grasping onto any aggregate as mine, me, or my soul results in suffering.

Do not worry if you do not fully understand this yet. This is profound stuff, which we will talk about again later in this book as you learn more about Buddhism. Think of this section as an introduction to a very deep person: it is good enough to just meet her now, and you will have plenty of chances to talk to her later.

How profound is this stuff? It is enough to trigger full enlightenment. In a particularly important discourse called the Discourse on the Characteristics of Not-self, the Buddha spoke on this topic.[16] This was his second discourse after his enlightenment, and it was delivered to the five original monks. The Buddha said:

> Any kind of form, or sensation, or perception, or volitional formation, or consciousness, whatsoever, whether past, future, or present, internal or external, gross or subtle, inferior or superior, far or near, all should be seen as it really is with correct wisdom thus: "This is not mine, this I am not, this is not my self."

With that, one becomes no longer enchanted by the five aggregates. With disenchantment comes liberation. At the end of the discourse, all five monks attained full enlightenment.

You may ask, what is the difference between "I" and "my self"? When the Buddha used the word *self* (*atta*) here, he meant it in a way that may be different from how modern people understand it. In the Buddha's time and place, one popular belief was we all have a core self that is permanent, unchanging, and inherently blissful. Many modern people call that the soul. During the Buddha's time, the word used to refer to this soul, *atta*, was the same word used for self, hence the translation to "self." But in this context, it should read as "soul."

The Buddha states that no one, not even God, or the universe, or nature, has a permanent, unchanging, and inherently blissful soul, and that none of the five aggregates, nor any combination of them, constitutes that permanent, unchanging, and inherently blissful soul. Instead, it is precisely freedom from any identification with a self that is release from suffering and the realization of true bliss. This is the teaching of **nonself** (*anatta*). It is one of the most important teachings in all of Buddhism.

There is an important nuance relating to grasping. While the English word *grasping* means "to hold tightly on," the Pali word, *upādāna*, also means "fuel."[17] This is the vitally important nuance that is lost when translated to English: whatever you grasp also fuels the one who is grasping. That which one grasps is also the basis of the one who grasps. The ancient Indian analogy is that of a fire. In the ancient Indian perspective, the fire "grasps" the fuel at the same time that the fuel sustains the fire.[18] A modern analogy is addiction. Addiction can be seen as grasping onto the substance one is abusing, but the very act of abusing that substance fuels the grasping itself. What makes this insight so vitally important is its consequence: once you release the grasping, you also let go of the fuel that supports the grasping itself. Therefore, the choice of releasing the grasping sets off a virtuous cycle that eventually removes the very support for the cause of your suffering.

Soryu says that you can also think of the five aggregates as being the fuel for the sense of self. When we try to use them as fuel for selfness, or as support for selfness, we are clinging to them. That is suffering right there. Most people have the opposite belief, they believe that grasping is safety. But the Buddha points out that grasping is actually suffering. Think of a drowning man grasping desperately onto a heavy sinking object, believing the grasping will provide him safety, when, in reality, real safety begins with letting go.

The most important consequence of this teaching is it shows you where your power lies. It turns out that you *can* choose not to grasp onto the aggregates as mine, I, or my self. That choice can yield freedom from all suffering. Later in this book, we will talk about how to develop the ability to make that choice.

You Already Have Gold in That Ball of Dung

If Soryu was giving a lecture on the Second Noble Truth, he would start by explaining that suffering is caused. That means it is not inherent, and not arbitrary, and that it is subject to cause and effect. And then, before he talks about the actual cause of suffering, he would say, "Let's pause and let that sink in: suffering is caused." He would stop talking, and there would be that long awkward silence. Yeah, it's a thing with Buddhist teachers, they like awkward silences—maybe they think it's funny or something.

Beyond being funny, Soryu drives home a fundamental point. People think the essence of the Second Noble Truth is craving (taṇhā), but it's actually not. The essence of the Second Noble Truth is that *suffering is caused.* The Buddha himself summarized the Second Noble Truth as *dukkha-samudaya,* which means "origin of suffering."[19] He didn't summarize it as craving; he summarized it as origin. Which means that while knowing the cause of suffering is important, knowing that suffering is caused is most important. That is the point Soryu tries to bring across with his awkward silence.

Inherent in the Second Noble Truth is another insight that carries profound significance in the practice of Buddhism: the realization that in order to eliminate suffering, we don't have to create anything new; we merely have to remove existing obstacles. The mind in its natural state is already pure, perfect, and free from suffering. However, there are conditions that cause it to suffer. For example, the Buddha said, "Monks, this mind is luminous, but it is defiled by external defilements."[20] In that sense, there is not a single thing we need to do to "upgrade" the already perfect mind; all we have to do is remove those conditions that cause suffering. Some Buddhist teachers humorously compared the original perfection of mind to a piece of gold hidden within a ball of cow dung. You don't have to create the gold—it is already there—all you need to get the gold is to wash away the dung.

Soryu has a complementary way of looking at it, and it relates to the five aggregates subject to grasping. He says you can think of them as five modes in which we can accumulate suffering.[21] Seen from this perspective, non-suffering is already available; we simply have to not accumulate suffering via any of those five avenues. Being a competitive tennis player in a former life, Soryu offers up a tennis analogy. There are five ways to lose: hit the ball into the net, too far to the right, too far to the left, too far long, or just miss the ball entirely. To win, all you have to do is to not do those five things.

Solve Problems Not by Creating More

The insight that you do not have to construct anything new to solve suffering also has a surprisingly powerful practical implication: that we can solve problems without creating new ones. This is an idea formulated by Soryu and a Buddhist master I know: Shinzen Young. The two are colleagues and friends, and in conversation one day made the astute observation that in the history of the world, every problem that is created by human beings started as a solution to a previous problem. There is an example I find quite amusing, which is known as the Great Horse Manure Crisis of 1894.[22] In those days, cities depended on horses for transportation of people and materials. Each horse produced fifteen to thirty-five pounds of manure a day, and they dumped it on the streets as they went. New York City alone had a hundred thousand horses producing two and a half million pounds of manure per day. Experts predicted that as cities grew, city streets would soon be buried under tons of horse manure. Oh, crap. What to do? The solution was the motorcar (applause!). Unfortunately, the invention of the internal combustion engine enabled a massive increase in our consumption of fossil fuels, to the extent that it contributes significantly to global warming, which is a major problem plaguing humanity today. So the next time you think about the internal combustion engine's contribution to global warming, know that it started as the solution to a previous problem, one that involves city streets being buried under horse manure.

This happens in an even more insidious way at a personal level: everything we do that causes suffering started as a solution to previous suffering. For example, if you are an alcoholic, you drink in order to feel better. If you do not drink, you feel very unpleasant, and your solution to this problem is to drink.

You do this even though you know that getting a drink will cause suffering to yourself and your loved ones. You took an action to solve a problem in the present that creates the problem in the future. That is what makes an addict. And we all suffer this at multiple levels. For example, many extra slices of chocolate cake have been unhealthily consumed (yes, I do plead guilty, Your Honor) and many wars have been started that resulted in millions of deaths because people were trying to solve the problem of having unpleasant feelings.

All solutions we formulate that later cause suffering have one thing in common: they all ignore the real cause of suffering, which is craving. In other words, all those solutions sidestep the real cause of the problem, and that is why they all turn out not to be real solutions. Imagine a hoarder whose house is full of old newspapers, used pizza boxes, used dental floss, rotting food waste, empty soda cans, and all sorts of other trash. There is so much trash she can hardly even walk inside her own house. The solution is simple and obvious: throw out the trash. Let's say instead of doing that, she puts silk brocades over her trash to solve the ugliness problem, applies perfume to solve the smell problem, and puts mouse traps all over the house to solve the rodent problem. No, it's not really going to work. Her house was already livable in its original state; it is currently unlivable only because she accumulated so much trash. The real solution is to take away the trash, not to add more stuff to solve the problems caused by the trash.

Guest artist: Natalie Tsang

In the same way, the mind experiences suffering only because it is defiled by craving. Any solution that ignores that cause not only leaves the original problem fundamentally unsolved, but creates more problems in the future.

The right solution is to clear out the craving. Doing that not only solves the problem, but has the happy side effect of not creating other problems.

What is it like to be free from craving and, hence, free from suffering? That's coming up next.

The Abbot's Commentary by Soryu Forall

Not everyone can lift a hundred-pound weight. Some people can, and some people can't. Some people will never be able to, however hard they try. Similarly, some people can lift a ten-pound weight, while others can't.

But everyone can put the weights down.

Suffering is caused and conditioned by craving. You don't need craving, and you don't need the suffering it creates. All you have to do is put it down.

Drop it. Cut it off. Abandon it. This alone is the end of suffering.

CHAPTER FIVE

Smells Like Nirvana

The Third Noble Truth

Try Explaining Dry Land to a Fish

Once upon a time, a fish and a turtle were friends. The turtle returned from a visit to dry land, and the fish had a lot of trouble trying to understand this "dry land" place where the turtle had been. So the fish asked a series of questions, such as, "Is it all wet?" "Can I move my fins about it and push my nose through it?" "Does it ever rise up in waves with white foam in them?" "Does it move in streams?" To every question, the turtle answered, "No." Finally, the fish confidently concluded, "In that case, dry land must be nothing." There was nothing the turtle could say in response, because any description the turtle could come up with was entirely beyond the experience of the fish.[1]

That is the central difficulty of this chapter: trying to describe something indescribable.

In his first discourse, the Buddha made the assertion that it is possible to end suffering by ending craving. This assertion is known in Buddhism as the **Third Noble Truth**. Specifically, he said,

> Now this, monks, is the noble truth of the cessation of suffering: it is
> the remainderless fading away and cessation of that same craving, the
> giving up and relinquishing of it, freedom from it, nonreliance on it.[2]

There is a one-word descriptor for the state of total freedom from all suffering: *nirvana*.[3] The biggest problem in describing nirvana is that nirvana
is basically indescribable. It is like the turtle trying to explain dry land to the
fish. It is also like trying to explain the taste of honey to someone who has
not tasted sweetness in his entire life; there is simply no way to satisfactorily
describe it. Actually, Soryu says it is incomparably harder even than that,
because in the analogy, you at least still have a frame of reference, which is
the experience of tasting, but nirvana has no frame of reference at all. The
Buddha says nirvana is "profound, hard to see, and hard to understand, . . .
unattainable by mere reasoning."[4]

The inherent problem in describing nirvana makes it easy for people to
mistake it to be "nothingness," in the same way the fish mistakes dry land
for nothingness. Fortunately, all hope is not lost. Sometimes it is possible to
understand an unobservable phenomenon by observing and understanding its
secondary, derivative aspects. One example is black holes. A black hole is a
region of space exhibiting such strong gravitational effects that nothing—not
even light—can escape from inside it. Since a black hole traps all light and all
electromagnetic radiation, there is absolutely no way to directly observe it.
However, you can infer the existence of a black hole in at least two ways. One
is by observing its gravitational effect on surrounding bodies. If a region of
seemingly empty space exerts strong gravitation on surrounding stars, then
it is likely a black hole is there. Another way a black hole is indirectly ob-
servable is through an effect called Hawking radiation. According to Stephen
Hawking's wildly popular *A Brief History of Time*, Hawking radiation happens when a matching particle and antiparticle pair is produced just outside
the event horizon of a black hole.[5] For example, let's say an electron and a
positron are produced; the positron may then be sucked into the black hole,
while the electron escapes and is observed as thermal radiation. In that way,
even though the black hole itself is observed to be a region of empty space,
radiation is produced in the space around it, and by observing the radiation,
you can infer the black hole.

In the same way, even though nirvana itself is unfathomable, indescribable, and not directly understandable to one who is not fully enlightened, there are some aspects of it that are almost describable and almost understandable to an unenlightened person, and the Buddha did talk about those. So while there is no way to fully understand nirvana until you achieve full enlightenment yourself, it is possible to derive some degree of approximate understanding based on a combination of your meditation practice and what the Buddha says about nirvana.

What Is Nirvana?

First, it's useful to know the literal meaning of the word *nirvana*. *Nirvana* literally means "going out," as in the extinguishing of a flame, so in that sense, *nirvana* means "extinguishing."[6] But what is extinguished in nirvana? The most obvious thing that is extinguished, of course, is craving. Indeed, the Buddha equates nirvana with the "ending of craving."[7] Nirvana is also the extinguishing of greed, hatred, and delusion (the original Pali words almost rhyme: *lobha, dosa, moha*), commonly known as the **three poisons**.[8] In relation to craving: greed relates to the grasping aspect of craving, hatred relates to the aversion aspect of craving, and delusion is a necessary condition for the arising of craving, so the extinguishing of delusion guarantees the extinguishing of craving both now and in the future.

The three poisons are also known as the **three fires**. Early in the Buddha's ministry, he met with a group of ascetics under the leadership of the three Kassapa brothers. After the meeting, the entire group of one thousand ascetics converted to Buddhism. The Buddha gave them a discourse, which was only the third one he had given. Those one thousand monks were all devoted to fire sacrifice before they became Buddhists, so the Buddha gave them a discourse based on the subject they were most familiar with: fire. It is the famous Fire Discourse.[9] He started with, "Monks, all is burning. . . . Burning with what? Burning with the fire of greed, the fire of hatred, and the fire of delusion." For that reason, greed, hatred, and delusion are also known as the three fires. Liberation from suffering, then, is the extinguishing of these fires. It was said that by the end of the discourse, all one thousand new Buddhist monks gained liberation. If the beer company Guinness had been keeping records at that time, that incident would have been recorded as the highest number of people reaching full enlightenment after a single discourse by the Buddha.[10]

"I'm trying to extinguish his greed, hatred, and delusion."

Nirvana is also often talked about as the escape from samsara. Back in Chapter 4, we described samsara as an endless cycle of suffering that entails repetitive cycles of birth, aging, death, and rebirth, including as gods, hell-beings, humans, animals, and ghosts. Nirvana is breaking free from that endless cycle. That is why in the ancient Buddhist texts, one who gains full enlightenment often declares, "Destroyed is birth, the holy life has been lived, what had to be done has been done, there is no more for this state of being."[11]

Since nirvana is escape from samsara, it's easy to mistake nirvana for annihilationism. Indeed, even during the Buddha's lifetime, some people claimed he taught annihilationism. He rebuked that directly, saying,

> I have been baselessly, vainly, falsely, and wrongly misrepresented
> by some recluses and brahmans thus: "The recluse Gotama is one
> who leads astray; he teaches the annihilation, the destruction, the
> extermination of an existing being."[12]

If nirvana is escape from samsara but is not annihilationism, that creates a vexing question (vexing for an unenlightened fool like me): When a fully enlightened one passes away, does that one then exist or not exist? To my surprise, I found the Buddha actually gave an answer to this question. It is in a context of a conversation between the Buddha and a wanderer called Vacchagotta.[13] Below is my rendering of the relevant parts.

Vacchagotta asked: Do you hold the view that when a fully enlightened one passes away, that he 1) exists, 2) not exists, 3) both exists and not exists, or 4) neither exists nor not exists?

Buddha replied: I hold none of these four views. Furthermore, these are all speculative views. Speculative views do not lead to liberation from suffering, hence I put them away.

Vacchagotta then asked in a different way: When a fully enlightened one dies, does he 1) reappear, 2) not reappear, 3) both reappear and not reappear, 4) neither reappear nor not reappear?

Buddha replied: None of the four applies.

Vacchagotta: Great, now I'm really confused.

Buddha: Let me ask you this. Suppose there is a fire. What does the fire burn in dependence on?

Vacchagotta: It burns in dependence on fuel.

Buddha: Suppose the fire dies out [because the fuel is used up]. Which direction does the fire go? North, south, east, or west?

Vacchagotta: None of the four applies.

Buddha: In the same way, a fully enlightened one is liberated from reckoning in terms of all five aggregates: form, sensation, perception, volitional formations, and consciousness. Hence, he is profound, immeasurable, and hard to fathom, like an ocean. Therefore, none of the four [propositions involving reappearing, or not reappearing, or both, or neither] applies.

Vacchagotta: Cool.

No, Vacchagotta didn't actually say, "cool." He instead praised the Buddha profusely and asked to be his disciple. I just decided to render two entire paragraphs of profuse praise with "cool."

The key point the Buddha makes is that a fully enlightened one after passing away cannot be fathomed in terms of existence or nonexistence, hence existence, nonexistence, both, and neither—all do not apply. If you find that confusing, here is some additional teaching that may reduce your confusion, or add to it, or, more likely, both (or neither). The Buddha once spoke about this topic in a different context. The Buddhist monk Kaccānagotta asked the Buddha for a clarification of "right view," and the Buddha said to him:

Most people in this world [except for the enlightened ones] depend upon a duality—upon the notion of existence and the notion of nonexistence. But for one who sees the origin of the world as it really is with correct wisdom, there is no notion of nonexistence in regard to the world. And for one who sees the cessation of the world as it really is with correct wisdom, there is no notion of existence in regard to the world.[14]

Medieval commentaries to the above passage clarify that "the notion of existence" (*atthita*) refers to eternalism ("I will forever be") and "the notion of nonexistence" (*natthita*) refers to annihilationism ("I will forever stop being"). Hence, the above passage points out the limits of the unenlightened mind, which is only capable of understanding phenomena in terms of existence or nonexistence.

How is one to understand this? Zen master Thich Nhat Hanh offers a beautiful analogy: think of the waves on the surface of the ocean.[15] If a wave sees only this wave as her individual self, she will see her own arising and ceasing, existing and nonexisting, birth and death. But if the wave can also experience water itself, then she also sees that there is a deeper reality that goes beyond both existing and nonexisting. That is not to say that the wave has a separate, larger "self" that is the ocean, but that the wave can *directly* experience the water that is beyond both her existence and nonexistence. That is a metaphor for nirvana.

Honestly, despite the Buddha's and my teachers' explanations, I still do not really understand what it means for one to be "unfathomable in terms of existence or nonexistence." It takes an enlightened one to fully understand that, and last I checked (which was 7:13 a.m. today), I'm not it. In the meantime, I just need to be content with partial understanding until my practice catches up.

Call Now and Get 50 Percent More Nirvana Absolutely Free

But wait, is there more? Is nirvana simply extinguishing (of greed, hatred, delusion, and all things uncool), or is nirvana also some reality? The ancient texts strongly suggest it is both extinguishing and some reality. As the wave analogy above suggests, the only way to understand nirvana is to look deeper into the reality beyond the surface.

First, the Buddha referred to nirvana as a dharma (or *dhamma*, in the Pali language). The word *dharma* here means "phenomenon," so nirvana is a phenomenon, an actual reality, not just a concept. In fact, the Buddha refers to *nirvana* as the "supreme dharma." More than that, the Buddha described it with these terms (the original Pali words in parenthesis): "infinite" (*ananta*), "unconditioned" (*asankhata*), "incomparable" (*anūpa-meya*), "supreme" (*anuttara*), "highest" (*para*), "beyond" (*pāra*), "ultimate goal" (*parāyana*), "refuge" (*tāna*), "security" (*khema*), "happiness" (*siva*), "whole" (*kevala*), "abodeless" (*anālaya*), "imperishable" (*akkhara*), "absolute purity" (*visuddha*), "supramundane" (*lokuttara*), "deathless" (*amata*).[16]

One of the key descriptors the Buddha used for nirvana is *unconditioned*. There are two types of phenomena, conditioned and nonconditioned. Conditioned phenomena are those that arise due to conditions. One example of a conditioned phenomenon is a chair. We have a chair because we have the right conditions: four legs, a seat, and a backing, put together in a certain configuration. Conditioned phenomena always change and cease due to change of conditions. For example, if the chair loses its legs, it is no longer a chair. The five aggregates (form, sensation, perception, volitional formations, and consciousness) are conditioned phenomena. Birth and death are conditioned phenomena.

The one and only nonconditioned phenomenon is nirvana. With reference to that, the Buddha said,

There is, monks, an unborn, unbecome, unmade, unconditioned . . .
therefore you know an escape from the born, become, made, and
conditioned.[17]

Elsewhere, the Buddha talked about nirvana as a "sphere" (āyatana), but
unlike anything that corresponds to our mundane experience. Because of that,
the description is full of negations, a lot like a turtle trying to describe dry land
to a fish ("not wet," "does not rise up in waves," etc.). The Buddha said,

> There is that sphere, monks, where there is no earth, no water, no fire,
> no air, no sphere of infinite space, no sphere of infinite consciousness,
> no sphere of nothingness, no sphere of neither perception nor non-
> perception, no this world, no world beyond, neither Moon nor Sun.
> There, monks, I say there is surely no coming, no going, no persisting,
> no passing away, no rebirth. It is quite without support, unmoving,
> without an object,—just this is the end of suffering.[18]

The two above passages get quoted a lot in books on Buddhism, but there
is also a less well-known one that reinforces them:

> The born, come-to-be, produced,
> The made, the conditioned, the transient,
> Conjoined with decay and death,
> A nest of disease, perishable,
> Sprung from nutriment and craving's cord—
> That is not fit to take delight in.
>
> The escape from that, the peaceful,
> Beyond reasoning, everlasting,
> The not-born, the unproduced,
> The sorrowless state that is void of stain,
> The cessation of states linked to suffering,
> The stilling of the conditioned—bliss.[19]

The Buddha also refers to nirvana as an "element" (dhātu); specifically,
he calls it the "deathless element" (amata-dhātu).[20] Mahācunda, one of the
Buddha's senior disciples, even suggests that nirvana is something so vivid

it can be experienced by the body; he calls it "touching the deathless element with the body."[21]

Finally, the Buddha calls nirvana "the greatest bliss."[22]

Four Stages of Enlightenment

The prospect of working toward full enlightenment can be very daunting. Fortunately, there is both good news and even better news. The good news is that the path toward full enlightenment can be broken down into four stages, and reaching stage one is far less daunting than reaching full enlightenment itself. The even better news is that, according to the Buddha, once you reach stage one, you are *guaranteed* to reach full enlightenment in the future—or your money back. Hence, for mere mortals like me, the seemingly unsolvable problem of reaching full enlightenment is greatly simplified to the still very challenging but actually solvable problem of reaching stage one.

According to the Buddha, there are ten fetters that hold us back from full enlightenment.[23] When these ten fetters are abandoned, full enlightenment results. These ten fetters are abandoned in four stages, known as the four stages of enlightenment.

In the first stage, one abandons three fetters: identity view, doubt, and the distorted grasp of rules and vows.[24] We will discuss in some depth what each of these three fetters means in Chapter 11. One who successfully abandons these three fetters arrives at the first stage of enlightenment and is known as a **stream-enterer (*sotāpanna*)**. Upon reaching this stage, one is guaranteed to arrive at full enlightenment in no more than seven additional lifetimes. In addition, if a stream-enterer is reborn, it will no longer be in a "state of woe." In other words, a stream-enterer who is reborn does so either as a human or a god, not as an animal or a hell-being.

In the second stage, one greatly reduces, but does not totally abandon, two fetters: sensual desire, and ill will. One who does that arrives at the second stage of enlightenment and is known as a **once-returner (*sakadāgāmī*)**. A once-returner will return to the "realm of the senses," which means being a human or a god, at most once before arriving at full enlightenment.

In the third stage, one totally abandons the fetters of sensual desire and ill will. Yes, sensual desire and ill will are so hard to abandon it takes two entire

stages of enlightenment just to accomplish that. One who abandons sensual
desire and ill will arrives at the third stage of enlightenment and is known
as a **non-returner** (*anāgāmi*). A non-returner will no longer return to the
"realm of senses" as a human or a god, but if a non-returner takes birth, it
will be in one of the "Pure Abodes" and the non-returner will arrive at full
enlightenment from there.[25]

Ajahn Brahm and I once both spoke on the first day of a multiday conference on Buddhism. After we got offstage, Ajahn Brahm told me that due to
his travel schedule, he could only come back one more day, and, as usual, he
made a joke about it. "I'm only coming back once; I'm a once-returner." And
I said, "I'm not coming back at all; I'm a non-returner."

The five fetters listed above are known as the five lower fetters. In the
fourth and final stage, one abandons the remaining five, known as the five
higher fetters. These five are: lust for form, lust for the formless, conceit,
restlessness, and ignorance. One who abandons all ten fetters arrives at full
enlightenment (yoohoo!) and is known as an **arahant**. Where does one go
from here? There is nowhere to go. You beat the game. No more suffering,
ever! In the ancient texts, one who arrives at arahantship declares that from
that moment on, "what had to be done has been done."[26]

The Four Stages of Enlightenment

STAGE	FETTER ABANDONED / REDUCED
stream-enterer	abandoned: 1) identity view, 2) doubt, and 3) distorted grasp of rules and vows
once-returner	greatly reduced: 4) sensual desire and 5) ill will
non-returner	abandoned: 4) sensual desire and 5) ill will
arahant (full enlightenment)	abandoned: 6) lust for form, 7) lust for the formless, 8) conceit, 9) restlessness, and 10) ignorance

The Five Higher Fetters Are Like a Subtle Final Boss

Guest artist: Natalie Tsang

The five higher fetters can actually be surprisingly subtle when operating at the level of someone getting close to full enlightenment. One story that illustrates this involves the last obstacles to full enlightenment for Anuruddha, one of the Buddha's ten main disciples.[27] Anuruddha was a fascinating character in his own right. He was a first cousin of the Buddha (their fathers were brothers) who lived a very pampered life. It was said that when he was growing up, he never heard of the phrase "no more" (*natthi*), because whatever he wanted, he was given.

According to one mythical story, Anuruddha was playing outside with some kids and wanted some cakes, so he sent his servant home to ask for cake from his mother, and Mom obliged. And then he asked for cake again, and again. After the third request for cakes, Mom got annoyed and returned an empty platter with the message, "no more cake" (*natthi pūvaṁ*). It was said that due to Anuruddha's amazingly good karma from his past lives, the gods could not stand to see him disappointed, so they put a delicious celestial cake on the platter for him. Anuruddha took one bite and determined that this "no more cake" is the most delicious cake he had ever had (it was divine, literally), so he repeatedly sent his servant back for more "no more cake," and the gods obliged every time.

When Anuruddha grew up, his cousin Prince Siddhattha became the Buddha, and Anuruddha and his brother Mahānāma decided that one of them should leave the house to follow the Buddha as a monk. Anuruddha volunteered to stay home because being a monk sounded hard, so Mahānāma informed him of the duties of a householder: "First the fields have to be plowed, then they must be sown, then water must be led into them, . . . etc. etc. etc. . . . And the same must be done every year." When Anuruddha heard that, he decided that's too much work and volunteered instead to become a monk. No, that's not why he became a monk, that was just my playful way of telling the story. In reality, Anuruddha asked an innocent question that led him to an important insight: "Does the work ever stop?" His brother replied, "No, there is no end to this work. Even when fathers and grandfathers pass away, the work is not to be stopped." With that, Anuruddha suddenly gained insight into the endlessness and meaninglessness of suffering in samsara and, consequently, gained determination to become a monk.

Happily, "Buddhist monk" turned out to be a great career choice for Anuruddha, because in a short span of time, he managed to perfect meditative concentration (the jhānas, which we will discuss in Chapter 8). He also developed a superpower called the "divine eye," which is the ability to see beyond the range of the physical eye. In Anuruddha's case, his divine eye was so powerful he could "survey a thousand world systems, just as a man standing on a high tower could see a thousand farmsteads."[28] In Buddhism, superpowers and miracles are nothing to be impressed by (a topic we will discuss in Chapter 13). Still, Anuruddha's divine eye was so powerful he was known and is remembered, even to this day, as the master of the divine eye. I bet he could always find Waldo.

Even with the mastery of meditation and the divine eye, however, Anuruddha could not reach full enlightenment. Something was holding him back. So Anuruddha asked his friend Sāriputta, the wisest of all the Buddha's disciples, "Friend Sāriputta, with the divine eye, which is purified and supernormal, I survey a thousandfold world systems. Energy is aroused in me without slackening; my mindfulness is established without confusion; my body is tranquil without disturbance; my mind is concentrated and one-pointed. Yet my mind is still not liberated from the taints through non-grasping."

Sāriputta replied, "Friend Anuruddha, when you think, 'With the divine eye, which is purified . . . ,' this is your conceit. When you think, 'Energy is aroused in me without slackening . . . my mind is concentrated and one-pointed,' this is your restlessness. And when you think, 'Yet my mind is still not liberated . . . ,' this is your remorse. It would be good if you would abandon these three qualities and stop attending to them. Instead, direct your mind to the deathless element."[29] Anuruddha did that and arrived at full enlightenment.

I tell this story to point out how subtle Anuruddha's restlessness was, and how even that was enough to hold him back. I have heard from at least two of my teachers that as their practice deepens and their minds get calmer and calmer, they keep discovering an even subtler layer of restlessness. In the case of Anuruddha, it wasn't like he couldn't sit still. His mindfulness, mental clarity, energy, tranquility, concentration, and one-pointedness were all already at very high levels of mastery. Someone at those levels can easily sit for hours in meditation in perfect mental stillness and bliss without any distracting thought, so you would think that such a person would have no problem with restlessness at all. But even with that, Anuruddha experienced enough residual restlessness to block him from full enlightenment. The same is true for all the other fetters; they can all be extremely subtle, and even that can hold you back from full enlightenment. Only when Anuruddha totally abandoned even the subtlest of his barriers was he able to break through to the final goal.

Streaming Nirvana

As mentioned above, one who gains the first stage of enlightenment is known as a stream-enterer. For that reason, one who begins the training can be poetically seen as one preparing to enter a stream. But what is the stream? The stream is the Noble Eightfold Path, and, therefore, a stream-enterer can be referred to as "one who possesses the Noble Eightfold Path."[30] But what is the Noble Eightfold Path? I'm glad you asked, because the Noble Eightfold Path is also the Fourth Noble Truth, and that is the topic of the next chapter.

The Abbot's Commentary by Soryu Forall

Imagine a man holding on to a chain attached to a stake in the ground. He has been circling that stake for years, walking thousands of miles without going anywhere. There is an end to his imprisonment, which will enable him to live a better life: he must let go of that chain.

In the same way, there is an end to suffering, which gives us happier and more meaningful lives: we must let go of the causes of suffering.

The Third Noble Truth says, "You can do it." It proclaims cessation as a truth: the cessation of suffering, which is the complete abandoning of craving. It is the end of greed, hatred, and delusion. This is the realization of nirvana.

Nirvana is the relinquishment of everything. It is the supreme joy. It is the supreme peace. It is clear and quick and bright. It is the supreme goal. Achieve this goal and offer your true life to the world.

CHAPTER SIX

Click Here to Uninstall Suffering

The Fourth Noble Truth

Do No Evil, Cultivate Good, Purify Your Mind

Once, the Buddha's attendant Ānanda asked the Buddha a deceptively simple question: What is the teaching of all buddhas past and present? That is kind of like asking, "What is the teaching of all geography teachers in the world?" It takes a deep and thorough understanding of the subject to give a very succinct yet complete answer. The Buddha's answer was surprisingly and brilliantly simple. He said,

> Not to do any evil, to cultivate good, to purify one's mind, this is the teaching of the buddhas.[1]

This is a good summary of Buddhism in general, and an especially good summary of the Fourth Noble Truth in particular.

In teaching the Four Noble Truths, the Buddha was said to have acted like a doctor who delivers his diagnosis in four parts. First, he explains the nature of your disease. Next, he tells you the causes of your disease. After that, he declares that a cure exists, and explains what a non-diseased state looks like. Finally, he gives you the prescription.

In the case of the Four Noble Truths, the disease is suffering (or more accurately, dukkha), the cause is craving, and the non-diseased state is nirvana. That leads us to the most important question: How? How do we cure ourselves of suffering to get to nirvana? The **Fourth Noble Truth** is the prescription that comes in eight parts, kind of like a traditional Eastern medicine consisting of eight medicinal herbs. It can also be thought of as a package of practices divided into eight parts. For that reason, it is unsurprisingly named the **Noble Eightfold Path**. It consists of these (with the original Pali words in parenthesis):

1. Right view (*sammā-diṭṭhi*)

2. Right intention (*sammā-saṅkappa*)

3. Right speech (*sammā-vācā*)

4. Right action (*sammā-kammanta*)

5. Right livelihood (*sammā-ājīva*)

6. Right effort (*sammā-vāyāma*)

7. Right mindfulness (*sammā-sati*)

8. Right samadhi (*sammā-samādhi*)[2]

That sounds about right, right?

Yes, the word *samādhi* is essentially left untranslated. Soryu and I tried our very best to use the English translation for every Pali word, but there is really no acceptable English translation for samādhi. Samādhi literally means "to put together," or "to collect." It is usually translated as "concentration," sometimes as "serenity" or "stillness." Unfortunately, all three translations are grossly inadequate, because each one captures only a partial meaning. Samādhi is all three and more. It is a state of mind that is calm, serene, and relaxed, and one-pointedly concentrated, meaning attention is perfectly stable and still. In addition, joy permeates the mind, equanimity is well established, and perception is clear. Most important, the mind in that state can cut through delusion like a sharp blade cutting through paper. Thankfully, the

Merriam-Webster Dictionary has an entry for samadhi (without the diacritics), which makes it an English word. So there; problem solved.

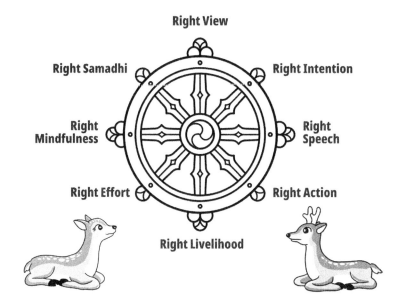

This chapter gives you an overview of each component of the Noble Eightfold Path.[3] In subsequent chapters, we will explore in depth how they lead directly to nirvana.

Right View

Right view is the "forerunner" of the Noble Eightfold Path, which is why the Buddha listed it first.[4] Having the right view guides the practice. Right view is like having the right map, while the other seven are like having a good vehicle. The right map guides you toward the right direction. It does not matter how good your vehicle is if you are heading the wrong way. So in that sense, right view may be the most important of the eight. OK, if it is that important, what is it? The Buddha said right view is knowing the nature of suffering, the causes of suffering, the nature of liberation from suffering, and the path to liberation from suffering.[5] In other words, knowing the Four Noble Truths.

To be fair, right view is actually a big topic. Sāriputta, the Buddha's wisest disciple, delivered an important discourse titled (get ready for a surprise . . . drumroll . . .) the Discourse on Right View, and it covers a host of topics: wholesome versus unwholesome, nutriment, the Four Noble Truths, aging and death, birth, being, grasping, craving, feeling, contact, the sixfold base, mentality materiality, consciousness, formations, ignorance, taints.[6] Phew. Not that there's anything wrong with Sāriputta's discourse; it's actually very good and very useful. But I think this was another genius move by the Buddha. The Buddha was able to reduce right view to a minimum set that everything else can be reduced to, and from which everything else can be derived, which is the Four Noble Truths. I think the difference between Sāriputta and the Buddha is that Sāriputta is a genius, whereas the Buddha is the genius among geniuses. It is not that the Buddha never elaborated on the topic; he did quite a lot. For example, he famously named sixty-two wrong views in one go in the Discourse on the Supreme Net, but when he had to, he could reduce the whole topic into three words in English: Four Noble Truths.[7]

We can think of the Four Noble Truths as the *teaching* of the Dharma, and the Noble Eightfold Path as the *practice* of the Dharma. Hence, by defining right view as the Four Noble Truths, the teaching (Four Noble Truths) ends with the practice, and the practice (Noble Eightfold Path) begins with the teaching, thus we get the additional benefit of fortifying the internal consistency between the teaching and the practice.

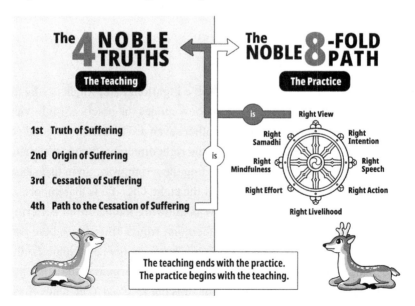

The **4** NOBLE TRUTHS — The Teaching

1st Truth of Suffering
2nd Origin of Suffering
3rd Cessation of Suffering
4th Path to the Cessation of Suffering

The NOBLE **8**-FOLD PATH — The Practice

Right View
Right Intention
Right Speech
Right Action
Right Livelihood
Right Effort
Right Mindfulness
Right Samadhi

The teaching ends with the practice.
The practice begins with the teaching.

Right Intention

Right intention means these three intentions: renunciation, non–ill will, and harmlessness.[8] They are the direct opposite of three intentions that result in suffering: unwholesome desire, ill will, and harmfulness. Renunciation does not just mean giving everything up and checking yourself into a monastery. It more generally refers to letting go, and it covers an entire spectrum, ranging from letting go of addiction, to letting go of unwholesome habits, to, yes, checking yourself into a monastery, all the way up to the letting go of samsara.

RIGHT INTENTION:

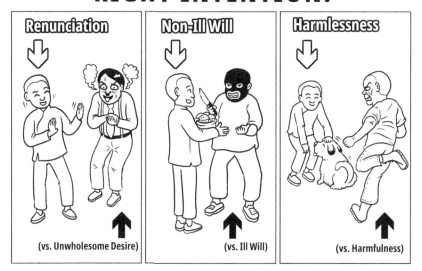

Renunciation	Non–Ill Will	Harmlessness
(vs. Unwholesome Desire)	(vs. Ill Will)	(vs. Harmfulness)

A beginner may think that renunciation hampers joy. Counterintuitively, all three parts of right intention, including renunciation, are designed to increase joy. They do so by trading in a less refined joy for a more refined joy. A childish example is when I was a child, I found a lot of pleasure in eating cheap sweets, but as an adult, I find them unsatisfying, so I give them up for high-quality chocolate. In a similar way, you will find in this book that the practice of Buddhism involves the discovery of deep sources of immense inner joy, and all three parts of right intention facilitate access to that inner joy. The greater the renunciation, goodwill, and harmlessness, the greater the access.

As compelling as that is, something else makes right intention more important: intentions beget thoughts, and thoughts change the inclination of the mind, either toward or away from nirvana. In one discourse, the Buddha talked about having two kinds of thoughts before his enlightenment: one arising from wrong intention, and the other arising from right intention.[9] He realized that thoughts arising from wrong intention "lead to affliction for myself and others, obstruct wisdom, cause difficulties, lead away from nirvana," while the other kind leads to the reverse. He further realized that "whatever one frequently thinks and ponders upon, that will become the inclination of his mind." Hence, he decided to abandon thoughts arising from wrong intention.

As usual, the Buddha has a delightful simile: "In the autumn, when the crops thicken, a cowherd would guard his cows by constantly tapping and poking them on this side and that with a stick to prevent them from straying into the crops. Why? Because he sees that he could be punished if that happens. In the same way, I saw danger, degradation, and defilement in the unwholesome thoughts." In addition to abandoning unwholesome thoughts, Siddhattha also cultivated the wholesome ones, the ones arising from renunciation, goodwill, and harmlessness. With that, the mental preconditions for arriving at nirvana were eventually established: "Tireless energy was aroused in me and unremitting mindfulness was established, my body was tranquil and untroubled, my mind concentrated and unified." That, my friends, is why right intention is important.

Soryu has a unique take on right intention. He thinks of right intention as the Buddhist edition of the "American Dream," as in, the ideal lives we want to aspire to. In the case of this "Buddhist Dream," it means three things: 1) to be delightfully happy whatever our physical and material circumstances, because our dream is to let go of everything; 2) to always have a joyful loving heart for all, because our dream is to never engage in hatred; and 3) to always be joyfully benefiting all, because our dream is to never harm anyone. In other words, a lifestyle of joy, meaning, and fulfillment is promised by the three ways of right intention.[10]

I'll say it again in case you missed the significance of it: one who lives a life of right intention lives a life of joy.

Soryu frames right view as a statement of facts—the way things are—and right intention as the dream of the good life—how we should behave in response to those facts ("right is" and "right ought," he half-jokingly calls them, or at least I think he is half joking), and the other six parts of the Noble Eightfold Path as the way to fulfill this "Buddhist Dream."

Right Speech

There is a very simple way to think about right speech: it is speech that gives rise to peace and happiness in self and others. In that sense, right speech is right intention as applied to speech; so as long as you maintain right intention while speaking, you basically have this covered.

As usual, though, the Buddha provided some useful practical guidelines. For monks, he prescribed right speech as abstinence from four things: false speech, divisive speech, harsh speech, and idle chatter.[11] The first three make immediate sense, the last one you may find a little curious. The reason for Buddhist monks to abstain from idle chatter is that they are supposed to practice preserving a certain degree of mental stillness and mindfulness at all times, and idle chatter interferes with that.

In a separate discourse, the Buddha talked about deciding whether something is worth saying based on two criteria: whether the words are truthful and useful.[12] Something is worth saying if and only if it is truthful and useful. In addition to that, the Buddha also advised to "have a sense of proper time" for speech based on whether or not it is endearing and agreeable. In other words, if something is truthful and useful but disagreeable, it is still worth saying; it's a matter of finding the right time to say it.

This topic came up during a conversation between the Buddha and a prince by the name of Abhaya. Abhaya invited the Buddha to his home for a meal, but his real intention was to try to humiliate him in front of an audience. Previously, the Buddha had said that an evil man by the name of Devadatta (whom we will talk about in Chapter 13) was destined for hell due to his evil actions, and when Devadatta heard that, he got angry. So Abhaya was planning to ask the Buddha whether he would utter any speech that would be "unwelcome and disagreeable to others." If the Buddha answered yes, Abhaya would say, "then you are no different from an ordinary person," and if the Buddha answered no, he would say, "you lie, because you said this and that about Devadatta." So, either way, he would refute and humiliate the Buddha.

After the meal, Prince Abhaya sat near to the Buddha and asked the question, "Venerable Sir, would you utter speech that would be unwelcome and disagreeable to others?"

Prince Abhaya at this time had a young infant (presumably his son) sitting on his lap. According to medieval commentary, this was a cheap debating trick. If Abhaya found himself losing the debate, he would use the infant as an excuse to abruptly end the debate and leave.

The Buddha knew what was happening, and he decided to use the infant as a teaching aid. He asked Abhaya, "If, while you or your nurse were not attending to this child, he was to put a stick or a pebble in his mouth, what would you do?" Abhaya answered, "Venerable Sir, I would take it out. If I could not take it out at once, I would take his head in my left hand, and crooking a finger of my right hand, I would take it out even if it meant drawing blood. Why? Because I have compassion for the child."

And the Buddha answered, "In the same way, if something is true and useful, I would say it even if it is unwelcome and disagreeable to others. Why? Because I have compassion for beings."

At the end of the conversation, the prince declared himself a follower of the Buddha.

Right Action

Like right speech, there is a very simple way to think about right action: it is action that gives rise to peace and happiness in self and others. In the same way, right action is simply right intention as applied to action.

As usual, the Buddha provided useful practical guidelines. He prescribed right action as abstinence from three things: killing, stealing, and sexual misconduct.[13]

The combination of right speech and right action gives rise to a set of guidelines that the Buddha recommends for ethical behavior called the **five precepts**.[14] These five precepts form the center of ethics and morality in Buddhism. They apply both to monastics and laypeople. The five precepts are:

1. To abstain from killing

2. To abstain from stealing

3. To abstain from sexual misconduct

4. To abstain from lying

5. To abstain from intoxicating drinks and drugs

The first three precepts are the practice of right action. The fourth is the one item in right speech that is so important the Buddha also named it as a precept. Those first four precepts are kind of obvious, really, but the fifth precept may be a surprise to some. In one discourse delivered to a large group of monastics and lay folks, the Buddha explained the purpose of abstinence from intoxicants in verse:

> Because of intoxication,
> foolish people do evil deeds,
> and they make other heedless folk do such deeds.
> One should avoid this basis of demerit,
> delightful to fools, causing madness and delusion.[15]

In modern parlance: we don't do intoxicants because intoxicants make people do bad stuff. Beyond that, however, there is a deeper reason why there is a precept concerning intoxicants, and that is the keen awareness in Buddhism of the close interrelationship between the mind, behavior, and suffering. For that reason, keeping the mind unclouded and uncompromised is an essential part of Buddhist practice.

There is a beautiful way to look at the five precepts, and that is as gifts. The Buddha says to think of observing the five precepts as giving **five great gifts** to oneself and others. By observing the precepts, he says, "the noble disciple gives to an immeasurable number of beings freedom from fear, enmity, and affliction. He himself in turn enjoys immeasurable freedom from fear, enmity, and affliction."[16]

In that spirit, modern Buddhist teachers like to emphasize the active aspects of the precepts. Each precept is not just a call to refrain from certain actions, it is also an opportunity to practice certain beautiful qualities. The great Zen master Thich Nhat Hanh, for example, lovingly encourages one to use the first precept (to abstain from killing) as an opportunity to practice compassion, the second precept (to abstain from stealing) as an opportunity to practice generosity, the third precept (to abstain from sexual misconduct) as an opportunity to practice true love, the fourth precept (to abstain from lying) as an opportunity to practice loving speech and deep listening, and the fifth precept (to abstain from intoxication) as an opportunity to practice nourishment and healing.[17] In other words, the five precepts are an opportunity for beautiful living.

But wait, there's more. The five precepts are the core of virtue, and virtue is a gift that keeps on giving. Just for laypeople alone, the Buddha lists five benefits of being virtuous:

1. A virtuous person does not lose wealth because of heedlessness.

2. A virtuous person gains a good reputation.

3. A virtuous person approaches any assembly confident and composed.

4. A virtuous person dies unconfused.

5. A virtuous person, after death, is reborn in a good destination.[18]

For those reasons, the Buddha declares a layperson who possesses the five precepts as one who dwells in self-confidence.[19]

Students of religion may be tempted here to equate the five precepts with "moralistic strictures," standards of conduct set for people by God. Being nontheistic, however, there is no such thing as moralistic strictures in Buddhism, given that there is no God to impose anything upon us. Instead, the reason we practice virtue in Buddhism is because virtue is highly conducive to our own happiness.

Buddhist monk and author Ajahn Munindo has a beautiful way of putting it. Paraphrasing the Buddha, he says, "It is wisdom that enables letting go of a lesser happiness in pursuit of a happiness which is greater."[20] In Buddhism, the practice of virtue is precisely that, having the wisdom to let go of the lesser happiness of non-virtuous indulgence for the greater bliss of blamelessness and confidence and, as you shall see later, the even greater bliss coming from compassion, samadhi, and nirvana.

Right Livelihood

The inclusion of right livelihood in the Noble Eightfold Path was a surprise to me. After all, I didn't think a great, world-transcending sage like the Buddha would give a bother about what people do for a living. In retrospect, however, it makes sense. One's livelihood is something one depends on for sustenance, so in that sense, it is literally a matter of life and death, and matters of life and death tend to have a disproportionate effect on one's behavior and mental state. Just saying.

Specifically, a problematic livelihood may require you to routinely compromise at least one of the five precepts, and that undermines your practice. A problematic livelihood may also fan the three flames of greed, hatred, and delusion (for example, if your job requires you to cheat little old ladies out of their life savings, or promote hateful racist propaganda, or tell big lies in order to protect certain companies from the legal consequences of destroying the environment). There is a painfully insightful modern saying, attributed to investigative journalist Upton Sinclair, that hints at how wrong livelihood can even make people stupid: "It is difficult to get a man to understand something when his salary depends on his not understanding it." For this reason, Soryu was not at all surprised that the Buddha included right livelihood in this list of eight essential spiritual practices. It is precisely in being willing to change one's livelihood that one gains the confidence to enter upon the transcendent aspects of the path.

Recognizing the outsize impact of one's livelihood, the Buddha prescribed right livelihood as one component of the Noble Eightfold Path. And once again, he gave specific guidelines. For laypeople, he recommends not engaging in these five trades: trading in weapons, living beings, meat, intoxicants, and poison.[21] For monastics, right livelihood means having very few material possessions, needing very little, and depending on the generosity of donors for basic needs such as food and clothing. In other words, the right livelihood for a monk is to subsist on alms. Even the very term *bhikkhu*, usually translated as "monk," literally means "mendicant." The Buddha also specifically forbade monastics from engaging in fortune-telling or selling lucky charms.[22]

To put it most simply, right livelihood for laypeople means livelihood that facilitates the weakening of greed, hatred, and delusion, and right livelihood for monastics means livelihood that facilitates the complete ending of greed, hatred, and delusion.

Right speech, right action, and right livelihood do not just create happiness for you and the people around you; they also play an essential role in your path to directly see nirvana. We will examine that in detail in Chapter 9.

Right Effort

In practicing right effort, one generates desire and makes an effort for four things:

1. the non-arising of unarisen unwholesome states

2. the abandoning of arisen unwholesome states

3. the arising of unarisen wholesome states

4. the maintenance and expansion of arisen wholesome states[23]

Just in case four things are too many for you to remember, the Buddha offers you a 50 percent discount on required memorization by asking you to remember only two things:

1. abandon the unwholesome

2. develop the wholesome[24]

This seemingly trivial teaching is the component of the path more empha- sized by the Buddha than any other. You can tell just by the number of times the Buddha talks about it. You might have figured out by now that Buddhism loves lists. And yes, lists beget meta-lists (lists of lists, try saying that quickly three times). The Buddha speaks about a meta-list of seven lists of things that help you reach enlightenment.[25] It is known as the thirty-seven aids to enlightenment.[26]

Effort (or one of its synonyms: energy and ardency) is the only thing that is explicitly mentioned in every one of the seven lists.[27] That's how important it is. No matter how powerful your car is, if you want to drive it home, you need fuel. In the same way, no matter how exquisite your understanding of the Dharma is, if you want to practice it, you need to apply energy. I hope this analogy drives the point home.

Right effort also denotes a total commitment to your practice while you are doing it. And yes, as usual, the Buddha has a wonderful analogy. He says, imagine there is a beauty queen singing and dancing onstage, attracting a large crowd. Imagine a man is ordered to walk within the crowd while carrying a bowl on his head filled to the brim with oil. Walking behind the man is a soldier with a sword, and if the man spills even one drop of oil, the soldier will immediately chop his head off. Imagine the intensity of mindfulness the man must be practicing while doing the task. The Buddha tells the monks to practice mindfulness of the body at that level of intensity and commitment.[28]

Guest artist: Natalie Tsang

Soryu has a thought-provoking way of getting across that point. He says:

> Right effort means that you throw yourself in, fully and completely, without hesitation, reservation, or compromise, to doing what is right and avoiding what is wrong, whether that be with your thoughts, words, or deeds. Do this and don't hold back.
>
> If you were in a street fight, would you make a half-hearted effort? Of course not. If you were giving birth, would you make a half-hearted effort? Of course not. You'd make a full effort. Why? Because that situation would matter.
>
> This situation right now matters. Every day of your life matters.
>
> Your life is short and precious. Take advantage of this precious

opportunity. Come to know the joy of right effort, the joy of affirming with every moment how much your life matters, the joy of shaking off all apathy and doing what you know is right for the benefit of all the world. Know this more deeply with each next day.

Right Mindfulness and Right Samadhi

The Buddhist system of meditation training is based on two pillars: serenity (*samatha*) and insight (*vipassanā*, literally: "clear seeing"). The basic premise is simple: it's good to have the right equipment for each task. If you need to see your own face, it's good to have a mirror. If you're doing microbiology, it's good to have a microscope. If you're doing astronomy, it's good to have a telescope. If you'd like to gain the wisdom necessary to liberate yourself from suffering, the rightly equipped mind wields serenity and insight.

The Buddha actually makes the importance of serenity and insight explicit. He says that if a monk wishes for enlightenment, he needs "to fulfill virtuous behavior, be devoted to internal serenity of mind, not neglect the jhānas (samadhi), be possessed of insight, and meditate diligently."[29] Serenity and insight are essential parts of the practice. In other separate discourses, the Buddha tells the monks that they should develop serenity and insight with the urgency of a man whose turban is on fire.[30] He also says monks who have already developed both serenity and insight should use them to reach enlightenment.[31]

As stated in Chapter 2, this combination of serenity and insight was a key innovation of the Buddha. Before Siddhattha became the Buddha, meditations for cultivating serenity (samatha) and its close cousin samadhi were already widely known and taught; we know that because Siddhattha himself learned those meditations from two famous teachers. A meditator begins with serenity to calm his mind, and when his mind becomes sufficiently calm, it becomes increasingly undistracted and blissful. Eventually, attention becomes so well collected the mind reaches samadhi. Siddhattha correctly realized that those blissful meditative states are conditioned, and therefore impermanent, and therefore cannot possibly be the ultimate solution to all suffering. However, he also correctly figured out that he could use that powerful state of mind to look deep into the nature of suffering, thereby gaining final freedom from all suffering. This was a genius move. Using that combination of serenity and insight, he gained full enlightenment and became the Buddha.

This standard method of serenity + insight is reflected in the last two components of the Noble Eightfold Path: right mindfulness and right samadhi. Right mindfulness includes practices that both calm the mind and develop insight. Right samadhi puts the mind into deep serenity and amps up its power to max-plus so it can be used with right mindfulness to develop profound insight.

The Buddha defines right mindfulness as the four establishments of mindfulness, which are mindfulness of the body, sensation, mind, and dharmas.[32]

Right samadhi is defined as the four meditative states known as the jhānas.[33] In the first jhāna, you are secluded from sensual pleasure and unwholesome states, and you experience what the Buddha calls "rapture and happiness born of seclusion." In the second jhāna, all thinking subsides, and because of that, the mind becomes placid and unified, and you experience what the Buddha calls "rapture and happiness born of samadhi." In the third jhāna, the mind becomes much more tranquil than the second jhāna, and with that tranquility, the mind abandons rapture and is left with a gentle happiness. With that, the meditator dwells "equanimous, mindful, and clearly comprehending." In the fourth jhāna, the mind abandons even that gentle happiness and rises beyond pleasure and pain. It also rises beyond being joyful for things being the way we want, or being dejected for things not being the way we want. Equanimity is perfected. In that state, the mind possesses mindfulness purified by equanimity. The Buddha calls it the "pure bright mind."

Right mindfulness and right samadhi are both major topics, each deserving its own chapter. We will discuss them in detail in the two subsequent chapters, and then talk about how they, along with the other six parts of the Noble Eightfold Path, arc directly to nirvana.

The Abbot's Commentary by Soryu Forall

It is strange that the word appearing most frequently in the context of the Noble Eightfold Path is also the one that gets the least attention: the word *right*. (Meng might joke in response, "I know, right?")

The Pali word translated to "right" is *sammā*. Sammā also means "correct," "complete," "whole," "proper," "perfect." It's a wonderful word. The path teaches us how to see and live correctly. But what is it that says what is right and what is wrong? That must be something deeper than doctrine. What is the source of correct doctrine?

The definitive Buddhist answer is that what leads to suffering is wrong, and what leads to the end of suffering is right. However, in Buddhism, we are not satisfied with a definition given in words. We strive to realize it, to know for ourselves what makes right right. What is it about the path that makes it sammā: right, correct, complete, whole, proper, perfect?

Practicing the path enables us to answer these questions. They are not answered with mere words. They are answered with our lives.

CHAPTER SEVEN

Don't Mind My Right Mindfulness

Exploring Mindfulness in Depth

Mindfulness, My Foot

Once upon a time, a talented student of meditation was granted an opportunity to meet a great Zen master. Eager to impress the master, right after sitting down the student proceeded to recite the list of his meditative accomplishments. After he finished his long monologue, the master smiled and said, "I only have one question for you. When you entered this room, which foot landed first? The left foot or the right foot?"

The student had no answer. He suddenly realized he had not even perfected basic mindfulness of the body. He bowed to the master and left the room. He would practice mindfulness diligently for ten more years before he would ask to see the master again.

In this chapter, let us take a deep dive into right mindfulness, starting with a definitive definition of *mindfulness* itself.

A Definitive Definition of *Mindfulness*

The Buddha famously said, "Mindfulness, I declare, is useful everywhere."[1] Mindfulness is one of the most important teachings in all of Buddhism. It is the main pillar of the meditative system taught by the Buddha.[2] Furthermore, it is the first of the seven factors of enlightenment, the balancing factor of the five spiritual faculties, one of the eight parts of the Noble Eightfold Path, and an accompanying factor of each of the other seven parts, and so on. The Buddha talks about mindfulness a lot.

Given the importance of mindfulness, you would think it'd be easy for me to give you a formal definition. I wish. Ancient texts never recorded the Buddha giving a formal definition of mindfulness in a clear expository manner. Instead, the texts give us numerous operational demonstrations of how mindfulness functions in the practice of Buddhism, and those of us who write books on Buddhism are left with the task of teasing out a definition (<grumble, grumble, grumble . . .>).

The Pali word *sati*, translated to "mindfulness," originally means "memory." Indeed, there are discourses where the Buddha uses the word *sati* to mean "memory."[3] However, according to Buddhist scholar monk Bhikkhu Bodhi, the Buddha more frequently uses *sati* to mean "attentiveness directed to the present"[4] or, more broadly, "lucid awareness of the phenomenal field."[5] In a sense, sati can be thought of as present-moment awareness, the presence of which helps us remember something easily forgotten: the present moment.

The best way to understand mindfulness functionally is in relation to two Pali words: *anupassanā* and *upaṭṭhāna*. *Anupassanā* is usually translated as "contemplation," but it literally means "close and repeated seeing" (*anu* means "close" or "repeated," and *passanā* means "seeing"), in other words, "to observe closely and repeatedly."[6] *Upaṭṭhāna* means "attendance, waiting on, looking after, service, care, ministering."[7] It literally means "standing near" (*upa* means "near," and *ṭhāna* means "standing"). To really attend to somebody means to fully make yourself present for them, so upaṭṭhāna is about fully establishing your presence. Functionally, *mindfulness* means both: "to observe closely and repeatedly,"[8] and "to fully establish your presence with the object of meditation" (such as the breath or bodily sensations).[9]

That is mindfulness. To practice right mindfulness, though, requires one other really important quality: wise discernment. This is reflected in the Buddha's use of the Pali word *pajānāti*, which means "to really know" (*jānāti* means "to know," and pajānāti is extra-strength jānāti), which is in turn related to the word for "wisdom," *paññā*. The Buddha's instruction here is to pajānāti every object of mindfulness. One place this wise discernment really comes to the fore is where mindfulness practice involves ethical considerations. For example, in one discourse, the Buddha instructed his disciples to practice right mindfulness by "mindfully abandoning" wrong intention, wrong speech, wrong action, and so on, and "mindfully acquiring and dwelling in" their right counterparts.[10] In this case, practicing right mindfulness requires us to wisely discern right from wrong. It is important to remember that mindfulness is not a passive state, it is a volitional activity.

Also important, just as tofu takes on the flavor of whatever seasoning it is cooked in, the object of mindfulness can cause the mindfulness practice to take on a different flavor. For example, when mindfulness is applied to the breath or bodily sensations, it is something akin to bare attention, but if mindfulness is applied to closely observing impermanence, it takes on a contemplative dimension, and if it is applied to a factor of the Noble Eightfold Path, say in mindfulness of right intention versus wrong intention, it takes on an ethical dimension.[11] If you ever hear Buddhist teachers arguing endlessly about whether mindfulness means bare attention or not, or other such matters, this is where it is coming from. That is why it is always useful for Buddhist teachers to study the early Buddhist texts.

In any case, all forms of mindfulness practices require three things: 1) to continuously attend to the chosen object of meditation with a fully established presence, 2) to observe it closely and repeatedly from moment to moment, and 3) to do so with wise discernment. This is true whether the object of meditation is sensation, a topic for contemplation, the present moment itself, or a memory about the past or a thought about the future.

Given all that is discussed, I would define *mindfulness* as "**remembering to pay attention, fully establishing presence with the object, closely and repeatedly observing it, and doing so with wise discernment**." Alternatively, I also like Soryu's shorter definition: "**remembering to pay attention, and remembering how best to pay attention**."

How to Establish Right Mindfulness

The Buddha's discourse on the establishment of mindfulness was recorded mainly in the Discourse on the Establishment of Mindfulness.[12] It's worth noting that entire books and PhD theses have been written on this one really important discourse.

To successfully establish right mindfulness, one needs these three other mental qualities besides mindfulness:

1. ardency

2. clear comprehension

3. putting away "covetousness and grief for the world"[13]

To be ardent is simply to be resolute and diligent in practicing **right effort**. Mahā Kassapa, one of the Buddha's top disciples, says: "A monk arouses ardor by thinking: 'If unarisen evil unwholesome states arise in me, or if wholesome states that have arisen in me cease, this may lead to my harm.' Thus he is ardent."[14]

The Buddha once gave a very useful definition of *clear comprehension* as: "**seeing and understanding the arising, presence, and passing away of sensations, thoughts, and perceptions**."[15] However, *clear comprehension* also more broadly means "**the type of awareness that develops wisdom**." Four Buddhist teachers I respect refer to it operationally as "full awareness" (Bhikkhu Ñāṇamoli),[16] "situational awareness" (Bhikkhu Sujato),[17] and "introspective awareness" (Dalai Lama and Thubten Chodron).[18]

Clear comprehension can also be thought of as the wise discernment aspect of mindfulness. Mindfulness and clear comprehension are practiced together as a pair. You may find that Buddhist teachers do not necessarily agree on where the exact boundary lies between mindfulness and clear comprehension, and there are even teachers who totally disregard the boundary and teach mindfulness + clear comprehension as a single thing. That is all fine, since both qualities are practiced in tandem anyway, and Buddhist teachers care far more about practice than theory.

The mental quality of "putting away covetousness and grief for the world" refers to a meaningful depth of samadhi that leads to the temporary abandoning of the five hindrances (which we will discuss in detail later in this chapter).[19] Here, you catch a glimpse of the close, mutually reinforcing relationship between right samadhi and right mindfulness: the stronger your practice of right samadhi, the more successfully you can practice right mindfulness, and vice versa.

These three mental qualities do not necessarily have to be present before you practice the establishment of mindfulness, because they grow as a consequence of the practice. In that sense, they form a virtuous cycle with the establishment of mindfulness.

The Four Establishments of Mindfulness

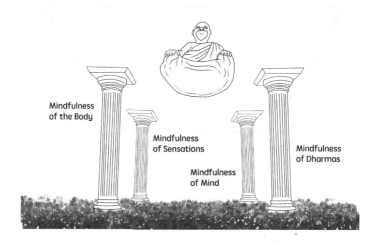

Like a chair constructed upon four legs, mindfulness is built upon four establishments, which are:

1. mindfulness of the body

2. mindfulness of sensations

3. mindfulness of mind

4. mindfulness of dharmas

Well, technically, that was not how the Buddha named them. He actually named the four establishments as the anupassanā-ing of (not "mindfulness of") body, sensations, mind, and dharmas. Remember, *anupassanā* means "close and repeated observation," often translated inadequately as "contemplation." However, many respected modern Buddhist teachers teach them as "mindfulness of [object]," which is also not incorrect, since the Buddha included the other key components of mindfulness in the actual instructions, namely presence (upaṭṭhāna) and fully knowing (pajānāti).[20] We decided to follow that popular modern convention, partly out of convenience and partly to avoid causing confusion.

Mindfulness of the Body

Mindfulness of the body constitutes a sizable part of the establishment of mindfulness. When I was a beginner, I was surprised how much importance the Buddha placed in the mindfulness of the body. He said, for example, that:

> Just as one who encompasses with his mind the great ocean thereby includes all the streams that run into the ocean, in the same way, whoever develops and cultivates mindfulness directed to the body includes all wholesome qualities that pertain to true knowledge.[21]

It's that important. Wow. I had naively assumed that for any spiritual practice, the mind and "spirit" would take center stage, while the body would have been a distant afterthought. But no, the Buddha puts mindfulness of the body right at the forefront of spiritual practice. I think the main reason is that Buddhism is, first and foremost, an insight tradition: Buddhism is concerned with developing the direct insight to see things as they really are, so as to understand the nature of suffering and liberation from suffering. A large percentage of our experience comes directly from the body. Therefore, one really cannot directly understand suffering and liberation from suffering without insight concerning the body. Another important reason to put mindfulness of the body first is that the body is very tangible, it has a physical presence, and it's therefore much easier to place attention on a bodily object than on something less tangible, like a mind object.

Furthermore, the meditative skills developed from mindfulness of the body are transferable to other establishments of mindfulness. For example, by attending to the breath, one can develop relaxation and attentional stability. Once developed, those same qualities can be applied to mindfulness of sensations or mindfulness of mind. In that sense, mindfulness of the body facilitates all other establishments of mindfulness, and that's why it eventually "includes all wholesome qualities that pertain to true knowledge."

The Buddha suggests six meditation practices relating to mindfulness of the body. The first, and possibly most important, is mindfulness of breath, important enough that the Buddha devoted an entire discourse to it (unsurprisingly titled the Discourse on the Mindfulness of Breathing) and explained how this one practice alone can lead to nirvana![22] The basic practice is surprisingly simple: know the breath at this moment, experience the whole body as you are breathing, and relax the body. That is all.

The second practice is also surprisingly simple, which is to just be mindful of your current posture. The Buddha specifically identifies four standard postures: walking, standing, sitting, lying down. The third practice is to engage in clear comprehension while in any posture and while performing any activity, including while falling asleep and waking up.

The next two practices examine the body in its component parts; in doing so, you see the unattractive aspects of the body, thereby cultivating nonattachment to it. One practice scans the body, noticing thirty-two parts of the body (head-hairs, body-hairs, nails, teeth, skin, flesh, sinews, bones, bone-marrow, kidneys, heart, liver, diaphragm, spleen, lungs, intestines, mesentery, contents of the stomach, feces, bile, phlegm, pus, blood, sweat, fat, tears, grease, spittle, snot, oil of joints, urine, and the brain) and seeing that it is full of "impurities" and unattractive aspects. Another practice examines the body as containing the four elements as defined in ancient India: earth, water, air, and fire and, once again, seeing its non-attractive aspects.

The final practice is kind of an extreme version of the previous two. It is called charnel ground contemplations. In ancient India, there were charnel grounds, which were places where human corpses were thrown and left to rot. This mindfulness practice is to go to those places, examine the corpses in various states of decay ("bloated, livid, oozing matter"), or see those corpses being devoured by birds, animals, or worms, or see skeletons or disconnected human bones and compare them to your own body and think, "My body too is of the same nature, it will be like that, it is not exempt from that fate." Yes, this is a very much in-your-face kind of practice; it forces you to face the shocking truth of your own inevitable death and horrifying decay. I know, truth sucks.

These last three practices are also known as *asubha* practices. Asubha literally means "not beautiful," but is often translated as "foulness" or "repulsiveness." Asubha practices are often prescribed as an antidote against lust, and against attachment to one's own body.

During the Buddha's time, there was a very beautiful and famous courtesan by the name of Sirima. Sirima was very sick, and as she was being carried around, a young Buddhist monk caught a glimpse of her. He thought to himself, "Even when Sirima is sick, she is very beautiful." He felt a very strong desire for her. That same night, Sirima died of illness. Four days later, her corpse started bloating and was infested with maggots. Taking advantage of the teaching opportunity, the Buddha asked King Bimbisara to announce that Sirima was available for a thousand coins. No man would take her for that price, or for five hundred coins, or two hundred fifty, or for any price, or even for free. The Buddha then told his monks, "Look at Sirima. When she was alive, many men were willing to give a thousand coins just to spend a night with her, but now, none would even take her for free. The body of a person is subject to deterioration and decay." And then he spoke in verse:

> Look at this dressed up body,
> a mass of sores, supported (by bones), sickly,
> a subject of many thoughts (of sensual desire).
> Indeed, that body is neither permanent nor enduring.[23]

When that young monk saw Sirima's body and heard the Buddha's words, he gained stream-entry.

Mindfulness of Sensations (*Vedanā*)

Guest artist: Natalie Tsang

Mindfulness of sensations, Lego style

The Pali word *vedanā* can be translated either as "sensations" or "feelings." In fact, I had a long debate with myself about which translation to use (and like all debates with myself, I ultimately won). *Vedanā* here includes the sensations generated by the contact of any sense object with any sense faculty.

It does not necessarily include emotions, however. Emotions are complicated processes with both feeling and thinking components, and *vedanā* includes only the feeling component of the experience of emotion.

Mindfulness of sensations is surprisingly short, simple, and powerful. The instruction really has only two parts:

1. Be mindful of whether a sensation experienced is pleasant, unpleasant, or neither-pleasant-nor-unpleasant.

2. Be mindful of whether that sensation is worldly or unworldly.

That's it.

You may wonder what it means for a sensation to be worldly or unworldly. The Pali word for "worldly," *sāmisa*, is closely related to the word for "flesh," *āmisa*. Hence, a worldly sensation is one related to flesh, and an unworldly sensation is one related to renunciation. Unworldly pleasant and neither-pleasant-nor-unpleasant sensations refer to experiences within the jhānas, but what is an unworldly unpleasant sensation? I'm not aware of any example given by the Buddha, but from a separate but closely related discourse, you can get an idea. Here, a disciple gains understanding of impermanence and unsatisfactoriness of all sensory phenomena. He then experiences a longing for the supreme liberations, and that longing causes grief. The Buddha calls it "grief based on renunciation."[24] Unworldly unpleasant sensation is the sensation associated with the grief based on renunciation. Soryu clarifies that this grief comes not from desiring to be enlightened, but from not having attained the goal yet, and being insecure about whether one will ever attain it.

How powerful is mindfulness of sensations? According to the Buddha, when one develops deep, piercing wisdom into the nature of sensation, and one is able to abandon 1) the underlying tendency to lust in regard to pleasant feeling, 2) the underlying tendency to aversion in regard to painful feeling, and 3) the underlying tendency to ignorance in regard to neither-painful-nor-pleasant feeling, one then cuts off craving. And by completely breaking through conceit, one has "made an end to suffering."[25] In other words, one reaches nirvana. Yes, there is a direct path from mindfulness of sensation to nirvana. The Buddha says, "Completely understanding sensations, one is without defilements in this very life."[26]

Yeah, wow.

Mindfulness of Mind (*Citta*)

Mindfulness of mind refers to awareness of the general state and level of consciousness, which is determined by its mental factors, such as lust, hate, and delusion. For that reason, the instruction for mindfulness of mind is about paying attention to mental factors. Specifically, the meditator understands if the mind is affected or unaffected by lust, hate, and delusion, and whether or not it is concentrated or liberated.[27]

The main purpose of mindfulness of mind is clear, honest, and objective self-examination. In a separate discourse, the Buddha calls it "being skilled in the ways of your own mind" and compares it to a young person, desiring beauty for himself or herself, looking at his or her own reflection in a clean bright mirror, examining the reflection for any dust or blemishes.[28] For that young person, looking at the mirror is helpful to increasing his or her own beauty. In the same way, self-examination is very helpful for a practitioner to grow in wholesome qualities.

"Can you teach my stepmother mindfulness? She is not using the mirror for self-examination."

The shift from mindfulness of the body to mindfulness of sensations, and then to mindfulness of mind, represents a gradual shift toward increasingly subtler objects of meditation. According to Bhikkhu Anālayo, another shift happens at mindfulness of mind: going from *what* is experienced to *how* it is being experienced. For example, in mindfulness of sensations, you are aware of a particularly pleasant sensation (the "what"), but in mindfulness of mind, you are aware of your state of mind while experiencing that pleasant sensation, for example, whether the mind is experiencing it with or without lust (the "how"). Another way to look at it: your state of mind is the underlying current of your experience at this moment, and mindfulness of mind brings attention to this underlying current. That is the most useful aspect of mindfulness of mind. It is what makes it such a good mirror for self-examination.

Mindfulness of Dharmas

The final foundation of mindfulness is the mindfulness of dharmas (*dhammas* in Pali, and *dharmas* in both Sanskrit and English). Dharmas here is often translated as "mental objects," which is an awful translation because at least two of the other establishments of mindfulness also include mental objects. I have also seen it translated as "phenomena," which, while technically correct, I find too broad for this context. Mindfulness of dharmas refers to the contemplation of experiences in relation to the universal laws surrounding the nature of suffering and liberation from suffering. My favorite translation of dharmas in this context is "conditions of being," but even that I find unsatisfactory. For these reasons, I decided it best to leave dharmas untranslated here.

Mindfulness of dharmas encompasses:

- The five hindrances

- The five aggregates

- The six sense bases

- The seven factors of enlightenment

- The Four Noble Truths

The five hindrances: This is a major topic. We will explore it in the next section below.

The five aggregates: Form, sensation, perception, volitional formations, consciousness. See Chapter 3.

The six sense bases: The six pairs of sense organs and objects, which are

Mindfulness of Dharmas

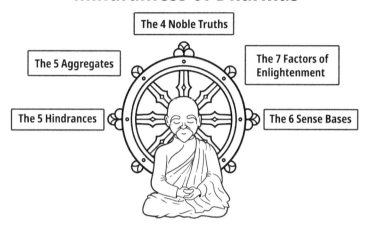

1) eye and visible objects, 2) ear and sounds, 3) nose and odors, 4) tongue and tastes, 5) body and tactile objects, and 6) mind and mental objects.[29]

The seven factors of enlightenment: The essential mental factors that lead to enlightenment.[30] They are: mindfulness, investigation of phenomena, energy, rapture, tranquility, samadhi, and equanimity. We will become well acquainted with each of them by the end of this book, and we will see a case study of how they come together to facilitate a spiritual breakthrough in Chapter 12.

The Four Noble Truths: You know, the nature of suffering, the origin of suffering, the cessation of suffering, and the path to the cessation of suffering.

According to Bhikkhu Anālayo, mindfulness of dharmas is unlike the other establishments of mindfulness in a very important way. The first three establishments provide objects for you to practice mindfulness on. In contrast, mindfulness of dharmas gives you the lenses through which you see all experienced phenomena, including the first three establishments of mindfulness.[31] For example, to apply these lenses when practicing mindfulness of breath, you can check for the five hindrances while trying to attend to the breath, and then contemplate the five aggregates in relation to the breath, and then contemplate how the sense bases relate to the experience of breathing, and so on. In doing so, eventually you will directly experience impermanence in its moment-to-moment glory, followed by lust fading away and cessation, leading in turn to letting go, resulting in enlightenment.[32]

Five Hindrances

Sensual Desire	Ill Will	Sloth-and-Torpor

Restlessness-and-Remorse	Doubt

The five hindrances are mental obstacles that hinder the mind from meditative concentration. Beyond that, they also hinder the mind from wisdom in general, which means that they don't just operate during meditation, they also operate in daily life. The five are:

1. sensual desire

2. ill will

3. sloth-and-torpor

4. restlessness-and-remorse

5. doubt[33]

Sensual desire can be understood as the lust for the "five strands of sense pleasure," which means objects that give pleasure to the five senses: pleasant sight, sound, smell, taste, touch. The pleasure arising from right samadhi, which does not depend on pleasing the five senses, is notably excluded from sensual desire.[34]

The best antidote to sensual desire is to develop the ability to experience the joy of the present moment when nothing is happening. One simple way to do that is whenever you are in an alert and relaxed state, notice that it is subtly pleasant. To be alert and relaxed is not a neutral state; it is a lightly joyful state. Once you are able to find that subtle pleasantness, give it your full attention and indulge in it for as long as you can. The more you do it, the more the mind becomes familiar with it and, consequently, the more easily you can find that subtle joy. Soon you will find yourself able to access it on demand, which means whenever you sit in meditation, with nothing happening at all, you can find that joy! With that joy, sensual desire will find it much harder to grab hold of you. Happily, this ability is mastered when you enter right samadhi (see the next chapter).

A complementary antidote is to attend to grasping and aversion. After every sensation, there is perception, and after perception, there can be either grasping or aversion. I suggest that the grasping and aversion is where the suffering is, and therefore, if you experience a sensation without grasping or aversion, then it can be experienced with no suffering (temporarily). The same with every thought and every desire. Therefore, the practice is to notice the arising of grasping and aversion when experiencing a sensation, a thought, or a desire, and then try to experience it without grasping or aversion. One way to reduce grasping is to meditate on the impermanent and unattractive nature of the object (also see "asubha practices" from earlier in this chapter). The more successfully you can do that, the less sensual desire can control you.

Ill will refers to mental states born of aversion, which include anger, hatred, resentment, jealousy, and envy. These feelings can be directed toward other people, objects, situations, or even oneself.

The antidote to ill will is loving-kindness. One highly effective way to do that is to cultivate the *joy of loving-kindness*. Try this exercise now: For the next ten seconds, bring to mind somebody you care about, and then wish for that person to be happy. Do you notice you were smiling when you did that? To be on the giving end of loving-kindness is intrinsically joyful. The practice is to wish people well a lot, and then bring full attention to that joy that accompanies loving-kindness. The mind loves this kind of joy, so the more you do this, the bigger loving-kindness expands in your mind and, the bigger it becomes, the more it pushes ill will away.

Sloth-and-torpor are actually two distinct mental states rolled into one hindrance. Sloth is characterized by dullness and lack of energy, while torpor is characterized by drowsiness and smothering unwieldiness.[35] Together, they describe a mind that is sleepy, saddled with mental inertia, and too "heavy" to wield.

The obvious solution to sloth-and-torpor is to increase energy. There are two things to increase: the quantity of energy and the quality of energy. A lot of us modern people are chronically sleep deprived, which means we simply do not have sufficient quantity of energy. Formal meditation puts us in a state of stillness and relaxation, and if a sleep-deprived body finds itself in a state of stillness and relaxation, what does it want to do? It desperately wants to fall asleep, of course. Which is why so many modern meditators have so much trouble staying awake during meditation. The simple solution: get enough sleep. There are complementary practices—for example, certain breathing techniques—that can give you a jolt of energy, but still, if you do not have enough sleep, nothing works better than simply addressing that.

If you already have enough sleep but still struggle with sloth-and-torpor, then you have to manage the quality of your energy. The best way to do that is to manage your motivation. For example, you can remind yourself how amazingly rare it is to be born a human being who is so extremely lucky that you get to learn the Dharma. Or remind yourself that you will surely suffer old age, sickness, and/or death someday, so if you don't work hard enough to directly see nirvana while you still can, you are going to be so damned screwed. Such reminders are a little like lighting a small fire under your own gluteus maximus—guaranteed to make you jump up with energy, but in a good way.

Restlessness-and-remorse are also two distinct mental states rolled into one hindrance, because they share the common feature of disquietude. Restlessness makes the mind unsteady, like wind makes a banner ripple, while remorse refers to regret and sorrow over what has been done (or not done) in the past.[36] Together, they describe a mind that is agitated and cannot be easily settled.

The best solution to restlessness is to develop the ability to experience the joy of the present moment, as we talked about for sensual desire. Whenever sitting is calmly joyful, restlessness is overcome.

Remorse is addressed by understanding that it comes from a good place:

two mental states called *hiri* and *ottappa*. The Buddha calls hiri and ottappa "guardians of the world," as if they are superheroes that keep the world in a good state.[37] Wow. So what are they? They are conscience and concern.[38] The Buddha says it is because people have conscience and concern that other people are protected from harm by them. Therefore, if everybody has those qualities, no harm would come to anyone. Furthermore, the Buddha also says that one who possesses conscience and concern acquires a whole host of other good things—including heedfulness, good friends, and virtue—that lead all the way to liberation from suffering.[39] If you have remorse, it means you are capable of conscience and concern, and that is a good thing.

There is one other compounding factor. See, the spiritual path is one of increasing wisdom and virtue, which means that if your practice has been going well, you are wiser and more virtuous today than you were before. But that also means that at one time, you must have been more foolish and less virtuous compared to today. Which means that very likely, something you did in the past must cause you remorse when viewed with the wisdom you possess today.

So the thing to recognize is that remorse comes from a good place: from the "guardians of the world" qualities of conscience and concern, combined with your spiritual growth over time. Once you recognize that, remorse becomes a motivation to be a much better person, so as to make up for the past and to create greater benefit to others for the future, rather than an excuse to beat yourself up. That is how to address remorse as a hindrance.

Doubt traditionally refers to the inability to place confidence in the Buddha, the Dharma, the Sangha (monastic community),[40] and the training, and, by extension, also the lack of confidence in one's current teacher.[41] It can also extend to doubt in oneself, meaning, even if you have full confidence in the teachings and the teacher, you have no confidence in your own ability to carry it out.[42] I find this perspective useful because it afflicts me a lot.

The Buddha strongly encourages intelligent probing of his teachings, so why is doubt listed as a hindrance? Part of the answer is there are two types of doubt: an unhealthy doubt that undermines practice, and a healthy doubt that informs the practice. The hindrance here refers only to unhealthy doubt. The main difference is in the underlying attitude. The attitude underlying healthy doubt is an open-minded, intelligent curiosity that seeks to understand and clarify, while the attitude underlying unhealthy doubt is a strong negative bias that foolishly cannot be moved by fact or reason. In Buddhism, doubt is overcome not with blind faith, but with much learning and investigation.[43] (We will talk more about doubt in Chapter 11.)

In addition, even healthy doubt can sometimes become a hindrance in a "wrong place, wrong time" situation. When you are learning to ride a bicycle, for example, if you are already on the bike pedaling wobblingly, it is precisely the wrong time to ask yourself, "Can the laws of physics actually enable me to balance on two wheels?" No, don't do that! What you need to do at that moment is to just pedal and try to keep balance. The question concerning the laws of physics is a good and correct one to ask, but not at the moment you are pedaling and wobbling. Asking it at that time is counterproductive because it interferes with the practice. In the same way, while you're in the middle of meditation practice, questions such as, "Is the human mind actually capable of calming down?" or "Is the Buddha an actual historical figure?" interfere with the practice and are, hence, counterproductive. They are good questions, and there are proper times to ask them, and the middle of meditation practice is usually not it.

As usual, the Buddha gives us delightful similes. The Buddha compares the five hindrances to strangler figs. A strangler fig tree starts its life as a seed dropped onto a host tree by a bird or an animal. It then grows roots all around the trunk of the host tree, all the way into the ground. Eventually, it envelops the host tree and strangles it to death. In the same way, the five hindrances encircle and strangle the mind and, in doing so, they weaken wisdom.[44] Yes, a gripping simile indeed.

In addition, the Buddha gives us a set of similes to help us understand each of the five hindrances. He compares the hindrances to a man in an assortment of crappy situations.[45] One afflicted with sensual desire is like a man taking on debt. Every debt must be repaid with interest or be extended (and incur even more interest in the future). In the same way, every sensual pleasure indulged must be repaid later with even more suffering through eventual loss, separation, or death, or it creates more sensual desire in the future. One who is free from sensual desire is like a man whose business prospered and who made enough money to pay off all his debts; he rejoices!

One afflicted with ill will is like a man who is sick. Ill will is like a serious disease; it causes you pain and destroys you from the inside out. One who is free from ill will is like a man who recovered from sickness; he rejoices!

One afflicted with sloth-and-torpor is like a man in prison, bounded and unable to do what he wants to do—a festival, for example, goes on near the prison and he misses the entire thing. One who is free from sloth-and-torpor is like a man released from prison; he rejoices!

One afflicted with restlessness-and-remorse is like a slave whose master forces him to do this or that. He has no agency or autonomy; he can't even rest when he wants to. One who is free from restlessness-and-remorse is like the slave released from slavery; he rejoices!

One afflicted with doubt is like a traveler lost in a desert where food is scarce and dangers abound. One who is free from doubt is like the lost traveler arriving safe and sound at the edge of a village; he rejoices!

Notice that every simile has one important thing in common? In every simile, when the man finds himself out of his crappy situation, he rejoices. Joy is his internal measure of success. This is an important point, because **freedom from the five hindrances is not a neutral state, it is a joyful state**. This joy born of freedom from the five hindrances is very wholesome, and as we will see in the next chapters, is an important propellant toward nirvana.

Is There Such a Thing as Wrong Mindfulness?

Yes, it turns out there is such a thing as wrong mindfulness. Every part of the Noble Eightfold Path has its "wrong" counterpart. For example, there is wrong view (versus right view) and wrong intention (versus right intention). Mindfulness is no exception.

Unfortunately, for those of us who write books on Buddhism, the Buddha also did not give a formal definition of wrong mindfulness. More challenging still, he never even spoke of wrong mindfulness as a topic on its own. I have found sixty-five discourses in the ancient texts where the Buddha mentioned wrong mindfulness, and in all sixty-five instances, he talked about it in the context of practicing all eight parts of the Noble Eightfold Path wrongly. For example, in one discourse, he said:

Monks, relying on the wrong way leads to failure, not success. How
so? Wrong view gives rise to wrong intention, which gives rise to
wrong speech, which gives rise to wrong action, which gives rise to
wrong livelihood, which gives rise to wrong effort, which gives rise
to wrong mindfulness, which gives rise to wrong samadhi. Wrong
samadhi gives rise to wrong knowledge, which gives rise to wrong
freedom. That's how relying on the wrong way leads to failure, not
success.[46]

Fortunately, it is pretty easy to figure out a definition of wrong mindfulness, because the Buddha gave us a big hint in a discourse where the Buddha taught that right view, right mindfulness, and right effort "run and circle
around" all of the other parts.[47] In other words, every part of the Noble Eightfold Path needs to be practiced alongside right view, right mindfulness, and
right effort, which obviously means that right mindfulness must be practiced
alongside right view and right effort. But what does that mean? Remember,
right view basically means knowing the Four Noble Truths, and that right
effort means commitment to developing the wholesome and abandoning the
unwholesome.[48] That means that to practice right mindfulness, you need
three things:

1. commitment

2. wise awareness that your final goal is total liberation from suffering

3. ethical considerations

One good example of wrong mindfulness is an assassin mindfully aiming
at his target, mindfully breathing, and then mindfully squeezing the trigger. Mindfulness in the execution of cold-blooded murder is obviously wrong
mindfulness. A more nuanced example involves practicing mindfulness at
work. If your intention is to make yourself a calmer person for your own
welfare and for the happiness of your customers, co-workers, and all living
things, then it can be considered right mindfulness. If your intention does not
include ethical or compassionate considerations, then it can be considered
wrong mindfulness.

Mindfully Getting Right Mindfulness Right

In summary, right mindfulness refers to the four establishments of mindfulness, which are:

1. Mindfulness of the body, consisting of:

   a. mindfulness of breathing

   b. mindfulness of posture

   c. practicing clear comprehension in any bodily activity

   d. mindfulness of thirty-two component parts of the body

   e. mindfulness of bodily experience in the context of the "four elements"

   f. charnel ground contemplations

2. Mindfulness of sensations

3. Mindfulness of mind

4. Mindfulness of dharmas, consisting of:

   a. the five hindrances

   b. the five aggregates

   c. the six sense bases

   d. the seven factors of enlightenment

   e. the Four Noble Truths

We use these to cultivate a mind that is clear, lucid, and free of the five hindrances, so that we may enter right samadhi, the subject of the next chapter.

The Abbot's Commentary by Soryu Forall

Mindfulness is said to be useful everywhere. That means we can always do it. We can practice it in every circumstance.

Too often, people think they need to hold a specific focus, such as the breath, in order to practice mindfulness. But we can experience everything with mindfulness. Are you experiencing pain? You may not be able to focus on your breath, but you can experience pain with mindfulness. Are you experiencing joy? You may not be able to focus on your breath, but you can experience joy with mindfulness. This experience, not a different one, is where we most easily establish mindfulness.

Mindfulness is relevant always. It is how we make this very moment into the next step on the path to the end of suffering.

CHAPTER EIGHT

Focus on Right Samadhi

The Fascinating Power of

Meditative Concentration

How a Draper Became a World-Changing Scientist

In the 1600s, there was a Dutch draper by the name of Antonie van Leeuwenhoek. Antonie cared a lot about the quality of his textiles. He wanted to see the quality of the thread better than anyone else could, so he developed an interest in lens making. Eventually, he became very good at making high-quality microscopes.

Happily for all of us, Antonie's interest quickly went beyond looking at textiles to exploring the natural world with his microscopes. Soon he was startled to see an entire world of tiny creatures milling about in a drop of water.[1] In the 1670s, he started publishing his observations of very small organisms such as mold and lice and, more important, bacteria and other unicellular microorganisms. He helped change the way people understood diseases. Today, we take for granted that diseases are spread by germs. This is called the germ theory of disease. During Antonie's time, however, germ theory was not widely accepted. As a consequence, practices we find shocking today were widespread; for example, doctors did not even wash their hands between touching corpses and delivering babies.

Thanks to Antonie's pioneering work, germ theory eventually gained ground, and that changed everything. Today, Antonie van Leeuwenhoek is remembered as the Father of Microbiology.

Without a microscope, it is possible to theorize that diseases are spread by tiny particles invisible to the naked eye. However, to actually be able to see bacteria and other unicellular microorganisms with a microscope changes everything.

Right samadhi is to a meditator what a microscope is to a microbiologist. Soryu says this analogy is especially apt given that, like a microscope, right samadhi reveals distinctions, is unbiased, and does not add to what is actually there. Right samadhi is a meditator's most important and most powerful tool. Without it, you can only theorize about the nature of the mind. Having right samadhi allows you to actually examine the depths of your mind in perfect calmness, clarity, and equanimity, without the obstruction caused by the five hindrances. You can then see the mind as it actually is. Right samadhi changes everything.

In this chapter, we will examine right samadhi.

The Noble Five-Factored Right Samadhi

Right samadhi refers to the four jhānas. The word *jhāna* literally means "meditation," but when the Buddha uses that word, he is referring to a specific collection of four increasingly refined states of meditative absorption. That is why you often see *jhāna* translated as "absorption" and, occasionally, as "meditation." I decided to leave *jhāna* untranslated. The four jhānas are imaginatively named the first jhāna, the second jhāna, the third jhāna, and the fourth jhāna.

The four jhānas offer powerful stepping stones toward nirvana. The Buddha speaks very frequently of the jhānas, but I find his Discourse on the Five Factors to be particularly helpful because he makes an explicit link between the jhānas and the "direct knowledge" that leads to nirvana, plus he gives colorful similes to illustrate his point.[2]

First jhāna

In the first jhāna, you are secluded from sensual pleasures and unwholesome states. That first jhāna gives you what the Buddha calls "rapture and happiness born of seclusion." That is an extremely important stepping stone for you as a practitioner, because it offers you the ability to reliably experience intense joy independent of sensual pleasures. Prior to this, you suffer from a reliance on sensual pleasure for joy, and in that sense you are a slave to sensual pleasure. When you arrive at the first jhāna, however, you realize that you don't need pleasant sensory experiences at all to be joyful; you can be ecstatically joyful just by sitting there with nothing happening.

To be fair, many seasoned meditators can already access a reliable stream of joy way before arriving at the first jhāna, but in my experience, that pre-jhāna joy tends to be subtle and not strong enough to, say, displace my craving for chocolate, whereas the joy in the first jhāna is intense enough to significantly focus the mind and for the mind to tell itself, "This is all I need right now; I need nothing else." Though highly focused, the mind is not totally unified at this point (that happens in the second jhāna), but it is sufficiently focused on the intense joy that, if you had never experienced jhāna before, may be the deepest meditative concentration you had ever experienced up to this point in your practice.

The pleasantness you experience starting from the first jhāna is why the Buddha calls the jhānas "pleasant abiding here and now." Modern people may call it "blissing out." But the first jhāna does something far more important than allowing you to bliss out: it gives you a *vital* insight that opens your door to nirvana. When you first learn Buddhism and read about the Buddha referring to sensual desire as a "fire" or "poison" that causes suffering, you may think it makes no sense at all. Satisfying sensual desire brings about so much pleasure, so how can sensual desire possibly be a cause for suffering? Surely it's a cause for happiness. Once you experience the rapture and happiness in the first jhāna, however, the Buddha's teachings on sensual desire suddenly make perfect sense.

First, you realize that this joy born of seclusion from sensual desire is more refined, sustainable, and satisfying than the joy that relies on fulfilling sensual desire. Second, and more important, you realize it does not have the same problematic side effects. Every shot of happiness that comes from fulfilling sensual desire necessarily plants a seed for future suffering in ways we talked about back in Chapter 3: no matter how many pleasant sensory objects we have, they eventually change for the worse (e.g., they get old, or decay), or we habituate to them (so even the very same objects become less pleasurable or even unpleasurable over time), or we will eventually lose them, or we lose the ability to enjoy them due to our own eventual sickness, frailty, or death. Worse still, fulfilling sensual desire reinforces one's reliance on and addiction to it. It is like scratching an itchy skin rash: you make it more likely that you'll need to scratch it even more. Worse still, scratching the rash does extra damage to it, and contributes nothing to its healing.

Hence, deriving happiness from sensual desire is like borrowing money from a loan shark who enjoys breaking knees: you get to enjoy the pleasure now, but you will surely pay much more than you get in the long term. Whereas experiencing happiness without sensual desire is like discovering that your rich grandparents left you a generous trust fund that gives you free money to spend every day. Once you realize you have that source of income, you would never want to borrow from a loan shark again, especially if the free money is more than what you can get from the loan shark. In the same way, once you have reliable access to rapture and happiness born of seclusion, you would understand why the Buddha calls sensual pleasure "low, vulgar, coarse, ignoble, and unbeneficial."[3] The mind then naturally begins to let go of sensual desire. Or, as the Buddha says, "If you always have water, you don't need a well."[4]

This is why the Buddha says the first jhāna is where sensual desire temporarily "ceases without remainder," along with ill will and cruelty.[5] That is also why he calls the jhānas the place where "Mara and his following cannot go" and where the meditator has "blindfolded Mara" (remember from Chapter 2 that Mara is the personification of all things bad).[6] The implication of this statement is that the first jhāna serves you in two fantastic ways: it is not just a pleasant abiding for you; it is also a safe refuge where you gain total safety from Mara. In the first jhāna, a meditator knows, "I am secure from danger and Mara cannot do anything to me."[7]

That is the reason the first jhāna is so important: it provides access to the inner joy that inclines the mind toward total freedom from lust and sensual desire, and thereby propels the mind toward wisdom and liberation from all suffering.

The Buddha's simile of the first jhāna puts that inner joy on center stage. He says, "Just as a skillful bath man might heap bath powder in a metal basin and, sprinkling it gradually with water, would knead it until the moisture wets his ball of bath powder, soaks it, and pervades it inside and out, in the same way, the meditator makes the rapture and happiness born of seclusion drench, steep, fill, and pervade this body, so that there is no part of this whole body that is not pervaded by it."

Second jhāna

The second jhāna builds upon the first jhāna. In the second jhāna, all thinking subsides, the mind becomes placid and unified, and you experience what the Buddha calls "rapture and happiness born of samadhi." This rapture and happiness is even more refined and sublime than in the first jhāna, but the most important contribution of the second jhāna is the strength of samadhi, which allows for placidity and unification of mind.

It is this unification of mind that turns the mind into a powerful force for breaking ignorance and developing wisdom. It is like trying to start a fire with sunlight. If you merely put tinder out in the sun, it's not likely to catch fire, but if you use a magnifying glass to collect sunlight into a tiny spot of tinder, then it may catch fire. It is also like uniting the mass of oppressed slaves against a tyrant's rule. When the slaves are disunited, they have no chance against the tyrant's oppressive regime, but once those slaves are united into a single force, then they can be free. In the same way, if you are dispersed internally, you are weak against Mara, but if your mind is internally unified, you become very powerful. The word *samadhi* literally means "to collect," and the second jhāna is where this collectedness of mind begins to become a true force of wisdom to be reckoned with.

The Buddha's simile of the second jhāna involves a lake: "Just as there might be a lake whose waters welled up from below with no inflow from any direction, and the lake would not be replenished by showers of rain, then the cool fount of water welling up in the lake would make the cool water drench, steep, fill, and pervade the lake, so that there would be no part of the whole lake that is not pervaded by cool water; so, too, the meditator makes the rapture and happiness born of samadhi drench, steep, fill, and pervade this body, so that there is no part of his whole body that is not pervaded by the rapture and happiness born of samadhi." Once again, rapture and happiness take center stage in this simile. The image of a lake that has no inflow from the outside, but wells up entirely from within, alludes to expanded breadth and depth of the inner joy, and to the experience of placidity and collectedness.

One key difference between the first two jhānas is illustrated in the similes. In the first jhāna, joy needs to be deliberately "sprinkled and kneaded in" until it saturates the body, while in the second jhāna, joy fills the body internally and spontaneously.

Third jhāna

The third jhāna builds upon the second jhāna. In the third jhāna, rapture fades away and you are left with happiness. The Pali words that are translated into "rapture" and "happiness" are *pīti* and *sukha*, respectively. *Pīti* is also translated as "exhilaration," "uplifting joy," or "energetic joy," and *sukha* is also translated as "bliss," "pleasure," or "non-energetic joy." Pīti and sukha are qualitatively different types of joy, with pīti marked by energy and excitement and sukha marked by a calm sense of pleasantness. In the third jhāna, the mind becomes much more tranquil than in the second jhāna, and with that tranquility, pīti becomes uncomfortably exhausting and grating, so the mind gently abandons it and is left with sukha. With that, the Buddha says, "the meditator dwells equanimous, mindful, and clearly comprehending." It is not that those factors were not present before, but that with increasing tranquility and unification of mind, those factors strengthen massively and become prominent enough to start taking the foreground.

Hence, the most visible contribution of the third jhāna is the tranquilization of mind that leads to the abandoning of pīti, but, more important, with a mind well pacified and unified, the factors of mind that lead directly to wisdom strengthen and come prominently into the foreground: equanimity, mindfulness, and clear comprehension, supported solidly by sukha. For that reason, the Buddha says one who dwells in the third jhāna is declared by the noble ones as: "equanimous, mindful, dwelling happily."

The Buddha's simile of the third jhāna is, "Just as in a pond of blue or red or white lotuses, some lotuses that are born and grow in the water might thrive immersed in the water without rising out of it, and cool water would drench, steep, fill, and pervade them to their tips and their roots, so that there would be no part of those lotuses that would not be pervaded by cool water; so, too, the meditator makes the happiness divested of rapture drench, steep, fill, and pervade this body, so that there is no part of his whole body that is not pervaded by the happiness divested of rapture."

This simile is similar to the second jhāna, but with one visible addition: the lotuses. Is there a significance to the lotus imagery? Very likely so, since the Buddha uses the lotus as the symbol for buddhahood itself. In a conversation with the brahmin Doṇa, the Buddha famously said in verse:

> As a lovely white lotus
> is not soiled by the water,
> I am not soiled by the world:
> therefore, O brahmin, I am a buddha.[8]

My own understanding, based on the description of the third jhāna, is that the lotuses in the simile allude to the wisdom factors coming to the fore. That is the most important contribution of the third jhāna.

As usual, Soryu offers a complementary but deeper and more nuanced understanding of the analogy. He thinks the key point about the analogy is aliveness (of the lotuses), and it is exactly this aliveness that is the wisdom. He points out in his usual poetic Zen style, "It's no longer that we are just doing what we learned we should. The path knows how to walk itself. It shifts from dead knowledge to living wisdom." In addition, because of that aliveness and wisdom, the joy also appears to expand: it is now experienced as if it is everywhere, both within and without, like the cool water that is both within the lotuses and also outside in every direction.

Fourth jhāna

The fourth jhāna builds upon the third jhāna. In the fourth jhāna, the mind abandons even sukha (happiness) and rises above and beyond pleasure and pain, joy and dejection. Equanimity is perfected. In that state, something extremely important happens: the mind now possesses mindfulness purified by equanimity. The meditator "sits pervading this body with a pure bright mind, so that there is no part of his whole body that is not pervaded by the pure bright mind." It is this mindfulness purified by equanimity that directly enables the penetration into the "direct knowledge" that leads to nirvana.

The Buddha's simile of the fourth jhāna alludes directly to this purity of mindfulness. The simile is one where a man, having taken a bath, "sits covered from the head down with a white cloth, so that there would be no part of his whole body that is not pervaded by the white cloth; so, too, the meditator sits pervading this body with a pure bright mind, so that there is no part of his whole body that is not pervaded by the pure bright mind."[9]

Jhāna teacher Leigh Brasington suspects this simile is more literal than most people think. He said when one enters the fourth jhāna upon establishing very strong concentration, one's visual perception is very bright, even with eyes closed. He said imagine on a very bright and sunny afternoon, pitching a small white tent in the middle of an open field, and sitting inside that tent: your visual sense will be dominated by white brightness in all directions, and that is the visual experience. Soryu agrees that the visual perception is very bright, yet somehow not blinding, but more important, the mind itself is bright. Every aspect of consciousness is bright, not just the visual field. The practice is to be sure that this bright mind pervades somatic experience.

Direct knowledge

The final step is to make use of this pure bright mind to acquire "direct knowledge." The way to do that is to attend to the object of interest with this turbocharged mind. This is a mind that is unified with perfect attentional mastery, sharpened with perfect mindfulness, pacified with perfect tranquility, and unencumbered by hindrances, pleasure or pain, like or dislike. This is the mind most perfectly conducive to wisdom.

With that power of mind, the Buddha says, "a meditator grasps well the object to be reviewed, attends to it well, sustains it well, penetrates it well with wisdom." He gives a simile of a person looking at another from a higher point of view, and because his point of view is elevated, he can see better. "Just as one standing might look upon one sitting down, or one sitting down might look upon one lying down—so, too, a monk has grasped well the object of reviewing, attended to it well, sustained it well, and penetrated it well with wisdom."

Guest artist: Angeleen Tan

Yes, it's true that the jhānas are a great place to be just to bliss out and enjoy a "pleasant abiding here and now." Indeed, when the Buddha was asked whether "an exclusively pleasant world" can be realized, he answered, "Yes, and that exclusively pleasant world is the fourth jhāna."[10] In fact, the Buddha even encouraged it. He said, "The four jhānas are called the bliss of renunciation, the bliss of seclusion, the bliss of peace, the bliss of enlightenment. This kind of pleasure should be pursued, developed, cultivated, should not be feared."[11] But far more important than that is using the jhānas to take the mind to a place where it is perfectly conducive to wisdom, and then using to gain direct knowledge into nirvana. The Buddha calls it the **noble five-factored right samadhi**: the four jhānas, and the gaining of direct knowledge using the fourth jhāna as the base of operations.

In summary, these are the five parts of the five-factored right samadhi, and the essential stepping stone each offers you on your path to nirvana:

1. In the first jhāna, you gain the life-changing ability to abide in rapture and happiness independent of sensual pleasures.

2. In the second jhāna, thinking subsides completely and mind becomes placid and unified.

3. In the third jhāna, mind becomes tranquil, rapture fades away, and wisdom factors (mindfulness, clear comprehension, and equanimity) come to the fore.

4. In the fourth jhāna, mind rises above and beyond all pleasure and pain, equanimity is perfected, and, most important of all, mindfulness is purified by equanimity. The Buddha calls it "pure bright mind."

5. Using this pure bright mind, gain wisdom and direct knowledge leading to nirvana.

The Buddha offered three similes relating to the end result of this process. The first is a jug full of water that has been set out on a stand; a strong man can easily tip it in any direction and spill the water. In the same way, a meditator equipped with the jhānas has a strong mind that can realize any insight as easily as the strong man can tip the jug. The second simile is similar: a square pond on level ground filled to the brim; a strong man can open any of the four walls and the water will rush out. The third simile involves a masterful charioteer riding a chariot harnessed to thoroughbreds, driving on flat ground; he can easily drive in whichever direction whenever he wants. A meditator equipped with the jhānas is like that masterful charioteer.

Guest artist: Angeleen Tan

In the same discourse, the Buddha states by applying your super-duper jhāna mind appropriately, you can "with the destruction of the taints, realize in this very life with direct knowledge the taintless liberation of mind and liberation by wisdom, and having entered upon it, dwell in it."

In other words, my friends, nirvana.

The Buddhist Path Is Filled with Joy

The Buddha is the greatest genius in the history of the world. One of his most important innovations, which is surprisingly less than prominent on the radars of many Buddhist teachers and scholars, is the central role of joy. The path to enlightenment can be long and hard, but can be made significantly easier if joy is a key part of it. Designing a training program this way is so challenging it takes a genius to pull it off, and the Buddha was that genius.

We get a glimpse of how successful he was in a conversation he had with King Pasenadi of Kosala. The good king visited the Buddha when they were both old men, not long before they would both pass away (this would, in fact, be the last time they would see each other alive). The king said to the Buddha that when he saw the ascetics from the other sects, they looked like they were miserable, wretched, and "leading the holy life dissatisfied." In contrast, the Buddhist monastics appeared to be "smiling and cheerful, sincerely joyful, plainly delighting, their faculties fresh, unexcited, unruffled, living by what others give, dwelling with minds like the wild deer."[12]

There are many discourses where the Buddha talks about joy in practice. One such discourse started as a conversation the Buddha had with a wise layperson called Pessa, known here only as "the elephant driver's son" (imagine if that is how history remembers you; so sorry, Pessa), who visited the Buddha with a friend.[13] After they left, the Buddha told the monks sitting around him, "Pessa is wise, and if he had stayed just a little longer to listen to what

I have to say next, he would have gained stream-entry." It sounds a bit like a comedy. What the Buddha talked about next was a road map of the joyful path.

It begins with a disciple hearing the Dharma, after which he makes a determined effort to live his life in accordance with the five precepts.[14] He gains "noble virtue," contentment, and a clear conscience. With that, he benefits from the first joy, the "**bliss of blamelessness**." Note that ethical behavior is not framed as a sacrifice, but as a source of bliss. I find it a fascinating idea in and of itself.

Next, the disciple practices what the Buddha calls "sense restraint," which he defines as "not grasping onto the signs (*nimitta*) and secondary characteristics" of perceived sense objects. Buddhist scholar monk Bhikkhu Anālayo clarifies that "signs" refers to first forming of an assessment of the sense object, while "secondary characteristics" refers to further association and mental proliferation based on that first idea. In other words, *sense restraint* does not mean "refraining from having sense input"; instead, it means "steering clear of mental proliferation and reacting in ways that are unwholesome."[15] In even more other words, *sense restraint* means "not making sense data into something that it is not." For that reason, with sense restraint senses actually become even clearer and more expansive, since the mind is not grasping onto things and distorting sense data. With that, the Buddha says the disciple experiences the next joy: "**the bliss that is unsullied**."

After that, the disciple practices mindfulness and clear comprehension, he meditates, he abandons the five hindrances, and he enters the jhānas. At this point, he experiences the joys relating to the jhānas, including the "**rapture and bliss born of seclusion**," "**rapture and bliss born of samadhi**," and the "**pleasant abiding of equanimity**" above and beyond pleasure and pain. Finally, the disciple uses the jhānas to reach enlightenment and he is now "hungerless, extinguished [the fire], and cooled, and **abides experiencing bliss, having himself become holy**."

Every few miles on the Buddhist spiritual path, there is a rest stop serving joy for free.

You may notice something fascinating: the further down the path, the more you let go of, and the greater the joy is. This leads us to a conversation in the ancient texts that sounds almost like comedy. Sāriputta, the wisest of all the

Buddha's disciples, was residing with a group of Buddhist monks. He spoke to them, "Friends, happiness is this nirvana. Happiness is this nirvana." The monk Udayi replied, "But friend Sāriputta, what happiness could there be when nothing is felt?" And Sāriputta replied, "Nothing is felt here, that is where the happiness is."[16]

The Joy of Right Samadhi Makes a Smooth Ride to Nirvana

The inner joy of the jhānas plays a very important role in the joyful path. In fact, the joy of the jhānas is one place where the genius of the Buddha shows up. See, since those states of right samadhi are inherently joyful, there must have been a level of fear that a meditator can become attached to them, get stuck there, and hence not be able to advance into higher wisdom. We know even Siddhattha (before he became the Buddha) had that concern because just before he decided to go into the jhānas on the night of his enlightenment, he had to ask himself, "Why should I be afraid of the inner joy brought about by the first jhāna?" And then he realized, "That joy has nothing to do with sensual pleasure or unwholesome mental states, so I should not be afraid of it." With that insight, he became willing to get into the jhānas in pursuit of wisdom.

In a conversation with a novice named Cunda, the Buddha addressed this issue head-on, and then some.[17] He told Cunda that the indulgence in the pleasure of the four jhānas is "entirely conducive to disillusionment, dispassion, cessation, peace, insight, awakening, and nirvana." Why? Because those pleasures are "detached from all sense desires and unwholesome mental states." He also told Cunda, "If the followers of the other sects were to accuse you [Buddhists] of living indulgent in the pleasures of the jhānas, you should tell them 'Exactly so!'" As if that was not shocking enough for novice Cunda, the Buddha added the kicker, "Anybody who lives indulging in the pleasures of the jhānas can expect one of four outcomes: he becomes a stream-enterer, once-returner, non-returner, or arahant" with the destruction of the fetters.[18] Cunda probably had to pick his jaw up from the floor.

Having said that, yes, it is possible to get attached to the jhānic joys and then get stuck in your spiritual progress. The Buddha warns about it; he calls it "being stuck internally," which is described as, "if a meditator's consciousness follows after the meditative joys and is tied and shackled by their gratification."[19] When the Buddha tells the monks to "indulge in the pleasure of the four jhānas," he means to do it without being tied and shackled by their gratification.

Soryu nonetheless makes the point that this isn't a great concern for two main reasons. First, while it is true that the pleasure of jhāna is more fulfilling than sensual pleasure, it is of its own nature far less addictive. Actually, in an almost funny way, that's the reason it is so hard for most people to enter it. Most of us are slaves to our addictions. Therefore, we get lost in the small pleasure of thinking, which is very addictive, rather than in the deep and vast pleasure of jhāna, which is much less addictive. Second, the pleasure of jhāna is healing. It releases us from our fixations and lets our bodies relax so that the tension that holds us captive can release. For these reasons, Soryu and I definitely disagree with modern teachers who warn students against practicing right samadhi for fear of being addicted to the pleasure of jhāna. To them, we say, "Dear friends, remember that the Buddha never said that right samadhi is optional. The sheer power of right samadhi to propel a student toward nirvana is far more advantageous compared to the small risk of the student getting stuck in it. Furthermore, that risk is highly manageable with a good teacher."

In another discourse, the Buddha frames the power of jhāna for enlightenment in a different way. He talks about a hard path to liberation (which he calls the path "through volitional exertion") and a comparatively easy path (the path "without volitional exertion"). The easier path is the one with the jhānas. He says:

> How, monks, does a person attain nirvana through volitional exertion?
> Here, he dwells contemplating in unattractiveness, repulsiveness,
> discontent, impermanence, perception of death. He dwells relying
> upon the five powers of a trainee: faith, moral shame, fear of
> wrongdoing, energy, and wisdom. These five faculties then become
> extremely strong in him: faith, energy, mindfulness, samadhi, and
> wisdom. Because of the strength of these five faculties, he attains
> nirvana.

> How, monks, does a person attain nirvana without volitional
> exertion? Here, he enters the four jhānas. Thereafter, he dwells relying
> upon the five faculties of faith, energy, mindfulness, samadhi, and
> wisdom. Because of the strength of these five faculties, he attains
> nirvana.[20]

Modern teachers interpret the above passage in one of two ways. The first
is that it is entirely possible to reach nirvana without the jhānas, but it is hard
and painful (unless you find volitional exertion to be fun, like Soryu does).
The second interpretation (the one favored by Soryu) is that right samadhi is
unavoidable on the way to nirvana, and you either experience it organically
for at least a short time before seeing nirvana or, if you choose, you traverse
the path with it. And since you will experience it anyway, you might as well
traverse the path with it, because it makes the path so much easier.

In either interpretation, the conclusion is the same: the scenic path through
the jhānas is more fun and much easier. The discovery of the scenic path is
pure genius.

This is not to say that the unpleasant things listed here by the Buddha on
the harder path are bypassed by those taking the easier path. For example,
the jhāna practitioner will still end up eventually having to contemplate un-
attractiveness, impermanence, perception of death, and so on. However, the
jhāna-equipped mind will find the process much easier and far more pleasant.
As you will see later in Chapter 12, when the modern student Susan, who had
mastered the jhānas at this point, fully experienced impermanence and all,
and described that experience as, "Both horrifying *and* the most pleasant and
wonderful experience of a person's life up to this point."

In that sense, the joy of right samadhi is like grease on an engine—you are
taking a trip to nirvana; that engine takes you there. As the engineer, you can
either grease the engine or not. If you do not grease the engine, it will grind,
overheat, and make horrible noises, and, worse, you risk a total engine break-
down. With grease, you still make the same journey using the same engine,
but the trip is much more pleasant.

Guest artist: Natalie Tsang

Soryu and I have both studied the entire corpus of the early Buddhist discourses, and we are not aware of even a single instance where the Buddha talked about his system of training without including right samadhi. In other words, there is not a single case where the Buddha said right samadhi was optional in the training. That leads me to believe that the Buddha was like the type of engineer who always greases his engines. That warms the heart of this old engineer.

I Can't Believe It's Not Nirvana

Guest artist: Natalie Tsang

There is an important teaching regarding samadhi that enjoys consensus among all Buddhist masters across all schools of Buddhism, which is that meditative experience and realization are different things. In other words, no matter how sublime your jhāna experience, that is most certainly not nirvana.

Siddhattha had a sense of it even before he became the Buddha. He was able to reach the sublime state of the base of nothingness and later the even more sublime base of neither perception nor non-perception, equaling or exceeding his teachers Alara and Uddaka, but he had the wisdom to know that just because he experienced those states did not mean he was liberated from suffering. For that, he needed to gain realization into the true nature of all phenomena. Because of that insight, he rightly continued his search until he became the Buddha. The sublime states are jumping boards to nirvana, not nirvana itself.

Ānanda gave a discourse that reinforced this point to a man called Dasama of Aṭṭhakanāgara. Ānanda said that a disciple can jump to enlightenment from *any* jhāna ranging from the first jhāna to the base of nothingness. He also added an important point: that jump can only happen with insight, specifically, in this case, the insight into the impermanence of the jhāna itself. When the disciple is in any jhāna, he considers and understands completely: "this jhāna is conditioned and volitionally produced, but whatever is conditioned and volitionally produced is impermanent, subject to cessation."[21] If he is steady in that insight, Ānanda says, he can gain enlightenment.

The main drawback of the jhānas is they are conditioned states, and when those conditions change, the jhānas fade away. Anything impermanent cannot possibly be nirvana. Mahā Koṭṭhita, one of the Buddha's top disciples, gave a number of delightful similes to illustrate this point.[22] It started with a monk called Citta Hatthisāriputta, who constantly interrupted the senior monks when they were discussing the Dharma. Mahā Koṭṭhita asked Citta Hatthisāriputta to please stop interrupting, to please wait until the senior monks had finished talking. Citta's companions were offended. They fought back, claiming that Citta was just as accomplished as the senior monks.

Thus began a discourse by Mahā Koṭṭhita to those junior monks to not judge a monk by his jhānas. He said, just because a monk can enter even the most sublime of jhānas doesn't mean he would never again fall back to a lesser life. He gave a number of similes. When the rain comes, the dusty crossroad is no longer dusty, but you cannot say that this crossroad will hence never be dusty again. There is a shallow pond with the clams and mussels, and pebbles and gravel. When there is heavy rain, they would all vanish under the increased water level, but you cannot say that, therefore, clams, mussels, pebbles, and gravel would never appear again. A man finished a delicious meal, and he became so full he has no desire for leftovers, but you cannot say that, therefore, food will never appeal to him again. And so on.

So what happened to Citta later? Just as Mahā Koṭṭhita had hinted, despite Citta's meditative accomplishments, he was still unenlightened, and he later became discontent and eventually disrobed and returned to a lesser life. Fortunately, there is good news. Citta did attain the jhānas during his time as a monk, and that powerful experience stayed with him even after he disrobed. Living as a layperson, he eventually remembered renunciation. He shaved his head and returned to the Buddhist order as a monk, and this time he gained enlightenment.

As important as right mindfulness and right samadhi are, virtue is just as important. It serves as their basis and infuses them with great power. In the next chapter, we will take a closer look at virtue before taking a deeper dive into the Dharma and exploring the final arc to nirvana.

The Abbot's Commentary by Soryu Forall

Samadhi changes everything. It is how we see directly and accurately, finding happiness and peace. It is how we accept into our own minds the clarity that resolves all delusion. It is how we accept into our own bodies the joy that heals all trauma. It is how we realize the truth rather than just believing in it.

This is very hard for modern people to believe. We have forgotten samadhi. We are lost in our heads and think that the spiritual path means that we figure out what is right and then try to make ourselves be that way. But that will never lead to deep truth or real joy.

It's like cooking a meal. If you want to cook a meal, you should go to the kitchen and use the stove. Don't go to the bathroom and use the toilet. Or it's like if you have to relieve yourself after a meal. You should go use the toilet rather than going to the kitchen and using the stove.

In the same way, if you want to awaken, enter samadhi. Don't just think about it.

CHAPTER NINE

By Virtue of Virtue
How Virtue Underlies All of Buddhist Practice

And Now You Have All Four Noble Truths

Let us recap the Four Noble Truths. In short, the Four Noble Truths are:

First Noble Truth: Birth, aging, illness, death, to be with what you do not want, to be separated from what you want, and to not get what you want are suffering (dukkha). Specifically, the five aggregates subject to grasping are suffering.

Second Noble Truth: Suffering cannot arise without cause, and a necessary cause is craving (taṇhā).

Third Noble Truth: The total cessation of craving leads to nirvana, the total cessation of suffering.

Fourth Noble Truth: The path leading to the total cessation of suffering is the Noble Eightfold Path.

A summary of the Noble Eightfold Path:

Right view: understanding of the Four Noble Truths

Right intention: the intentions of renunciation, non–ill will, and harmlessness

Right speech: abstinence from false speech, divisive speech, harsh speech, and idle chatter

Right action: abstinence from killing, stealing, and sexual misconduct

Right livelihood: livelihood in accordance with the above

Right effort: the effort to abandon the unwholesome and develop the wholesome

Right mindfulness: the four establishments of mindfulness

Right samadhi: the four jhānas

After the Buddha delivered the first discourse, in Buddhist parlance, the "Wheel of Dharma" was set in motion by the Buddha. That is why that discourse is known as the Discourse on Setting in Motion the Wheel of Dharma.[1]

At the end of that discourse, Koṇḍañña attained stream-entry. He became the first of the Buddha's disciples to "see the dust-free, stainless vision of the Dharma." From that moment on, he was honored as Añña Koṇḍañña—Koṇḍañña Who Has Understood. Which is very nice, except that English-only speakers would now think his name is Anna.

With that, the three most precious pieces of Buddhism were now assembled: the **Buddha** (teacher), the **Dharma** (teachings), and the **Sangha** (monastic community of practitioners). Together, these three are known as the **Triple Gem**. A Buddhist is someone who takes refuge in the Triple Gem. For that reason, the Triple Gem is also known as the **Three Refuges**.

Virtue, Samadhi, Wisdom

In a discourse called the Discourse of the Great Forty, the Buddha taught that you can think of the first seven parts of the Noble Eightfold Path as being the "support and requisites" for the last one, right samadhi.[2] He also suggested that there is some semblance of a linear causal relationship between them, namely that right view leads to right intention, which in turn leads to the next one, and so on. However, it's not a strict linear relationship; the eight parts also support each other. For example, in that same discourse, the Buddha said that right view, right mindfulness, and right effort "run and circle around" all the other parts, meaning, for example, that you really cannot practice right action if you do not also practice at least right view, right mindfulness, and right effort.

You can think of right view, right effort, and right mindfulness as the cavalry in an ancient army and the others as the infantry. The cavalry protects the army's vulnerable flanks. They also periodically scout ahead to protect the army from ambush, and periodically survey the rear to protect the army from a sneak attack. In that sense, the cavalry "runs and circles around" the whole army. In the same way, right view, right effort, and right mindfulness run and circle around the Noble Eightfold Path: they provide the vigilance, protection, and situational awareness that enable the entire Noble Eightfold Path to do its job.

Guest artist: Natalie Tsang

The main lesson is that the eight parts are mutually reinforcing and that all eight parts need to be practiced. None of them are optional for the path toward nirvana.

If eight items are too many for you to remember, and you wish there were only three items to memorize, you are in luck; I have just the solution for you. There is a very popular way of presenting the Buddhist path, which is to structure it in three stages: virtue, samadhi, and wisdom,[3] known as the **threefold training**.[4] It is very popular perhaps because it is easy to remember three items, and also because it lends itself mightily well to a very understandable system of practice. First, you practice living an ethical life by practicing virtue. Next, you develop your mind with meditation by practicing samadhi. Finally, you cultivate wisdom.

This makes sense because, at a minimum, one living a genuinely virtuous life is less likely to be haunted by afflictive mental states such as hatred, guilt, and shame. But beyond that, one can also begin to feel happy about having the courage to make wise choices and live in increasingly beautiful ways. This type of joy eventually transforms into confidence, most importantly, the confidence to walk the path to liberation. Furthermore, one's mind becomes more conducive to inner peace and joy. That creates a strong foundation for the practice of samadhi. When samadhi becomes sufficiently strong, one begins to develop penetrating insight into phenomena. And using that penetrating insight, one can cultivate wisdom.

The Buddha put it quite simply: "When samadhi is imbued with virtue, it is very fruitful and beneficial. When wisdom is imbued with samadhi, it's very fruitful and beneficial."[5] While everything we have said in this book so far is meant to explain the Buddha's first discourse, this quote is the summary of his last discourse, delivered shortly before he passed.

There is a really nice way to map the Noble Eightfold Path onto the three-fold training, which was suggested by the Buddha's disciple Dhammadinnā. Dhammadinnā was the wife of Visākha, a wealthy merchant. They both became disciples of the Buddha, and, eventually, Visākha became a non-returner and Dhammadinnā became a Buddhist nun who attained arahant-ship, which means the wife was fully enlightened while the husband was still one step behind. In other words, the wife was spiritually more advanced than the husband, which is probably true of most married couples in all of history. In a conversation between them, Dhammadinnā suggested that the Noble Eightfold Path can be mapped onto the threefold training in this way:[6]

virtue: right speech, right action, right livelihood

samadhi: right effort, right mindfulness, right samadhi

wisdom: right intention and right view

Dhammadinnā's discourse was soon reported to the Buddha, and he gave it his highest seal of approval, saying, "I would have explained it the same way." It remains a very popular way to frame the Noble Eightfold Path. First, practice right speech, right action, and right livelihood to cultivate virtue; then practice right effort, right mindfulness, and right samadhi to cultivate samadhi; and, finally, you cultivate right intention and right view.

You might go, "But wait! Something is wrong." Earlier in Chapter 6, I quoted the Buddha saying that you start with right view and all the other seven parts are guided by it, but now I'm saying that right view comes at the end, as a result of the other parts. Which is right? They are both right, because as we said earlier in this chapter, all eight parts mutually support each other in various ways. Right view guides the other seven parts, and the other seven parts also strengthen right view. If, say, you get better at your practice of right mindfulness and begin to clearly see the interplay between pleasure and suffering in your daily experience, that then informs your understanding of the Four Noble Truths, which informs right view. For that reason, right view can be said to be the forerunner of the other seven, or the end result, or both.

In addition to the main lesson (that all eight parts of the Noble Eightfold Path are mutually reinforcing and that none of them are optional), there is an important secondary lesson here as well: that in learning the Dharma and Buddhism, it is important not to hold any teaching too tightly. Think of it as applying the spirit of the Middle Way to the teachings themselves, even the ones that came directly from the Buddha. If teachings appear to conflict, it is important to first understand why they appear to conflict. In very many cases, you may find that they are simply different ways of slicing and dicing the same thing, so what appears to be conflict at first is just a different way of framing the same facts.

The Awesome Power of Virtue

If I ever give you the mistaken impression that virtue is merely the preparation for meditation, and that meditation is the "real Buddhism," then you should scold me and call me funny names. In truth, virtue is a powerful and essential component in every step of the training.

Virtue is inherently life-changing

First, virtue is life-changing in and of itself. Even if you cultivate no samadhi and no wisdom, if you cultivate only virtue, that alone creates its own sustainable source of happiness. Better still, it works on a number of levels. Take the simple virtue of generosity. On the lowest end of the spectrum, if nothing else, the Buddha reminds you that practicing generosity makes you dear to people, and helps you gain a good reputation.[7] Beyond that, you bring benefit to others and you feel better about yourself. Even beyond that, it helps you cultivate kindness and compassion and, therefore, *directly* helps purify your mind of ill will. But even beyond that, it weakens your craving and strengthens your ability to let go, and therefore makes a *direct* contribution to your journey to nirvana.

All virtues possess a similar spectrum of life-changing benefits, ranging from totally worldly stuff like improving your social standing, to helping you gain inner happiness, to helping purify your mind—all the way to helping you arrive at nirvana. All that *and* it benefits people around you. So if you do nothing except cultivate virtue, and even if you cultivate only a single virtue, it will bring happiness to you and the people around you.

Virtue sets you up for samadhi

Beyond its inherent value, virtue also very importantly sets you up for samadhi, and it does so in two ways. First, it gifts to you a mind that is largely clear from gross mental afflictions such as lust, envy, anger, hatred, and regret. It is like a farmer clearing the ground of rocks and large stones before plowing; it makes the process a lot smoother. In the same way, the more your mind is free from gross mental afflictions, the more easily it can get into samadhi. Second, inner joy is highly conducive to samadhi. The Buddha even says that the direct cause for samadhi is happiness, specifically the type of gentle happiness that comes from wholesome sources that are not polluted by afflictive mental states such as lust or anger.[8] Virtue is a bountiful source for that type of happiness. Hence, the more virtue you have, the more wholesome happiness you possess that then turbocharges your samadhi.

Virtue helps you relinquish craving

Compelling as that might be, virtue works on an even deeper level. Remember how in the Second Noble Truth, the Buddha identified craving as a necessary cause of suffering? Virtue turns out to be an awesome power tool when it comes to relinquishing craving, by providing you with an honest, objective measure of how well you are really dealing with craving. That is because behavior can be observed far more objectively than inner mental states. Let me give you an example. Say you enjoy killing mosquitoes but, inspired by virtue, you want to closely observe the first precept to refrain from killing even mosquitoes. Let's say you learn meditation for a while, and then I ask you a self-perception question, "Do you feel that your craving for swatting mosquitoes is weaker now?" It is remarkably easy to fool yourself. What if, instead, I ask you a behavioral question, "Are you now able to stop swatting mosquitoes?" This question has a very objective answer, because you either swatted a mosquito or you did not; there is no space for subjective interpretation. In that sense, behavior is the most objective aspect of the mind.

Now, because you are trying to not swat mosquitoes, you have to address the underlying strands of craving that make you want to swat them. The main one is the craving to avoid the physical discomfort of itchiness from mosquito bites. So much discomfort! And then maybe there are subtler strands of craving, such as the feeling of power and the pleasure of "revenge" experienced when swatting mosquitoes. In addressing all those strands of craving, you need to deepen samadhi to the point where that sensation of itchiness is experienced merely as sensation, and no longer as suffering, at least during formal meditation.

In short, in this process, you start with trying to fulfill the virtue of not killing even mosquitoes, and you end with cutting various strands of craving and reducing your own suffering, with the number of mosquitoes you do or do not swat from now on as the convenient measurement of progress.

This process works for anything at the intersection of virtue and craving, such as consuming alcohol and drugs, the temptation to lie, or steal, or give in to sexual misconduct.

Why is that important? There is a popular saying, "You can't manage what you can't measure." In organizational management and in engineering, the first step in managing any process is to measure it. In relinquishing craving, the best measure of how well you are doing is how it shows up in behavior change. The better you can measure it, the better you can manage it.

Virtue gives you the struggle to enable growth

Once upon a time, a young boy witnessed a butterfly struggling for hours to break free from its cocoon. Eager to help, the boy took a pair of scissors and cut a large slit on the cocoon. The butterfly emerged, but it was unable to fly. Why? Because the butterfly needed that struggle in order for its wings to be filled with blood and to gain strength. Without the struggle, the butterfly will emerge unable to fly.

Many processes in nature require struggle to facilitate growth. The butterfly is only one example. Another example is physical training. To grow bicep muscles, you have to do bicep curls to the extent that you struggle to do the next repetition. The body then responds by growing the muscles.

Struggle turns out to also be highly conducive to spiritual growth, and virtue provides that struggle. Anybody who sincerely tries to practice virtue soon learns that it is a struggle. Once upon a time, there was a city where police corruption was rife. One year, the lone uncorrupted police inspector was assigned a few fresh graduates from the police academy. He asked each of them in turn, "Will you be able to always do your job with the utmost integrity?" Everyone confidently shouted back, "Yes, sir!" Everyone except Sam. Sam answered, "I don't know, sir; I will try, but it sounds really hard." The police inspector shook his head. Everybody laughed. Years later, every single one of those fresh graduates turned corrupt, except for Sam. The old police inspector went to see him and said, "Do you remember the question I asked you on the first day you reported to me? That was the day I knew I could trust you, because you said doing your job with the utmost integrity sounded really hard. That meant that, unlike the others, you were actually going to try. I know that because I have been doing this for decades, and every day of upholding the highest integrity is still very hard for me."

It gets worse. Those who persist in perfecting their virtue also soon learn that things are not usually black and white, and no matter how virtuous they already are, they will find it a continuing struggle, often with no good solutions. Take, for example, the very first precept: the precept to abstain from killing. At first, I was like, pffff, easy-peasy, I have never killed anyone or anything in my life, except occasional bugs. There, done, I'm home free! But wait, are bugs not sentient life? Well, of course they are, duh. What about all the meat and fish I eat? Is life not taken on my behalf? OK, but what if I become vegetarian? And then one of my Tibetan Buddhist teachers reminded me that agriculture involves killing a lot of "pests" as well, therefore, merely by eating, I am responsible for secondhand killing. It turns out there is no good answer. For that teacher, her answer was the solemn recognition at *every* meal that, "As long as I have to eat, some other sentient beings will die. Therefore, I dedicate my life to my own liberation and the liberation of all sentient beings." I find that a beautiful answer.

Soryu says as beautiful as that answer is, that is not the main point. Like the butterfly in the cocoon, the main point is the struggle itself. It is the aspiration to live a completely virtuous life, no matter how "unrealistic" it may appear, and the willingness to face, with brutal honesty, this question: What is my inner obstacle to complete virtue? That question is important because its answer illuminates the next stubborn strand of craving to cut. Or, more accurately, that obstacle illuminates the next growth opportunity. Here again, virtue helps you to relinquish craving. Every time another strand of craving is weakened or cut off, samadhi and wisdom deepen, you become happier, and you live a more virtuous life. If you follow your commitment to living complete virtue, you will then have to struggle with the next obstacle, which presents the next growth opportunity, and so on. That is how the continuous struggle toward complete virtue continuously offers up new opportunities for spiritual growth.

It is not just eating. Constructing buildings also causes loss of life and environmental damage. Same with using products or taking transportation. And then there are livelihood-related questions such as: Should I continue working in the arms industry, or in an industry that contributes to environmental destruction? To be clear, Soryu does eat food, live in a building, wear clothes, own a laptop, and use transportation (I checked). It is not that we stop doing those things. It is that we are always aspiring to live a life of maximum virtue, even if we do not know how to overcome the obstacles to it, and that we are always willing to experience that difficult struggle internally to achieve maximum virtue. The more honest that struggle, the more spiritual growth is facilitated.

Soryu offers us a deep point to contemplate. He says:

> The depth of the struggle predicts the depth of the realization. The more you struggle, the more deeply you will awaken. You may need to take this on faith right now, but I assure you that to struggle in this way allows you to realize a new kind of joy, and that joy facilitates realization. The joy we can experience from struggling with ethical questions is greater than any joy anyone in the world can ever experience through getting what they desire. Because we experience this joy, we enter deep samadhi. Because we enter deep samadhi, we discover wisdom. Because we discover wisdom, we are liberated. The depth of joy predicts the depth of wisdom. Therefore, the depth of struggle predicts the depth of realization.

Virtue shows you that you can walk the path

Virtue is so powerful in so many areas it is hard to pinpoint one thing and say, "This is the most important thing it does for you." But if I have to choose, this could be it: it shows you that you are indeed capable of walking the path.

I was a prominent member of a movement to make mindfulness widely accessible in secular settings. A few of my friends started a very noble project to teach mindfulness, for free, to women in highly disadvantaged backgrounds who lost their jobs. The idea was that maybe if they learned mindfulness, it would help them do better in job interviews. At the end of the course a few weeks later, many of the women offered their testimonials. One testimonial was so powerful it brought people to tears, and it didn't even have anything to do with job-hunting. The woman simply said, "Since I started learning mindfulness, I no longer beat my kid."

A powerful feature of the Buddhist practice is it gives you the ability to live more virtuously. In the case of this woman's story, there is no doubt that she would rather not beat her kid, but rising to that virtue was too hard for her. Once she practiced even just a few weeks of relatively shallow mindfulness practice, she developed the ability to rise to that virtue. It was life-changing for her, and for her child.

So the practice allows you to become more virtuous. That virtue then gives you the confidence that you can do the practice. This is a virtuous cycle.

There are many people who understand and accept the Dharma, but choose not to practice it anyway. That is because they have a deeply held belief that they are incapable of walking the path, and, therefore, they will not even try. That is where virtue comes in. It shows you that you can do it, and it does so in two ways.

First, virtue shows you that you have more power than you knew. The woman in the story above, for example, found that she had the power to not beat her kid, which was way more power than she imagined she had. Let me share another example. Imagine that you had an addiction to snacking (this example, by the way, is based on the embarrassing true story of one of this book's two coauthors, and it is not Soryu). You went to see a doctor and he informed you that you were developing health problems, and that you had to cut down on your snacking by at least half. Ouch. You obeyed your doctor's orders because you were too afraid to, you know, die. Six months later, your blood tests showed that those health problems were gone. Whoa. Besides better health, you gained something else: self-confidence. By being able to halve your snacking for six whole months, you showed yourself that you have *some* power over desires. You proved that you do not have to always be the slave of your desires. You have the power to transcend yourself. That gives you confidence.

In life, it is often very easy to know the right thing to do; the hard part is actually doing it. For example, when I was addicted to snacking, I *knew* for certain that the right thing to do was to drastically cut it down, but actually doing it was too hard. Same with lying to get out of trouble, and a whole host of other stuff. The gift that virtue gives us here is every time we succeed in doing the right thing, it gives us more confidence that we have the power to transcend ourselves. And confidence in being able to transcend oneself is one of the most important conditions for staying on the spiritual path.

I discovered my own power in a similar way as the woman in the story. When I first started doing the practice, my motivation was entirely utilitarian: all I wanted was escape from misery. And then I discovered that not only was the practice able to do that, but it had the totally surprising "side effect" of making me a better human being. I did not ever imagine myself becoming a better person. I saw myself as a useless weakling in the face of temptation and my worst impulses. But there I was, with every little bit more practice, becoming less weak, less useless. It was like when I was a kid, I was a skinny weakling bullied by the bigger boys, but the better I became at karate, the less of a weakling I became, and I gained confidence in my training and in myself.

The second thing virtue does for you is show you that you are, in truth, a good person. Look, we all want to be happy, and for many of us, the most obvious path to being happy is to do things that feed us with sensual and egoistic pleasures, often at the expense of virtue. Imagine that one day, you find that being virtuous gives you more happiness than that. For example, pretend you were a selfish person, and then you tried being charitable, and then you realize after a while that being charitable makes you significantly happier. What does that say? It says that *you* are a better person than you imagined, because you are, by your very nature, the type who gains more happiness being charitable than being selfish. It says that your original assumption about your nature may be wrong. Whatever story you spun to malign yourself, it turns out that you are, at your very core, a good person. The self-narrative then goes from "I am a lousy person incapable of enlightenment who is better off just indulging" to "I am an imperfect but fundamentally good person, a work in progress, continuously learning to expand and express my goodness." That changes everything. Virtue gives you that gift.

Later, in Chapter 12, we will share the true story of the spiritual journey of a modern seeker on her path to directly seeing nirvana, and one thing that may surprise you is how often she got stuck. In every case, one of the most important things that got her unstuck was her training in virtue. That is because virtue demands self-honesty, and yields self-confidence, so the deeper her training in virtue, the stronger those two qualities. Every time she was stuck on her spiritual path, she needed total self-honesty to assess her situation and the self-confidence to say, "I can move forward." And that was how her training in virtue helped get her unstuck every time.

Actually, virtue is essential in everything

If you are already sold on the awesome power of virtue, given everything we said, this is the part where we go, "But wait, there is more!"

Virtue is not just an amazingly powerful tool on your spiritual path; it is an essential element of the *entirety* of your spiritual path. This is expressed beautifully in a later Buddhist text, that states that if you deepen your virtue sufficiently, you cease being an "ordinary worldling," and you become an admirable person.[9] If you deepen your virtue further, you can upgrade from being a worldling, because you are walking a path that will lead you to a heavenly realm after you die. If you deepen your virtue even further, you can use it as a basis to gain enough samadhi and wisdom to gain stream-entry. And then, if you deepen your virtue even more still, it is the basis of enough samadhi and wisdom to gain full enlightenment.

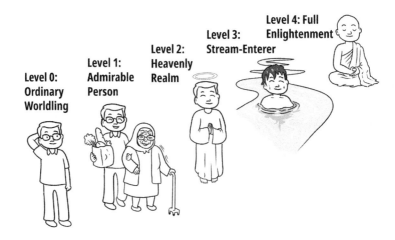

Level 0: Ordinary Worldling

Level 1: Admirable Person

Level 2: Heavenly Realm

Level 3: Stream-Enterer

Level 4: Full Enlightenment

If you remember only one thing about virtue, remember that virtue gives us the bliss of blamelessness, and that **the bliss of blamelessness can be cultivated far beyond what sensual pleasure can offer us**. Once you are able to do that, everything else eventually falls into place.

The entire spiritual path is by virtue of virtue.

By Transforming You, Virtue Transforms Society

Back in Chapter 6, I mentioned that the reason we practice virtue in Buddhism is that virtue is highly conducive to our own happiness. It gets even better. In addition to increasing your own happiness, your practice of virtue creates ripple effects that benefit the entire society.

First, of course, there is right livelihood. Remember that right livelihood is a part of the Noble Eightfold Path and, therefore, a non-optional part of a sincere Buddhist's practice. Which means, for example, that no sincerely practicing Buddhist may engage in fraud or corruption, or poison the land or water. Obviously, people practicing right livelihood benefit society.

And then there is generosity, a virtue the Buddha repeatedly emphasizes. When the Buddha talks about virtue, he very often singles out generosity for extra mention. For example, in one discourse, the Buddha talks about five kinds of wealth: faith, virtue, learning, generosity, and wisdom.[10] Note that generosity is not subsumed under virtue, but is instead listed as a separate item of equal importance.[11] Also note that, fascinatingly, generosity is considered a kind of wealth, not a reduction in wealth.

There is so much emphasis on generosity because it is closely related to right intention. Remember from Chapter 6 that right intention refers to the intentions of renunciation, non–ill will, and harmlessness? When one properly practices generosity, one practices all three parts of right intention at once: one delights in relinquishment, thereby practicing renunciation, and one devotes to being charitable out of kindness to others, thereby practicing non–ill will and harmlessness.[12] Therefore, in a practical sense, generosity is the virtue that can lead to all other virtues. That is why it is so important. Separately but relatedly, there is a popular teaching in Buddhism known as the ten perfections, which are ten qualities every sincere Buddhist practitioner tries to perfect: generosity, virtue, renunciation, wisdom, energy, patience, truthfulness, determination, loving-kindness, and equanimity.[13] Unsurprisingly, generosity is the first perfection.[14]

Given the outsize importance of generosity, it is a key virtue that every sincere Buddhist aspires to. Obviously, the more generous people are, the more society itself benefits. Just this one thing alone can have a transformative effect on society.

There is still more. Buddhism may appear to be very solitary; most people's idea of a practicing Buddhist is somebody sitting alone under a tree. While that image is not incorrect, it is also true that Buddhism has a very heavy communal emphasis. You can tell simply by textual volume: the Buddha devoted a significant percentage of the monastic code to maintaining communal harmony, and he gave numerous discourses on the topics of friendship, good relationships, duty to each other, and creating and maintaining communities where monastics "dwell in concord, harmoniously, without disputes, blending like milk and water, viewing each other with eyes of affection."[15]

Many of those discourses are applicable to us laypeople living in modern societies. For example, the Buddha taught four ways of sustaining favorable relationships:[16] giving, endearing speech, beneficent conduct, and impartiality.[17] In other words:

1. When somebody needs a gift, I give them a gift.

2. When somebody needs kind words, I give them kind words.

3. When somebody needs concern or assistance, I give it to them.

4. When somebody needs to be treated fairly, or as an equal, I do it for them.

In later Buddhism, these four ways gained even more prominence. In Mahayana Buddhism, for example, they became a core part of the training of a bodhisattva, the model of an ideal practitioner.[18]

Imagine having a large number of people practice these four ways. What a huge effect it would have on society.

But wait, there is even more. The most important thing about the Buddha's teachings on relating to others is that they are a vital part of the core spiritual training. If you buy into the impression that Buddhism is exclusively solitary, you might think that "real Buddhism" is sitting alone under a tree, while relating to others is what you do in your free time. In fact, it is quite the opposite. The Buddha's attendant Ānanda once told the Buddha that he realized "half of the holy life is good friendship." He was in for a surprise. The Buddha said to him, "No, Ānanda, the whole of the holy life is good friendship."[19]

What people think the holy life is like

What the holy life is actually like

Meditating alone all day

Noble friendship

Why is good friendship so important? The reason is good friendship is what helps to get you on the path and to stay on the path. The Buddha says, "Just as dawn is the precursor of the rising of the sun, good friendship is the precursor for the arising of the Noble Eightfold Path. When a monk has a good friend, it is to be expected that he will develop and cultivate this Noble Eightfold Path."[20] In one discourse, he even names good friendship as "the first vital condition for the development of the factors of enlightenment."[21]

How is good friendship able to do all that? First, a good friend is a good person who is virtuous, learned, energetic, mindful, and wise.[22] In addition, a good friend is pleasing, respected, esteemed, patient with you, supports and helps you, does not forsake you,[23] gives "deep talks," and does not enjoin anyone to do what is wrong.[24] When you have friends like that, you can be expected to 1) become virtuous yourself, 2) receive the good teachings, 3) arouse energy for abandoning the unwholesome and cultivating the wholesome, and 4) gain wisdom.[25] Yes, Soryu can testify to the importance of good friendship with his own experience, both as a trainee and as a teacher.

And that, my friends, is how good friends get you on the path, and how to stay on the path. That is why good friends are the whole of the holy life. Of course, part of the practice is to be that good friend for others. Happily, good friendship is something you can receive and give at the same time.

Yes, of course, there is more (how did you guess?). The communal teachings of the Buddha are not just about supporting each other's practice; they are more broadly about benefiting all sentient beings. The Buddha instructs all to practice both for their own welfare and also the welfare of others.[26] So in a sense, a practicing Buddhist strives not just to be mindful, but also to be heartful.

At the heart of heartfulness are the four qualities commonly referred to as the four immeasurables, or as the *brahmaviharas* ("supreme abodes").[27] They are:

loving-kindness: the wish for all to be happy

compassion: the wish for all to be free from suffering

altruistic joy: selfless joy at the happiness of others

equanimity: being unperturbed by the ups and downs of life[28]

These heartfulness qualities are not just really nice to have, they are liberating too. In meditation, the immeasurables can deliver you straight into jhāna. If, while your mind is deeply imbued with any of the immeasurables, you also gain deep insight into impermanence, it can deliver you all the way to final enlightenment.[29] That is how powerful the immeasurables are.

The main point is that Buddhist practice must involve deep concern for others. As usual, the Buddha has a very nice way of putting it; he says practice can be seen as "protecting others by protecting yourself," and "protecting yourself by protecting others."[30] The way you "protect others by protecting yourself" is to practice the four establishments of mindfulness. The way you "protect yourself by protecting others" is to practice the heart qualities, such as the four immeasurables. A good practitioner must do both.

Therefore, a sincere Buddhist practitioner benefits society, because part of his or her training necessarily includes highly prosocial things like generosity, promoting communal harmony, giving, speaking kindly, cultivating heartful qualities, having deep concern for others, and being a virtuous person in general. Therefore, merely by practicing what the Buddha taught, you will create a ripple effect that can transform society. That is why Soryu and I are eager to make Buddhism understandable and accessible to all. The more people who choose to practice, and the deeper their practice, the more goodness there will be to ripple all over the world.

You Should See the Right View Again

I once walked into a beach house with a stunning panoramic view of the ocean, and I made a joke, "This house is very Buddhist: it possesses right view." Jokes aside, right view is far more important to the Buddhist path than first meets the eye (yes, pun intended, and you should have seen it coming).

There is a very nice symbol of Buddhism as a wheel with eight spokes representing the Noble Eightfold Path. One thing I like about this symbol is that it alludes to the importance of all eight spokes. The wheel only turns properly with all of them. If one of those cost-cutting corporate executives tries to cut off a spoke and its corresponding one-eighth of the wheel "to realize 12.5 percent in cost savings," it's not going to work. As the wheel turns, all eight parts of the Noble Eightfold Path contribute to your journey toward full enlightenment.

Another thing I like about the symbol is, for the wheel to make a complete turn, it ends where it begins. Completeness is where beginning and end meet, and the place where it both begins and ends is right view. In Chapter 6, the Buddha defines right view as "understanding the Four Noble Truths." With this definition, you start your journey with an approximate understanding of the Four Noble Truths, which guides you along your way, and you arrive with a complete understanding of the Four Noble Truths.

In the Discourse of the Great Forty (which we came across earlier in this chapter), the Buddha offers a complementary alternative definition of right view.[31] Here, he identifies two types of right view: mundane right view and transcendent right view. Mundane right view is what you start your journey with, and transcendent right view is what you end the journey with. The Buddha defines mundane right view as:

> There is what is given and what is offered and what is sacrificed; there is fruit and result of good and bad actions; there is this world and the other world; there is mother and father; there are beings who are reborn spontaneously; there are in the world good and virtuous recluses and brahmins who have realized for themselves by direct knowledge and declare this world and the other world.

This definition says three things:

1. Actions have consequences, especially ethical ones, including across lifetimes.

2. There is still a mundane world, so do not use Buddhism to deny the mundane world even as you work toward transcending it.

3. There is a path, and there are wise and virtuous teachers you can learn from.

These three insights have a profound impact on your practice. The first point is a statement on empowerment. It says that everything you do has a direct consequence on your eventual enlightenment. Every thought of generosity, every act of compassion, every word of kindness, every decision to let go, every intention to do the right thing, every second of meditation practice, every moment of samadhi and mindfulness—they all have consequences.

Not a single thing you think, say, or do is inconsequential. That is your power. Recognize your power. Realize enlightenment is well within your power.

The second point reinforces the first point with a special emphasis on responsibility. There is a world you live in. There are suffering beings populating all corners of samsara. Even as you progress toward full enlightenment and begin to transcend this world, remember there are still mother and father and other sentient beings, and you have responsibility toward them.[32] This sense of responsibility usually shows up most vividly in your practice of kindness, compassion, and virtue, but it also permeates your entire practice.

The third point reminds us that we are all very fortunate because we have a path, and there exist wise teachers in the world who can guide us. Learn from them. Walk the path.

Understanding these points can make a huge difference in your progress along the path. That is why mundane right view is so important for the practitioner. In this same discourse, the Buddha emphasizes that right view leads *each and every one* of the other components of the Noble Eightfold Path.

Soryu has taught many students, and he has observed that the degree to which a student understands mundane right view consistently predicts the degree of their success on the path. Soryu keeps saying he does not know how to emphasize strongly enough the importance of mundane right view. I do not know either, but I do know how to make a joke about a beach house being Buddhist for possessing right view, and I hope that every time you remember that joke, you remember the profound importance of mundane right view.

Eventually, the student reaches full enlightenment and gains transcendent right view, which the Buddha describes as "right view that is noble, taintless, supramundane." It is, he says, the completion of investigation, the perfection of wisdom, and the full understanding of the Four Noble Truths.

Where's My Nirvana, Dammit?

When I started learning Buddhism, I learned about the Noble Eightfold Path, and I learned about nirvana, and I learned that the Noble Eightfold Path is supposed to result in nirvana. But I could never understand how one leads to the other. What is the arc between the Noble Eightfold Path and nirvana? I mean, I understood that it was a good thing to live ethically, practice meditation, and so on. But I could not for the life of me see how doing all those things would result in liberation from all suffering, and I could not get anybody to give me a straight answer. That was a source of frustration for me for a long time. Now that I'm a big boy, all grown up and writing a book on Buddhism, I cannot not give you an answer. So my pain, your gain.

In the next chapter, we will take a deeper dive into the Dharma, and then we will examine what a modern real-life journey to nirvana can look like.

The Abbot's Commentary by Soryu Forall

Life is hard. But virtue makes it fun.

It's like saying that tennis is hard. But getting better at tennis makes it fun.

Virtue is the process of getting better at life, so it makes life fun.

This is hard to understand because so often, we think that *being* better at tennis is what makes tennis fun. But actually, the process of *getting* better is even more fun. It is a process that continues even when we are old and can't beat anyone at tennis anymore.

A good life is a path from the joy we have now to greater, deeper, more trustworthy joy. Virtue is how we find this way, this path of getting better at life, this real and true fun. It continues all the way to Buddhahood.

CHAPTER TEN

Dude, Where's My Karma?

A Deeper Look into the Dharma

Those Giant Heads Turn Out to Have Bodies

There is an island in the southeastern Pacific Ocean called Easter Island that is famous for having hundreds of statues of giant heads carved from stone. Some of my friends make jokes about them, but I tell them, "Whatever you say, those statues still come out a-head." What many people do not know is those statues actually have bodies. The statues are installed with the bodies buried in the ground up to the shoulders, which is why most photographs of them give the impression that they are only giant heads. When scientists dug them up, they discovered that not only do those giant heads come with giant bodies, but those giant bodies are decorated with intricate carvings. A giant stone head is impressive enough, but when you dig the whole thing up, you discover how much more impressive it really is.

In this chapter, we are doing a similar thing: we are digging deeper into the Dharma. The Four Noble Truths are impressive enough, but underlying them is an entire body of foundational teachings. When taken as a whole, it gives you an even more complete picture of Buddhism.

Three Marks of Existence and Four Dharma Seals

One theme that consistently comes up in Buddhism is **seeing things as they really are**.[1] Buddhism is about total liberation from all suffering, and the way to do that is to fully understand cause and effect relating to suffering, and that begins with seeing things as they really are.

One discourse where this came up was when the Buddha compared the hindrances to looking at one's own reflection in a bowl of water under non-ideal circumstances.[2] Sensual desire is compared to a bowl of water mixed with dye. Ill will is compared to a bowl of boiling water heated over a fire. Sloth-and-torpor is compared to a bowl of water covered with water plants and algae. Restlessness-and-remorse is compared to a bowl of water stirred by the wind, rippling, swirling, churned into wavelets. Doubt is compared to a bowl of water that is turbid, unsettled, muddy, placed in the dark. In each case, if a man was to examine his own facial reflection in the water, he would not see his reflection as it really is.

In the same way, with a mind obstructed by any of the hindrances, one cannot see phenomena as they really are. One will then not understand what is "really for one's own good and the good of others."[3] Hence, only with the absence of the five hindrances can we begin to develop true insight and wisdom. That is why, in a separate discourse, the Buddha says the five hindrances are "nutriment for ignorance."[4]

Another discourse where this came up was when the Buddha talked about seeing as it really is, the arising and cessation of the five aggregates. To be able to do that is knowledge, and not being able to do that is ignorance.[5]

So what do you discover when you see things as they really are? You will recognize the **three marks of existence**:

> **impermanence**: all conditioned phenomena are impermanent

> **dukkha**: all conditioned phenomena are dukkha (unsatisfactory, suffering, or causes of suffering)

> **nonself**: all phenomena, whether conditioned or unconditioned, are nonself[6]

All phenomena are conditioned, with a single exception: nirvana. Nirvana is the one and only unconditioned phenomenon. Hence, all phenomena with the exception of nirvana are impermanent and dukkha. All phenomena *including* nirvana are nonself.

These three marks are so important they can almost be said to define Buddhism. As Buddhism evolved, there arose an idea called the **Dharma seals**. See, some large number of years after the Buddha passed, Buddhism spread widely, and there were many schools and sub-schools of Buddhism, some of which also absorbed local customs, practices, and beliefs. So how do we know which is "true" Dharma and which is not? The standard, which appears to enjoy consensus among all schools of Buddhism, is to measure against the four Dharma seals, the first three of which are the three marks of existence, and the fourth is nirvana.[7] If a school of Buddhism brings forth insight into the three marks of existence, and also leads to nirvana, then it can be said to be true Dharma.

IMPERMANENCE	**DUKKHA**
NON-SELF	**NIRVANA**

Dukkha Due to Formations

The Buddha's teachings on dukkha ("suffering") is somewhat more nuanced than we talked about in Chapter 3. In an important discourse, the Buddha clarified that there are three types of dukkha:[8]

1. dukkha due to physical or emotional pain
2. dukkha due to "formations"
3. dukkha due to change[9]

The first and third seem obvious, and there appears to be consensus among all Dharma teachers on what they mean. "Dukkha due to pain" simply means when you're in pain, you're suffering. Like, duh. "Dukkha due to change" means if you are not in pain now, things are going to change and you will suffer later. We are familiar with this by now.

The middle one, "dukkha due to formations (*saṅkhāra*)," is the one that is nuanced because it is open to interpretation. It is one of those frustrating cases in the ancient texts where the Buddha said something in a discourse to his disciples, and presumably everybody understood, so he did not elaborate. *Saṅkhāra*, usually translated as "formations," literally means "together-making" or "together-doing," so *saṅkhāra* can mean "that which has been put together" or "that which puts together."[10] You can poetically say that *saṅkhāra* is both a noun and a verb: it points to both what has been constructed, and the *process* of constructing it. For that reason, Soryu prefers the translation "constructions."[11]

An authoritative interpretation of "dukkha due to formations" comes from the highly influential fifth-century Indian Buddhist scholar Buddhaghosa in his book the Visuddhimagga. He interpreted it as dukkha due to all phenomena being "oppressed by rise and fall" even when you are in a state of equanimity.[12] The problem with this interpretation is the third type of dukkha, "dukkha due to change," is entirely a subset of it, and that's why Buddhaghosa had to swap their order in his book (presumably that is the reason; he did not say). I myself find his explanation very unsatisfactory.

I know of three other complementary interpretations of "dukkha due to formations" that make more sense to me. My favorite refers to it as suffering due to the oppression of having to maintain things in a (temporarily) pleasant state. For example, if you have a body or a relationship or a social status or a possession you are happy with, you need to put in a lot of time, effort, and expense to maintain it, and that is dukkha. This interpretation aligns the three types of dukkha into a very nice logical continuum. In this continuum, dukkha is:

1. You are in pain (physical or emotional).

2. If you are not in pain, you have to maintain the conditions to keep you not in pain.

3. You will eventually lose.

To put it in a funnier way: pain sucks, having to fix it sucks, and no matter what you do to fix it, it will eventually fail, and that sucks. This is why liberation is the only true solution.

Another interpretation of "dukkha due to formations (saṅkhāra)" requires saṅkhāra to be interpreted as "mental formation," which is a valid interpretation that occurs frequently in the ancient texts. In this interpretation, after experiencing physical or emotional pain, the mind laments and ruminates, constructing a host of painful thoughts involving "why me?," "this should be happening," and "this should not be happening" in reaction to the initial pain, thus multiplying the suffering.

In the ancient texts, the Buddha compared this type of suffering to being hit by two arrows.[13] Experiencing pain (physical or emotional) is like being hit by an arrow. In reaction to pain, many people also lament and ruminate, which the texts describe as, "he sorrows, grieves, and laments; he weeps beating his breast and becomes distraught." That doubles his suffering. The Buddha compares that to being hit by a second arrow, and, according to medieval commentaries, the second arrow is only an inch or so away from the first, which means the second arrow inflicts far more pain than the first one. The Buddha taught that with the right mental training, it is possible to be totally free from at least that second arrow of suffering. Hence, in this interpretation, the dukkha due to (mental) formations is this second arrow.

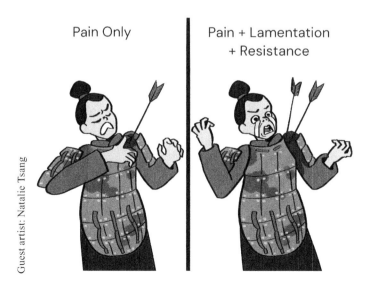

Pain Only

Pain + Lamentation
+ Resistance

Guest artist: Natalie Tsang

The third interpretation of dukkha due to formations is actually quite profound, and it is one that has been articulated by some masters I know of, including the Dalai Lama and our very own Soryu.[14] This one requires us to recognize that basically everything we experience in the world is a "formation" (saṅkhāra), which means that everything arises from conditions and ceases when those conditions end, and therefore, they can never truly be relied on. Relying on them is like a drunk man trying to stay upright by relying on an unstable stack of heavy barrels; he's not going to have a particularly good time. This, of course, relates closely to the etymology of *dukkha* as "unstable" or "not standing well."[15] Fundamentally, reliance on formations is always unsatisfactory, always arises from the ignorance that all formations are unreliable, and always ends in suffering.

Based on the above interpretation, Soryu ties together all three types of dukkha this way:

> We go broke, we get sick, we are betrayed. We experience pain. Therefore, we are insecure.
>
> We work hard to keep things good, to create things to protect ourselves. But this work does not ultimately work, and these things fall apart. Therefore, we are more deeply insecure.
>
> Everything is unstable. Everything outside of ourselves is unstable. Everything inside of ourselves is unstable. We have nowhere to stand. Therefore, we are even more deeply insecure.
>
> This is suffering.

In any case, whichever interpretation of "dukkha due to formations" you choose (or all of them), the above makes clear that dukkha is, in its broadest sense, the inherent unsatisfactoriness that arises from grasping to *any* phenomenon.

It's Cause and Effect All Over Again

There is an important theme you see over and over again in Buddhism, and that is the central importance of cause and effect. All of Buddhism can be said to revolve around the one vital insight that suffering has causes, and that if you take away any necessary cause of suffering, then suffering ceases.

A deep understanding of cause and effect is so fundamental to Buddhism that it can even serve as a proxy for stream-entry (the first stage of enlightenment). One story that illustrates this is the stream-entry of Sāriputta and Moggallāna, the Buddha's chief disciples.[16] Sāriputta and Moggallāna were best friends and earnest seekers of the truth. They promised each other that whoever finds "the deathless" first will quickly inform the other.

One day, the monk Assaji was in Rājagaha begging for almsfood. Assaji was one of the five original disciples of the Buddha, and by this time he was already fully enlightened. Sāriputta saw Assaji and was immediately impressed. He approached Assaji and asked, "Venerable Sir, your features are serene; your complexion is pure and bright. Who is your teacher and what is his dharma?"

Assaji explained that his teacher is the Buddha and he uttered this short four-line summary of the Dharma:

> Of those things that arise from a cause:
> The Buddha has declared the cause,
> And its cessation.
> This is the teaching of the great master.[17]

Upon hearing those words, this dustless, stainless Dharma-vision arose in Sāriputta: "Whatever has the nature of arising, also has the nature of ceasing." There and then, Sāriputta gained stream-entry.

Sāriputta immediately set out to look for Moggallāna. Moggallāna saw Sāriputta coming from a distance and could immediately tell that something profound had changed in him. He asked Sāriputta, "Friend, your features are serene; your complexion is pure and bright. Can it be that you have attained the deathless?"

"Yes, friend, I have attained the deathless."

Sāriputta taught Assaji's four-line summary to Moggallāna, and Moggallāna too attained stream-entry right there and then. They both went to see the Buddha to join his sangha. When the Buddha saw them coming from a distance, he declared to the other monks, "These two will become my chief disciples." Within weeks, both would attain full enlightenment.

There are three important places where cause and effect show up very prominently: the teachings of karma, dependent origination, and emptiness. We will explore them in the rest of this chapter.

Karma Is What Our Parents Taught Us at Six

The teaching of karma can be profound, but its central core is surprisingly simple. *Karma* literally means "action." The Buddha gives a clear, concise definition for *karma*:

> It is volition, monks, that I call karma. For having willed, one acts by body, speech, or mind.[18]

In other words, **karma is volitional action**. The most important thing about karma is that all karma has consequences, known as *kamma-vipāka* (literally, "maturation of action") or *kamma-phala* (literally, "fruit of action"). As the Buddha puts it:

> Beings are owners of their actions (karma), heirs of their actions; they originate from their actions, are bound to their actions, have their actions as their refuge. It is action that distinguishes beings as inferior and superior.[19]

Soryu made a funny comment, "The basic teaching of karma is that your actions have consequences; that's it. It's just what our parents tried to teach us when we were six."

The Buddha's definition of *karma* is straightforward and easy to understand. The part that is hard to grasp is the result of karma (kamma-vipāka). There are just too many hidden variables. Furthermore, results of your karma can interact amongst themselves, thus creating new complexity. For example, when you have a lot of good karma, it can render a trifling of bad karma ineffective. The Buddha compares it to putting a lump of salt in a bowl of water versus in a large, clean river. The same amount of salt can render the bowl of water too salty to drink, but does not do that to the river.[20] In the same way, an evil person may suffer a lot from a trifling of bad karma, but the exact same trifling of bad karma may have very little effect on a highly virtuous person (unfortunately for optimization-eager engineers, the Buddha did not teach a mathematical formula to calculate how much virtue versus how much bad karma).

Even more confounding for us mere mortals is that the results of karma can happen across lifetimes. The Buddha said, "The result of karma is threefold: to be experienced in this very life, or in the next rebirth, or on some subsequent occasion."[21] For those of us who are unable to see one or more of our previous lifetimes, it severely limits our data-collection ability for fully understanding karma. Even seeing some number of previous lifetimes is not enough. The Buddha said there were yogis who developed the ability to see past lives, but since some karma does not ripen until many lifetimes later, these yogis got confused.[22]

For those reasons, the Buddha said that only a fully enlightened one can fully understand the result of karma, and for the rest of us, it is an "inconceivable matter" and trying to conceive it would "reap madness or frustration."[23]

You might think that the Buddha's teaching on karma was something that was already popularly taken for granted in his time and place, but no, that is incorrect. Contemporary with the Buddha in ancient India was a group of famous teachers who taught an entire spectrum of teachings relating to karma.[24]

For example, Pūraṇa Kassapa taught that there is no such thing as morality. He said if one mutilates, tortures, harms, oppresses, murders, steals, or lies, one does no evil, and even if one were to go on a mass-murder rampage and "reduce all the living beings on this earth to a single pile of flesh," one still does no evil at all. Yeah, what a [insert pejorative epithet].

Makkhali Gosāla taught strict fatalism and denied cause and effect. He said there was no such thing as self-determination, and that "beings are defiled or purified without any cause or condition."

Ajita Kesakambala taught materialistic annihilationism. He said that we are all only physical material, and that after we die, there is no afterlife at all. Soryu jokes that Ajita was like a modern-day Western thinker, and no, Soryu doesn't mean it as a compliment.

There were, of course, teachers who taught that the only way to purification was to burn off all your past karma, and the way to do that was by torturing yourself. There were also teachers who taught that volition had no effect on karma, that the same karma was created whether a deed was performed intentionally or unintentionally.

The Buddha did not just conveniently pick up his teachings from the popular culture around him. On the contrary, his teachings courageously rebelled against the popular views of his time, including those of the priestly caste, Brahmanism. His teaching on karma was based on his own deep, careful investigation.

How to Karma Without Your Self

Back in Chapter 4, we stated the Buddhist teaching of nonself. That leads to two questions about karma that confound many people studying Buddhism, which turn out to have answers that are surprisingly understandable. The two questions are:

1. How can actions have consequences without a self to experience them?

2. Without a permanent soul, how does rebirth even work?

To answer the first question, we just need to be clear what the Buddha actually taught about nonself: he taught that no one has a permanent, unchanging, and inherently blissful soul. During the Buddha's time, the word that's used to refer to this soul, *atta*, is the same word used for self, hence this teaching is known as "nonself" (*anatta*).

Therefore, nonself does *not* mean there is no experience of selfness. There certainly can be an experience of selfness (ask me how I know) that arises with the five aggregates as conditions. It is this experienced selfness that creates karma and inherits its consequences. We know this from day-to-day experience. For example, in a funny way, if this experienced selfness conditioned by five aggregates identified as "I" were to say something nasty to another arisen experienced selfness identified as "my wife," it is guaranteed that this experienced selfness identified as "I" will suffer the consequences of that karma very quickly.

Soryu likes to explain it with a bit more depth: this experience of selfness is dependently arisen, and it depends on grasping. This grasping produces karma. Karma later conditions birth. The person who is born out of this karma experiences its results.

The second question is a bit of a royal pain, and we know that because that same vexing question was asked by a king. Many years after the Buddha passed, Alexander the Great from Greece invaded India and left behind a line of Indo-Greek kings in the region of Bactria (around modern-day Afghanistan). One of those kings was called Milinda (also known as Menander). According to the ancient text titled Milindapañha (literally, "Milinda's Questions"), Milinda had a series of conversations with the arahant Nāgasena. Near the end of those conversations, the king declared himself a Buddhist "for as long as life shall last."[25] Here is the relevant part of their fascinating conversation (slightly abridged):

The king asked, "He who is reborn, Nāgasena, does he remain the same or become another?"

"Neither the same nor another."

"Give me an illustration."

"Now what do you think, O king? You were once a baby, a tender thing, and small in size, lying flat on your back. Was that the same as you who are now grown up?"

"No. That child was one, I am another."

"If you are not that child, it will follow that you have had neither mother nor father, nor teacher. Is the mother of the embryo in the first stage different from the mother of the embryo in the second stage, or the third, or the fourth? Is the mother of the baby a different person from the mother of the grown-up man? Is the person who goes to school one, and the same when he has finished his schooling another? Is it one who commits a crime; another who is punished?"

"Certainly not. But what would you, Sir, say to that?"

The elder replied: "I should say that I am the same person, now I am grown up, as I was when I was a tender tiny baby, flat on my back. For all these states are included in one by means of this body."

"Give me an illustration."

"Suppose a man, O king, were to light a lamp; is it the same flame that burns in the first watch of the night, and in the second, and the third?"

"No."

"Then is there one lamp in the first watch, and another in the second, and another in the third?"

"No. The light comes from the same lamp all the night through."

"Just so, O king, is the continuity of a person or thing maintained. One comes into being, another passes away; and the rebirth is, as it were, simultaneous. Thus, neither as the same nor as another does a man go on to the last phase of his self-consciousness."

"Give me a further illustration."

"It is like milk, which when once taken from the cow turns, after a lapse of time, first to curds, and then from curds to butter, and then from butter to ghee. Now would it be right to say that the milk was the same thing as the curds, or the butter, or the ghee?"

"Certainly not; but they are produced out of it."

"Just so, O king, is the continuity of a person or thing maintained. One comes into being, another passes away; and the rebirth is, as it were, simultaneous. Thus, neither as the same nor as another does a man go on to the last phase of his self-consciousness."

"Well put, Nāgasena!"[26]

The essential insight, as we quoted Shinzen Young describing back in Chapter 4, is: **"the experience of self is a process, and there is no thing in that process that is a self."** Just like the flame in a lamp: at every moment, the flame is different from the one in the previous moment, yet every moment of the flame and its heat create the conditions for the next moment of the flame to arise. Hence, even though each moment of the flame is different, there is a direct chain of causation that produces the continuous *process* of a flame that lasts throughout the night.

In the same way, the self at every moment is different from the self in the previous moment, but every moment of self and its karma create the conditions for the arising of self in the next moment. Hence, even though every moment of self is different, there is a direct chain of karmic causation that produces the continuous *process* of a self that continues through this lifetime and across lifetimes.

And that, my friends, is how karma and rebirth function without a permanent soul. It is surprisingly understandable.

Dependent Origination:
The Full Causal Chain of Suffering

The place where the theme of cause and effect really shows up in a big way is in the teaching of dependent origination (*paṭicca samuppāda*), in which the Buddha explains in detail how karma functions without a self. This teaching has a general expression and a detailed expression. The general expression is these four lines:

> When this exists, that comes to be;
> With the arising of this, that arises.
> When this does not exist, that does not come to be;
> With the cessation of this, that ceases.[27]

The detailed expression of dependent origination is a causal chain with
twelve items that presents a complete picture of what causes suffering and,
therefore, how to resolve it. The causal chain, where each item creates the
conditions for the next, is:

1. ignorance (*avijjā*)

2. formations (*saṅkhāra*)

3. consciousness (*viññāṇa*)

4. name-and-form (*nāmarūpa*)

5. six senses (*saḷāyatana*)

6. contact (*phassa*)

7. sensation (*vedanā*)

8. craving (*taṇhā*)

9. grasping (*upādāna*)

10. becoming (*bhava*)

11. birth (*jāti*)

12. old age (*jarā*) and death (*maraṇa*)

If it does not make a lot of sense to you, fret not; the explanation turns
out to be quite understandable. The standard explanation extends the twelve
items over three lifetimes: where 1) and 2) relate to the previous life, 3) to 10)
relate to the present life, and 11) and 12) relate to the next life.

Here is how it works. The narrative begins in the previous life, and it begins with 1) ignorance. *Ignorance* is defined as "not knowing suffering, not
knowing the origin of suffering, not knowing the cessation of suffering, not
knowing the way leading to the cessation of suffering."[28] In other words,
ignorance is not knowing any part of the Four Noble Truths. It can also be
thought of as not seeing reality as it actually is; specifically, not understanding that all conditioned phenomena are impermanent, subject to suffering,
and possess no essence of selfness. Due to this ignorance, we continue creating 2) formations, defined here as things formed by body, speech, or mind.
Doing so produces karma.

That leads us to the present life. The karma produced in the previous life ripened as 3) consciousness for this life, starting as "rebirth consciousness," which arises at rebirth and continues as a process for a lifetime (like the lamp in the previous metaphor). Consciousness must function with other mental and material aggregates as its objects/fuel/basis (take your pick), which together give us both body and mind. Hence, consciousness conditions 4) name-and-form, sometimes translated as "mentality and materiality," which includes other aspects of mind and a physical body. With that, we gain 5) the six senses. Those six senses allow us 6) contact with physical objects and thoughts, which gives us 7) sensations. With that, we have desire for pleasant sensations and aversion for unpleasant sensations, which means we have 8) craving. Craving conditions 9) grasping, specifically toward four things: sensual pleasures, views, rituals, and a doctrine of self. Due to our grasping, we 10) become again when we die.

That brings us to the next life. With the wanting to become, we take 11) birth. And taking birth means, yeah, we are subject to 12) old age, death, and "this entire mass of suffering."[29]

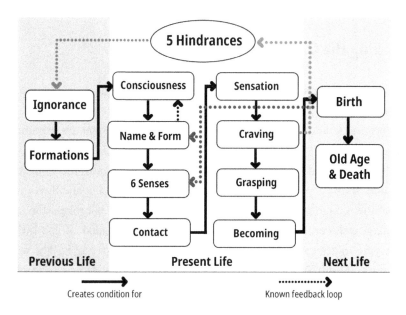

One really important feature about this chain is the existence of feedback loops. One, for example, is the tight feedback loop between consciousness and name-and-form; they both depend on and condition each other.[30] *Birth*, which the Buddha defines here as "the manifestation of the aggregates, the obtaining of the sense bases," creates an obvious feedback loop with name-and-form and six senses.[31]

Another major feedback loop is to be found between ignorance and craving. When craving is strong, the five hindrances are also strong, and when the five hindrances are strong, you cannot clearly see things as they really are; you are hindered from the full understanding of the Four Noble Truths, and so ignorance is strong. That is how craving conditions ignorance. This feedback loop is the reason you can end suffering either by eliminating ignorance or craving: you weaken one, you weaken the other; you take one down, you take down the other.

While dependent origination is usually presented as a chain, given feedback loops, it can be more accurately thought of as a web.[32] One important implication is there is no "first cause." If you just think of it as a chain, you may mistakenly think ignorance is the "first cause." In reality, ignorance also has causes, the most direct ones being the five hindrances.[33] Everything is just part of a beginningless web of cause and effect.

Breaking the Causal Chain of Suffering

The most important thing about the teaching on dependent origination is it provides the answer to how to end suffering. If your understanding of dependent origination does not lead to ending suffering, then you are missing the entire point.

The way to break suffering is surprisingly straightforward: there are strategic nodes in the dependent origination web you can work on, and through *any one* of them, you can break ignorance. Once ignorance is broken, the entire causation web comes crashing down and suffering is ended. It is a little bit like trying to destroy the Death Star in the first *Star Wars* movie. The way to destroy the Death Star is to blow up its reactor core, and one way to reach the reactor core is via a thermal exhaust port. That is why if you can fire even a single proton torpedo into a thermal exhaust port, you can take down the entire Death Star. Hence, the almost intractable problem of destroying the Death Star is reduced to the still-challenging but much easier problem of clearing your way to a thermal exhaust port and firing a proton torpedo into it.

In the case of ending ignorance and suffering, the most powerful access point is craving. Craving is something you can take direct action on and, as we stated in the previous section, once you weaken craving, you directly weaken the five hindrances, which then directly weakens ignorance, which in turn further weakens craving. You then ride that virtuous cycle until ignorance is destroyed, and then suffering ends. Soryu explains it in a complementary way: As you reduce craving more and more, you eventually reach a point where there is not enough craving to sustain ignorance. When that happens, ignorance breaks enough for you to clearly see that craving causes suffering. That motivates you to reduce craving even more. Eventually, with the complete elimination of craving, there is also the complete elimination of ignorance and the end of suffering.

What is the Buddha's teaching on ending suffering by breaking craving? That is right, it is the Four Noble Truths! In that sense, the Four Noble Truths can be seen as one derivative of dependent origination, albeit the most concise, most understandable, most practicable, and most powerful one, which is why the Buddha emphasized it so much and so often.[34]

This insight answers a question that vexes almost every sincere Buddhist student I know. See, in the Four Noble Truths, the Buddha teaches that craving causes suffering, but in dependent origination, he teaches that ignorance causes suffering. Which is it? Dammit, which is it? Once you understand the intimate, codependent relationship between craving and ignorance, you can clearly see for yourself that the answer is: both.

Craving is not the only access point; the Buddha also spoke about others. For example, in the Discourse on the Observation of Dualities, the Buddha stated that, "Whatever suffering arises, all is caused by grasping. With the complete ending of all grasping there is no arising of suffering."[35] He then stated the same regarding ignorance, consciousness, contact, sensation, craving, and other mental phenomena. The complete ending of any one of those things leads to the end of suffering.

Occasionally, the Buddha gave an entire discourse focusing on a single access point as the way to end suffering. For example, this is an entire discourse:

> Monks, there are these three sensations: pleasant, painful, neither-painful-nor-pleasant.

A disciple of the Buddha, mindful,
Concentrated, comprehending clearly,
Understands sensations
And the origin of sensations,
Where they finally cease,
And the path leading to their destruction.
With the destruction of sensations
A monk is hungerless and fully quenched.[36]

One key lesson here is the same one you encounter over and over in the study of Buddhism: there are many doors to liberation. There are many legitimate and effective doorways to the ending of ignorance and suffering. Hence, if you encounter a discourse that says, "This is the way out" and another that says, "That is the way out," know that they are not mutually exclusive. They are like the green "exit" signs surrounding the cinema, every one of them points to a legitimate way out. As long as it eventually ends ignorance, it is legit.

Dependent origination is one of the most important teachings in Buddhism. It can even be said that dependent origination encapsulates all of Buddhism. Sāriputta quoted the Buddha as saying, "One who sees dependent origination sees the Dharma; one who sees the Dharma sees dependent origination."[37]

Dependent origination is a teaching that is profound and complete enough that if you understand it fully, you can derive the rest of Dharma, including its most important and most powerful derivative: the Four Noble Truths. Now you have learned both. You are so lucky.

Emptiness Is So Full

There is a very important teaching closely related to dependent origination and nonself that gained a position of preeminence in many schools of Buddhism: the teaching on emptiness (Sanskrit: *śūnyatā*; Pali: *suññatā*).[38]

The person most credited for expanding and formalizing the teaching of emptiness is the great second-century Buddhist master Nāgārjuna, whose work had a deeply profound influence on Buddhism. Thanks to him, emptiness became a huge thing (I'm pretty sure there is a pun in there somewhere). His most famous book is titled Mūlamadhyamakakārikā ("Fundamental Verses on the Middle Way"). I'm going to use the common abbreviation "MMK" out of compassion for the person narrating our audiobook. Buddhist teacher Leigh Brasington jokes that the whole *MMK* reads like somebody's debate notes.

Emptiness, as espoused by Nāgārjuna, in essence refers to essence-less-ness (yes, there is a pun somewhere here too). It means that all phenomena are empty of essence of self, empty of inherent existence. Nāgārjuna did not make it up; the Buddha had already famously stated that, "all phenomena are nonself (anatta)," with *nonself* here meaning "not having a separate, permanent essence."[39] Sāriputta also clarified that seeing all phenomena as "empty of self or of what belongs to a self" will result in "liberation of mind through emptiness."[40] So Nāgārjuna was just expanding on the Buddha's teachings.

Emptiness means that there are multiple streams of dependent origination processes going on all the time, and all phenomena, including all physical objects, arise and cease merely as the result of these process streams and their interactions. A popular half-humorous, half-poetic way some modern Buddhist teachers articulate this teaching is: all nouns are really just slow-moving verbs. The noun *mountain*, for example, is really just a collection of very slow-moving geological verbs.

One major consequence of emptiness is the interdependence of every-thing. If you recognize all phenomena as the interaction of multiple streams of dependent origination, then you gain insight into how everything is inter-dependent on everything else in order to manifest. Zen master Thich Nhat Hanh famously calls it "interbeing."

In *MMK*, Nāgārjuna gave many examples of emptiness. One example: in the simple act of moving, the mover and the movement are not the same thing, yet there is really no such thing as a mover without movement, nor movement without the mover, therefore movement and mover must occur together, and therefore you cannot say they are separate phenomena.[41] He gave many other examples relating to seeing, hearing, and so on, but they are all of the same nature, just replace "mover/moving" above with "see-er/seeing," and so on.[42] He also gave the example of fire on fuel, making essentially the same argu-ment that fire and fuel are codependent: it is the fuel that enables the fire, but it is also the fire that makes the fuel fuel.[43]

More important, Nāgārjuna examines the self itself with the same lens:

> If the self were the aggregates,
> It would be arising and ceasing as they do.
> But if self were different from the aggregates,
> It would not have the characteristics of the aggregates.[44]

In other words, this is the realization that self too is empty of essence, and is dependently originated with the five aggregates. And from here, Nāgārjuna leads us to some profound practical consequence: the full understanding of the emptiness of self leads to freedom from "I" and "mine," which leads to free-dom from the unceasing and compulsive proliferation of thoughts (Sanskrit: *prapañca*; Pali: *papañca*), which leads to freedom from "action and misery." And then, "action and misery having ceased, there is nirvana."[45] Whoa.

Nāgārjuna devoted Chapter 18 of *MMK* to the exploration of the emp-tiness of self. Leigh Brasington has a rendering of its conclusion that is not strictly literal to the original text, but expresses the content faithfully in a beautiful way:

> You are not the same as or different from
> Conditions on which you depend;

You are neither severed from
Nor forever fused with them—
This is the deathless teaching
Of buddhas who care for the world.[46]

The teachings on emptiness are truly profound. The Buddha says if people fail to study the "teachings dealing with emptiness," Dharma will decline.[47] While the many teachings on emptiness are ultimately based on the realization of nonself, they offer a vast array of subtlety and wonder. We hope this short introduction encourages you to eventually take up a deep study of emptiness.

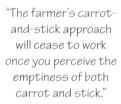

"The farmer's carrot-and-stick approach will cease to work once you perceive the emptiness of both carrot and stick."

Two Levels of Truths, When One Just Isn't Enough

Out of Nāgārjuna's *MMK* comes another teaching that had a profound and long-lasting influence on Buddhism: the idea of the two levels of truths. The way Nāgārjuna puts it:

The Buddha's teaching of the Dharma is based on two truths: a truth of worldly convention and an ultimate truth. Those who do not understand the distinction drawn between these two truths do not understand the Buddha's profound truth. Without a foundation in the conventional truth the significance of the ultimate cannot be taught. Without understanding the significance of the ultimate, liberation is not achieved.[48]

To understand this, we need a modern-day analogy: physics. You and I operate in a reality where solid things such as tables and chairs exist, matter is different from energy, particles are different from waves, space and time are uniformly distributed, and all motion deterministically obeys Newton's laws. Go down to the subatomic level, however, and everything operates in an entirely different reality. Matter is energy, particles are waves, space and time are bendable (and even collapsible, as in a black hole), and quantum mechanics is probabilistic rather than deterministic. I joke that at the subatomic level, Newton's laws become Newton's suggestions. Also, at that level, there is really no such thing as a solid object. Atoms are comprised almost entirely of space, and the only reason your table feels solid to you is that the lattice of atoms forming the table exert forces on the lattice of atoms forming your hand, and that's why the table exhibits the illusion of "solidity."

In other words, nature operates simultaneously on two separate levels of reality, each following its own starkly different set of physical laws. In physics, just as in the two levels of truth in Buddhism, without a foundation in classical physics, the significance of quantum physics cannot be taught, and without understanding quantum physics, you cannot be said to truly master physics.

The teaching of two levels of truth was alluded to by the Buddha, but never actually explicitly articulated. In the oldest texts, the Buddha was never known to have said anything like, "Monks, there are these two levels of truth: conventional truth and ultimate truth." The closest he came to that was saying some of his discourses are of explicit meaning (*nītattha*), while others require interpretation (*neyyattha*), and that you misrepresent him if you explain a discourse whose meaning requires interpretation as a discourse whose meaning is explicit, or vice versa.[49]

The Buddha tried to make all his teachings widely understandable and practicable, so he almost always taught at the level of conventional truth, which is why almost every time we quote him, you don't have much of a problem understanding. There were, however, times when the Buddha was clearly speaking at the level of ultimate truth, and it was very often when he was talking about nirvana, which has no frame of reference at all in conventional truth and, therefore, cannot really be spoken about at the level of conventional truth. The clearest example so far is the discourse from Chapter 5, where he said, "For one who sees the origin of the world as it really is with correct wisdom, there is no notion of nonexistence in regard to the world. And for one who sees the cessation of the world as it really is with correct wisdom, there is no notion of existence in regard to the world."[50]

The Buddha also often referred to himself in conversation, and there was at least one instance where he made explicit that he used self-references only as a convenience, as "designations in common use in the world, which the Tathāgata uses without misapprehending them."[51] I'm guessing it's akin to a nuclear physics professor who is keenly aware that her table has no real nature of solidity at the subatomic level, but uses it as a convenience anyway.

The existence of two levels of truth is the reason why, sometimes, statements about the truth can sound completely nonsensical. For example, if your physics professor states true statements regarding quantum physics such as "matter is energy; energy is matter," and if you only know classical physics, then not only does what she says sound nonsensical to you, it also contradicts what she taught you as truth in Physics 101. Yikes! Happily for you, things will start making sense once you complete the classical physics classes and start studying quantum physics.

In the same way, as you explore Buddhism, you may start coming across teachings such as this in Nāgārjuna's *MMK*:

> Everything is real,
> and is not real,
> and is both real and not real,
> and is neither real nor not real.
> This is Lord Buddha's teaching.[52]

Later Buddhist texts, including the *MMK*, are rife with such deep but seemingly nonsensical teachings. In contrast, early Buddhist texts, which this book is heavily based on, are very understandable, because the Buddha took care to speak at the level of conventional truth. It takes genius to teach the most profound Dharma, but it takes extraordinary super-genius to teach a Dharma powerful enough to bring people all the way to full enlightenment using the understandable language of conventional truth. The Buddha is that extraordinary super-genius, by far the greatest genius in all of human history, which is why he could do it. The good news is we have him. The bad news is his level of genius is so rare we only have one of him.

Hence, if you come across such teachings—for example, "there is no aging and death, and no end of aging and death"—and if they sound nonsensical to you, don't worry about it.[53] Don't feel bad about putting them aside for now. As your mindfulness and samadhi deepen, and as you approach nirvana, those things will start to make sense and, at some point, become useful to you.

And remember, even after you have fully realized the emptiness of self, you may still have to file tax returns.

The Abbot's Commentary
by Soryu Forall

Karma is power. You have power because your actions have consequences. You have the power to change the world, and you have the power to change your life. You use this power at all times. Even if you decide not to use it, that very decision is an exercise of your power, with consequences that cannot be avoided.

This is not about self-blame or self-exaltation. This is about accepting the precious nature of this moment, of this decision, right now, as the beginning of the future. Whatever you do now will have consequences that will impact your future choices, and this will continue all the way to your complete enlightenment.

Therefore, if you believe in anything, believe in this: "What you do matters."

CHAPTER ELEVEN

How to Nirvana Yourself

Seeing Nirvana Directly

How a Little Dragon Found the Sea

Once upon a time, a god dropped a dragon pearl into a pond deep inland by accident. The pearl later transformed into a little baby dragon. As he got older, he learned that he was actually a sea dragon, so the only way he could grow into a full adult was to be in the sea. But he looked all around and the sea was nowhere to be found. What to do? Fortunately, a wise old tortoise told him, "All you have to do is to find your way to a stream, then flow with the current, and you will eventually reach the sea. Trust me."

The little dragon was overjoyed. He could not even begin to figure out how to find the sea, but he knew where the closest stream was. So he made his way to the stream and entered in. Once he entered the stream, he flowed with the current and it brought him to a river, and then, eventually, the river current brought him to the sea. And there he grew into a mighty dragon and lived happily ever after.

The moral of the story is, in order to reach the sea, all the little dragon had to do was to enter a stream. The immensely difficult problem of finding the sea was reduced to a far easier problem of finding and entering a nearby stream.

That, my friends, would be how you can reach enlightenment. This chapter shows you a way.

Entering the Stream Makes You Cool

We learned back in Chapter 5 that the Buddhist path to enlightenment is defined in four stages. It is no accident that the first stage is called stream-entry. Ancient Buddhist texts poetically compare the journey toward full enlightenment as a gentle flow from the stream into the river and then into the sea.[1] When one enters the stream, one will gently flow to the river and eventually to the sea of full enlightenment. That is why one who has entered the first stage of enlightenment is called a stream-enterer (*sotāpanna*).

Stream-entry may be the most important stage for somebody embarking on the journey toward enlightenment. The reason is very simple: there is no guarantee that you will actually get to stream-entry, but once you reach stream-entry, you are *guaranteed* to reach full enlightenment within seven more lifetimes, according to the Buddha. Hence, anybody who wants to embark on the path toward full enlightenment has only to worry about reaching stream-entry. It is a bit like getting a degree from Harvard (or the university of your choice). If you are not in Harvard but want a degree from Harvard, you don't really have to worry about final-year or third-year coursework; you only have to worry about getting into Harvard. Once you are in, as long as you pass the exams, you are guaranteed to eventually earn your Harvard degree. Getting in is the key.

There is one important place where the Harvard analogy breaks down, and that is selectivity. Harvard is very selective; only about 5 percent of applicants are admitted each year. In contrast, stream-entry is not selective at all; 100 percent of all who want to join the club and who work hard enough to satisfy the entry criteria will be admitted. In that sense, it is more like becoming a marathoner. There is no limit to how many marathoners there are in the world; there is no admissions committee to decide whether you can be called a marathoner or not; as long as you are sufficiently healthy and train hard enough to be able to run 26.219 miles, you are a marathoner. Yes, it is very challenging; yes, not everybody has the motivation; yes, there are people with preexisting medical conditions who should not train without close medical supervision, but by and large, anybody can do it.

In the same way, stream-entry is very challenging, not everybody has the motivation, and some people need more expert supervision than others, but it is within the reach of anybody willing to do what is needed. And since stream-entry is within the reach of everybody, then, by extension, so is full enlightenment and total liberation from all suffering. That, I think, is the best news ever. Ever!

Stream-entry has the additional benefit of significantly reducing suffering. Once, the Buddha took up a little bit of soil with his fingernail and then told his disciples that before stream-entry, one's suffering is comparable to the great earth, while after stream-entry, one's suffering is reduced to the amount represented by the soil in the Buddha's fingernail.[2] Whoa. To be fair, the Buddha probably took into consideration that the suffering of a stream-enterer is limited to a maximum of seven more lifetimes, while the suffering of a non-stream-enterer is unbounded, but still, whoa.

But wait, there's more: stream-entry also benefits the people around the stream-enterer. That is because a stream-enterer abandons six types of de-filements: denigration, domination, envy, jealousy, hypocrisy, and fraud.[3] Imagine a world where all corporate and political leaders are stream-enterers: no more denigration, domination, hypocrisy, or fraud! I think it is for all these reasons that the Buddha declares stream-entry as "far better than being in heaven, or ruling supreme over the entire universe."[4] Whoa. That is why Soryu and I dream of creating a world where stream-entry is widely under-standable, accessible, and practicable to all.

All You Need to Break Are Three Fetters

The most technical definition of stream-entry is the total abandonment of the first three lower fetters: identity view, doubt, and the distorted grasp of rules and vows.

The first fetter, identity view, means identifying the self with any of the five aggregates (form, sensation, perception, volitional formations, and consciousness).[5] Happily for us, the Buddha offered a very precise technical definition for identity view. There are four possible views on each of the ag-gregates that relate to the self. Using the example of form, the four views are:

1. Self is form.

2. Self owns form.

3. Self is contained within form.

4. Form is contained within self.

If you apply these four views to all five aggregates, you end up with twenty views, since four times five equals twenty. For those who would like them all spelled out, the twenty views are:

- Self is form; self owns form; self is contained within form; form is contained within self.

- Self is sensation; self owns sensation; self is contained within sensation; sensation is contained within self.

- Self is perception; self owns perception; self is contained within perception; perception is contained within self.

- Self is volitional formations; self owns volitional formations; self is contained within volitional formations; volitional formations are contained within self.

- Self is consciousness; self owns consciousness; self is contained within consciousness; consciousness is contained within self.

The fetter of identity view means holding at least *one* of the twenty views. Therefore, the abandoning of identity view is the abandoning of *all* twenty views above.[6]

Soryu often defines the five aggregates as the five ways identity can be assumed. I think his definition beautifully summarizes the fetter of identity view.

The second fetter, doubt, traditionally refers to a lack of confidence in the teachings of the Buddha.[7] Specifically, it refers to the type of doubt that undermines practice. There are two types of doubt in relation to the teaching: healthy doubt and unhealthy doubt. The type of doubt that leads one to question and investigate the teaching in order to understand it more deeply is healthy; it is not a fetter. In contrast, the type of doubt that leads us away from investigation and prevents us from following through on the practice is unhealthy, and it constitutes a fetter.

To illustrate, let's consider the case of physical fitness. Suppose you want to be physically healthy and fit, and suppose you read in magazines that, according to scientists, exercise can lead to physical health and fitness. If you have healthy doubt, you first ask yourself, "Is that true?" You then read the scientific literature to investigate. As part of your investigation, you also try to understand how exercise works (for example, that running increases your VO_2 max [your maximum lung capacity for oxygen], and that resistance training builds up your muscles). But that is not enough, you actually try exercising to see for yourself if the claims in the literature are true. In a few weeks, you find yourself more physically healthy and fit, and you find that your initial skepticism and the effort you put into understanding exercise actually help and motivate you in your training. That is healthy doubt.

In contrast, let's say you are closed-minded, and let's say you hold this attitude that "all scientists are wrong." So you decide that if scientists say exercise can lead to physical fitness, it must be wrong. You do not take the time to investigate their claims. Worse still, you do not even take the time to think about your original assumption that "all scientists are wrong." Therefore, you do not exercise, and so you do not gain physical health or fitness. That is an example of unhealthy doubt, the type of doubt that leads you away from the practice.

In Pali, at least two words are translated into English as "doubt": *kankhā* and *vicikicchā*. Kankhā includes both healthy and unhealthy doubt, while vicikicchā refers only to unhealthy doubt.[8] Only vicikicchā is the fetter.

The third fetter is "distorted grasp of rules and vows."[9] There are, however, many other translations. For example, I've seen it translated as "attachments to rites and rituals," "attachment to precepts and practices," and "indulgence in wrongful rites and ceremonies." This fetter refers to the belief that merely performing certain rituals or obeying certain rules and vows is by itself *sufficient* to liberate one from suffering. Shinzen Young explains it quite brilliantly as: the belief that rules and regulations can provide more spiritual support than they really can. Soryu puts it in a more amusing way: it is like expecting rituals and rules to do all your spiritual work for you.

The fetter is probably easier to understand in the cultural context of the Buddha's time and place, where many people performed daily religious rituals (for example, repeating certain words, burning certain items in front of certain idols, or taking a bath in a holy river) in the belief that doing that alone will liberate them from all suffering.

The Buddha taught, instead, that suffering arises from mental factors such as greed, hatred, and delusion, and, therefore, the only way to gain liberation from all suffering is to completely abandon the mental factors that lead to suffering. Rites, rituals, rules, habits, and vows provide us important support for the practice toward abandoning those mental factors, but they are also merely supporting factors, not the main active ingredient. The failure to recognize that is the fetter.

The Buddha did not specifically elaborate on this fetter, but his teachings on at least three occasions illustrate it. The first involves bathing in a holy river. Once, the Buddha was giving a lecture when a man named Sundarika Bhāradvāja was in the audience. Sundarika believed that bathing in a holy river can "give liberation, give merit, wash away one's evil action," so he asked the Buddha if that was true.[10] The Buddha was like, no dude, it doesn't work that way. The Buddha then taught him the practice of "inner bathing" as the means for liberation, which means cultivating qualities including virtue, inner peace, inner joy, meditative concentration, kindness, and compassion. There is a funny but apocryphal story often told by Buddhist teachers: The Buddha was taking a walk one day and saw a group of holy men bathing in a holy river. He asked them why they were doing it, and they told him that by submerging themselves in the holy river, liberation can be gained. The Buddha told them, if one can really gain liberation by submerging in a holy river, then the ones most liberated would not be you, the holy men, it would be the fish and prawns in this river.

Buddhist monk and author Nyanatiloka Mahāthera has a very nice paraphrase of the Buddha's teaching on this topic:

> The man enmeshed in delusion will never be purified through the mere study of holy books, or sacrifices to gods, or through fasts, or sleeping on the ground, or difficult and strenuous vigils, or the repetition of prayers. Neither gifts to priests, nor self-castigation, nor performance of rites and ceremonies can work purification in him who is filled with craving.[11]

The context of the Buddha's teaching on the third occasion was shocking to me. Here, two ascetics came to see him, a naked "ox-duty ascetic" and a naked "dog-duty ascetic."[12] What are they? The ox-duty ascetic wore horns on his head, tied a tail to his backside, and went about eating grass together with the cows. Similarly, the dog-duty ascetic performed all the actions typical of a dog. And they were naked. Yeah, wow. They both did that in the belief that doing so would lead them to liberation. Fortunately for them, they respected the Buddha enough to come talk to him.

The ox-duty ascetic asked the Buddha what would be "the destination" for the other guy, the dog-duty ascetic. The dog-duty ascetic similarly asked what would happen to that other guy, the ox-duty ascetic. First, the Buddha shocked them by telling them that the ox-duty ascetic, in the best case, after he died would be reborn as an ox and, in the worst case, would be taking up residence in the hell realm, and similarly with the dog-duty ascetic. They both started crying. The Buddha then taught them that, ultimately liberation arises from intentions and actions. At the end of this discourse, both ascetics abandoned their animal practices and became disciples of the Buddha.

If you go around naked wearing horns on your head and a tail on your backside and live like a cow believing that doing so will bring you to nirvana, that's not going to happen. And that, my friends, is no bull.

Stream-Entry Is Seeing Nirvana

The total abandonment of the first three fetters is only one definition of a stream-enterer. There is a complementary definition, perhaps a more important one: **a stream-enterer is one who has clearly seen nirvana**, but is not yet able to enter it fully due to residual grasping.

One illustration came from a wise Buddhist monk named Nārada, who lived during the Buddha's time. He admitted to two fellow monks that even though he had personally seen nirvana, he had not yet "destroyed the taints" within himself, and he was therefore not yet an arahant. He further explained with an analogy: Suppose there is a well in the desert, but it had neither a rope nor a bucket. A thirsty man would come along, look down into the well, and he could clearly see the water, but he was not able to "make bodily contact with it."[13]

To be a stream-enterer, you do not have to see nirvana a lot; even one clear glimpse can be enough.[14] To explain it, let's use a prison analogy. Suppose there was a population of people who spent their entire lives in a huge prison building with no windows. Well, there was one window, but it was permanently closed, and it was painted black so nobody could see outside. One day, while a prisoner was cleaning the walls, he leaned on that window and accidentally flung it open. Immediately, prison guards rushed to close it back up. Imagine if you were that prisoner. You would catch one clear glimpse of the outside world. You would see for yourself there is such a thing as a sky, there exists a world without walls, there is such a thing as freedom. You are still inside the prison, you still see only walls and ceiling, but having had one glimpse of the outside, you will no longer believe that the inside of the prison is all there is to this world. In the same way, having caught a glimpse of nirvana, you will no longer believe that samsara is all that there is.

This is how a stream-enterer is totally free from doubt. Having seen nirvana, he no longer has any doubts in the teaching and the path. It is like someone in a vast desert with a map looking for a city. He looks around and all he sees is sand, and he experiences doubt. But if there is a hill nearby, and he climbs the hill and sees the city in the distance with his own eyes, exactly where the map says it should be, he will be free from doubt.

One key implication of directly seeing nirvana is you no longer need to rely on anybody, including even the Buddha, to tell you the true nature of phenomena, because you can already see it for yourself. That is why one who attains stream-entry is described as "having become independent of others in the Teacher's Dispensation." There is a really nice story that illustrates this point.

During the Buddha's time, there was a man named Sura. Sura gained stream-entry while listening to the Buddha give a discourse, and then returned home. Mara was dismayed to see one more person leaving his grasp, and so he decided to try to turn this one back. Mara assumed the form of the Buddha and came to Sura's home. Sura was tricked and invited him in with delight. Mara then told Sura that he had not considered carefully before giving his talk, and thus made a mistake. The mistake was that he said that the five aggregates are impermanent; but now, after reconsidering, he has realized that the five aggregates are actually permanent. Sura easily called Mara's bluff. Having attained stream-entry, Sura already saw for himself that all five aggregates are impermanent, so he could easily tell this must be Mara in disguise. Sura added that even a thousand Maras could not shake his faith, which is unshakable like Mount Meru. Mara then disappeared. This story is not found in the oldest texts but in a medieval commentary, so its veracity is not watertight, but it is definitely illustrative.[15]

Another definition of a *stream-enterer* I have heard from a living Buddhist teacher is one from Shinzen Young. He defines *stream-entry* as "the complete realization that there has never been a thing in me called a self." This definition makes perfect sense to me too. It sounds like a simplified rendering of the fetter of identity view, and it makes sense to me because the first fetter is the linchpin among the first three fetters: if you break it, the other two will eventually break. If you can penetrate so clearly into the nature of self that you no longer hold any of the twenty identity views, then you will soon also have no doubt in the teachings and will no longer believe that rites and rituals are sufficient for liberation from suffering. However, the reverse is not true: if you break any of the other two fetters, there is no guarantee that the first fetter will automatically break. You may not believe in the power of rites and rituals, and you may have absolute confidence in the teachings of the Buddha, but still, those things alone do not guarantee that you will develop the mental clarity to penetrate into the true nature of self.

I think this is why the Buddha gave a precise technical definition for the fetter of identity view, but did not do so for the other two. That, and the other two are more easily understandable.

Soryu has a way of articulating the power of stream-entry that I find particularly inspiring. I'm going to quote him here:

> Before stream-entry, all your thoughts and actions tend toward
> defilements, and you find your journey toward full enlightenment to

be a confused, uphill struggle. After stream-entry, all your thoughts and actions naturally tend toward nirvana, so you find your journey toward full enlightenment to be straightforward and aided by nature. It's not that one makes no more mistakes; it's that each mistake tends to push us back in the right direction, rather than sending us even further from it.

In that sense, reaching stream-entry is like reaching the summit of a hill. Before it, your journey requires struggle, but after, you let nature do some of the work for you. There are still a lot of things you need to work through after stream-entry, yes, but you now proceed in the easy direction. It's as if you have to fight to remain ignorant, rather than fight to become free of ignorance.

This metaphor also illustrates why the journey before stream-entry can take so much longer than after it. Imagine that the journey up the summit, and then down from the summit to the other side, are both roughly the same distance. On the uphill part of the journey, people tend to meander up, down, and across the side of the hill. They try to walk up, but then they think it would be much easier to walk down. Because they walk back and forth, they end up walking one hundred miles to cover a one-mile distance. On the other side of the hill, though, people can see the destination and it is in the direction aided by gravity, so even though they may lose the trail and get confused, they nonetheless walk not much further than one mile to cover the same one-mile distance. That is why the Buddha can guarantee that once you have reached stream-entry, you will reach the final goal within a relatively short time.

The ancient texts poetically call the moment of gaining stream-entry the "arising of the Dharma-eye." It also comes with a lovely stock description. Here, for example, is the description of that moment for the householder Upāli, one of the Buddha's disciples. As the Buddha was instructing him, the texts say,

> While the householder Upāli sat there, the spotless immaculate vision of the Dharma arose in him: "All that is subject to arising is subject to cessation." Then the householder Upāli saw the Dharma, attained the

Dharma, understood the Dharma, fathomed the Dharma; he crossed beyond doubt, did away with perplexity, gained intrepidity, and became independent of others in the Teacher's Dispensation.[16]

This is all great, but it would be even more useful for us to see what it is like for a modern person to gain stream-entry. That is coming up in the next chapter.

The Power of Nonselfness

We end this chapter with a short story that illustrates the sheer power of the realization of nonselfness. It is so powerful it can result even in full enlightenment. This famously happened to a man called Bāhiya, who was not even a disciple of the Buddha at the time.

Bāhiya was venerated in his community, so much so that he mistakenly thought of himself as being enlightened. A god who was a close friend of Bāhiya and fellow meditator in a past life, desiring his welfare, appeared to him to tell him that, no, he was really not enlightened, and advised him to seek out the Buddha. To Bāhiya's credit, he quickly understood and left immediately to see the Buddha.

When Bāhiya saw the Buddha, the Buddha was on his alms round collecting his breakfast. Bāhiya rushed over to the Buddha to ask for teachings, and the Buddha said, "Now is not the right time; we have entered the town for alms." Bāhiya asked a second time and got the same answer. And then Bāhiya asked again a third time, insisting with utter urgency, and out of compassion the Buddha acquiesced and taught him this:

> Bāhiya, you should train yourself thus:
> In reference to the seen, there will be only the seen.
> In reference to the heard, only the heard.
> In reference to the sensed, only the sensed.
> In reference to the cognized, only the cognized.
> That is how you should train yourself.
> When for you there will be only the seen in reference to the seen, only
>   the heard in reference to the heard, only the sensed in reference to

the sensed, only the cognized in reference to the cognized, then,
    Bāhiya, there is no you in connection with that.
When there is no you in connection with that, there is no you there.
When there is no you there, you are neither here nor yonder nor
    between the two.
This, just this, is the end of suffering.[17]

When Bāhiya heard that, he immediately gained full enlightenment and
became an arahant, right there on the spot! If Guinness was keeping records
at that time, Bāhiya would have held the world record as the fastest ever to
gain full enlightenment. Good thing Bāhiya gained full enlightenment there
and then, because he was killed by a charging cow later that same morning.

The Abbot's Commentary by Soryu Forall

To see the Dharma is enlightenment.
Enlightenment is seeing through self.
Seeing through self ends suffering.
The Dharma is that which ends suffering.

Have you seen the Dharma?

CHAPTER TWELVE

A Hero's Journey to Nirvana
A Nirvana Case Study

A Hero's Story

Helena was the most talented warrior of her generation. She made a solemn vow to retrieve a mythical stone of immense power, called Storm Maker, from a faraway island. The Storm Maker is said to endow its owner with the power to make rain, and that would allow Helena to end their great drought. She was given their best ship, and she assembled an elite crew of the best sailors and warriors.

Off they sailed. There were teething problems: an occasional rope breaking, water seepage, arguments among the crew, but everything was quickly taken care of. Soon they encountered enemies, but led by Helena, they easily defeated them. And then, one by one, they defeated vastly more powerful enemies: entire fleets of pirates, demons, and a magically animated skeleton army. More important, with each battle Helena became an even more powerful warrior. Before this journey, she was already the most talented warrior of her generation, but now she felt invincible, and for good reason. Her fame spread far and wide.

They arrived at a beautiful paradise island populated by a tribe of friendly, attractive people, led by a kind chieftain who warmly welcomed them. The crew lived on the island for many weeks. The desire arose in all of them to abandon their mission and live there for the rest of their lives. Helena almost gave in to that temptation too. Only when she was reminded of her solemn vow, and the plight of her people, did she decide to continue her mission.

That was the first surprise: the first great enemy that almost doomed the mission was not pirate fleets, or demons, or fighting skeletons; it was pleasure and complacency.

The crew continued the journey. They spent many weeks in open water with nothing much to do. Then, many, many more weeks passed. The mystery island was nowhere to be found. Maybe it would never be found. Worse, on most days there was nothing much to do all day except to train, and train, and train some more. By this time almost everybody wanted to give up and return to the paradise island. Ultimately, though, the crew decided to soldier on. This was the second surprise: the next enemy that almost doomed the mission was the seemingly endless tedium and drudgery of the journey.

The one small break from all that tedium came at the expense of Helena. While the crew was painstakingly searching the islands, they found an old woman trapped inside a deep hole in the ground. While Helena was trying to rescue her, she slipped and fell in. Worse, she disturbed the ground and caused the hole to cave in on itself, thereby sealing off the entrance. Helena was carrying very little food and water, and she gave it all to the old woman. It took days for her crew to rescue them. It was a mini-adventure that did nothing for the mission except to provide the crew a story with which to entertain themselves.

And then things took a sudden steep upturn. The crew found the mystery island where Storm Maker was hidden. As they searched for it, Helena met a strange old man who tested her and, approving of her character, gave her an immensely powerful magic sword. This enabled her to defeat even more powerful enemies than any mortal human had ever faced: a dragon and an archdemon. Nothing at this point could stop her. The completion of her mission was at hand.

Helena's final and most powerful enemy emerged: herself. At the moment she found Storm Maker, it found her, and it already knew how to use her against herself. Its powerful magic conjured a duplicate of Helena, which was like her in every way, except more powerful. Helena was already the most powerful warrior in the world, slayer of a dragon and an archdemon. There was no way she could defeat an even more powerful version of herself. She wanted to give up. She could only give up.

Fortunately, as Helena was leaving in despair, she met the wise old man again. He informed her that her hesitation was what powered her magical duplicate. The more she hesitated, the more powerful the duplicate became. The only way to defeat the duplicate was to charge at her, with no hesitation at all. That took Helena all her faith, all her courage, and all her determination. And she did it.

That was her final enemy.

Except, as we shall see, it was not her biggest challenge.

Helena finally approached the altar on which Storm Maker was enshrined. She lifted it. She could feel its sheer power. With exultation, she carried it home. When she arrived, everybody cheered for her. The drought would finally be over!

Helena climbed the highest mountain. She held up Storm Maker. Rain clouds gathered. And then, nothing. There was no rain. No matter how hard Helena tried, no matter what she did, she could not generate rain. Nothing worked. Forty days and forty nights later, Helena was completely out of ideas. All she had was panic and despair.

In her despair, that old woman she rescued from the hole in the ground suddenly appeared in front of her and transformed into a glorious goddess.

The goddess told Helena that the gods needed to know if Helena was worthy. By giving the old woman all her food and water, Helena showed she had selfless compassion, and because of that, she was worthy. "Worthy of what?" Helena asked. "Worthy of the answer," the goddess replied. And then the goddess spoke in a riddle, "To lose everything is to lose losing everything." And then she disappeared.

Helena thought she understood the riddle, maybe. She decided to drop Storm Maker into the deepest part of the sea, so there was no chance of ever getting it back. As she was on her ship ready to drop Storm Maker, the crew asked, "Are you sure?" "No, I am not sure," she replied, "but this is the only way to completely lose." She took a deep breath and dropped Storm Maker into the sea. It sank. Nothing happened. All hope was lost. She was completely helpless.

Amazingly, while being completely and perfectly helpless, she found complete and perfect trust. Unable to do a single thing, she was calm. There was nothing more to do.

Suddenly, a giant waterspout formed over the sea. It sucked water high up to the sky. Thick rain clouds started to form. And then it rained, drenching the land. The long drought was finally over. It turned out that Helena did precisely what she needed to do, because Storm Maker could only be fully activated when its owner had totally given up all control.

Helena's entire people were saved, and everybody lived happily ever after.

The reason I made up this story is that this chapter centers on the true story of how one of Soryu's students arrived at the breakthrough to the Dharma, the Dharma that saves all beings. Helena's mythical story demonstrates the heroism such a journey requires.

The Journey to Nirvana Is a Hero's Journey

To break through to the Dharma means to arrive at stream-entry. The most important question is: How do we, normal people in the modern world, arrive at stream-entry?

The standard answer, which is also the correct answer, is to understand and practice the Four Noble Truths. When I was a novice learner, that correct answer did not help me one bit. Worse still, I got more frustrated every time

I heard it. I did not see how practicing virtue and meditation, for example, would get me the spiritual breakthrough I need to reach stream-entry.

What would be really helpful would be to see how a modern person like ourself did it. Thankfully, we have Soryu. I asked Soryu to anonymously relate the story of how one of his students followed the path to an initial glimpse of liberation, partly as an inspiring example for everybody, but, more important, to give us a real, tangible, understandable idea of how everything we learn and practice in the Four Noble Truths comes together to enable a spiritual breakthrough.

Soryu is willing to share the story of one of his students, Susan (not her real name). But before he does that, he wants to make sure we do not think he is presenting a "road map to nirvana." That is because road maps give a few wrong impressions. First, they give the wrong impression that there is only one path to nirvana, while in reality, there are multiple paths, some of which suit some people more than others. Second, people wrongly assume there are steps and stages to be taken in a strictly linear order, while in reality, there are many feedback loops, and the order of certain steps is usually swappable, so things are really much more nuanced. Third, road maps do not account for individual differences. They appear to suggest that each step is roughly as challenging for each person, but in reality, some individuals can get indefinitely held up by certain steps until a skillful teacher helps them break through, while others breeze by those steps (only to be completely caught up in a different step while some other people breeze by).

With that caveat in mind, here is the story of how Susan arrived at initial insight. You will see that Susan's journey ties together everything we have talked about in this book. It begins with aspiration, mundane right view, a commitment to ethics, and the practice of right mindfulness. An important milestone of her journey is overcoming the five hindrances, which is life-changing in and of itself. It also enables her mastery of the jhānas, and the maturing of the seven factors of enlightenment, the combination of which enables her spiritual breakthrough.

And, yes, there are places where Susan feels invincible, for good reason, places where she feels defeated, also for good reason, and places where her journey gets sabotaged by the most unexpected "enemies." If her story reads like a hero's journey, that is because it actually is. Every journey to spiritual breakthrough is a hero's journey.

(Credit where credit is due: Susan's story was produced from long interviews with Soryu, and a very large percentage of what you read here are verbatim recordings of Soryu's carefully crafted words. So if you like the upcoming sections, that's where it's coming from. I wrote the Helena story, though. You're welcome.)

Susan's Excellent Adventure, Part I: Early Victories

Guest artist: Natalie Tsang

Susan was a resident trainee, living and training with others full-time, receiving teachings of the Dharma, living in a strict monastic routine, and meditating five to fifteen hours per day depending on the schedule. Susan's journey could be described in ten steps.

Step 1: Gaining early confidence and mundane right view

At the start of Susan's heroic journey, she appeared quite unheroic. Well, "annoying" might be a better descriptor. Soon after she arrived, she started trying to fix others, occasionally in anger. For example, she told others they weren't doing enough with their lives, that they should label food differently, mop the floor with more mindfulness, be more considerate of her feelings. Yet her behavior was seen as somewhat endearing by the community. Why? Because such behavior is normal for beginners: they have enough self-confidence to aspire for enlightenment, but not yet enough to actually strive to that end, so they try to fix others instead. Fixing others requires less self-confidence than cultivating one's own mind. What she needed was to develop that self-confidence.

She needed to cultivate positive inner states, and positive outer behavioral patterns. She began by working on her own behavior, because, as we have seen in Chapter 9, behavior is the objective aspect of the mind, so she could use it to measure her progress. This meant embarking on a continuous struggle to live ethically, dealing with gross personality issues and deepening her skillful relationships. This was supported by, and led to, understanding mundane right view.[1] Therefore, she started to gain the confidence to be willing to struggle with her own mind.

Practicing this way offered her a realization that initially shocked and dismayed her: that karma does not take a break. She realized that every action, every word, every thought has consequences, so her virtue must never take a break either. The good news is that soon enough, she started to enjoy the struggle, like an athlete who enjoys playing against people with superior ability, or a software engineer who enjoys the challenge of a difficult problem. She realized that this struggle to deepen one's virtue can be fun, a fun that leads to the ease of self-confidence. This simple sentence summarizes her transformation that occurred in this stage. Better still, that type of self-confidence is one with humility. From then on, her practice became more fulfilling and enjoyable.

You might wonder why she couldn't do this before. The main thing she did not have before was community. A monastic setting provides a community that creates the right conditions to support the trainees in a) living in compassionate relationship with all living things and b) accepting the importance of every small thing we do. That provides fertile grounds for accelerated spiritual growth.

Pretty soon, Susan's confidence grew into a magnificent aspiration for enlightenment out of compassion for all. That changed everything.

Step 2: Becoming skillful at basic mindfulness by making it physical

It did not take long for Susan to discover that she needed more than this initial confidence. She saw that however hard she might try to make herself kind and conscientious, underlying tendencies in her mind took over in every moment that lacked mindfulness. These were, to be blunt, pretty common. The only solution was to strengthen her mindfulness. Realizing that, sitting meditation made increasing sense to her.

Fortunately, at about the same time, a shift happened in her attitude toward meditation that may appear small but is actually very significant: she stopped seeing meditation as a way to get a big experience. Instead, she approached it as a way to purify and cultivate her mind. Surprisingly, it wasn't as fun at first, but she soon learned why. As long as she still held on to a consumer mindset, thinking that meditation is like a price we pay for marvelous experiences, meditation done correctly is not fun. Once she uprooted that view, every meditation session was exciting. Hours of sitting were no longer the price to be paid, but were like the path up a mountain, which is enjoyable and beautiful in its own right. Because of this, she no longer tried to make the price as low as possible, but instead tried to make it as high as possible. Why? Because there is nothing in the entire world better than this path. **The path of letting go is more joyful than anything in the world**. There is only one thing more joyful, and that is beyond the world.

What most surprised her in this step was the fact that the best way to purify her mind was to make meditation completely physical. The beginning of this was the ability to use walking, eating, chores, and other bodily activities as the foundation of mindfulness. Soon enough, mindfulness became even more concrete, as she learned to control her mind by keeping it on the breath. She learned to keep her mind focused whether it liked it or not. She realized she liked it. The fact that she liked it while her mind did not was early evidence that she was not her mind.

Furthermore, because her mind was following her breath, her breath began to control her mind, rather than the other way round. She was astonished to discover that her breath already knew how to be relaxed and energetic, and self-conscious awareness was not needed to force it to be that way. The breath was playful and had a great understanding of the best way forward. In this way, she learned to perfect the posture, feel the sensations in the body relating to the breath, calm the body with the breath, energize the body with the breath, and practice full mindfulness of the body.

Step 3: Beginning to overcome the hindrances to wisdom

Susan now felt she was getting "really good" at meditation. In the previous step, the five hindrances were already beginning to break down for her. But now she was much more skillful: her breath itself could purify her mind of the hindrances. More impressively, that process kept working whenever she was breathing (which is to say, all day long) and not only when she was doing formal meditation.

But wait, there was even more. She was not only purifying her mind of the hindrances; she was also cultivating their positive counterparts.

a) She used her breath to purify sensual desire, and then continued that process until she could abide in the aspiration to relinquish birth and death.

b) She purified any ill will she had toward anyone at all (including herself) and then found, where she least expected it, compassion for all beings.

c) She purified the habit of being stuck in ruts and, bursting out of that exhausting state, found a new and endless energy throughout her body.

d) She finally, after years of helpless slavery to anxiety, was able to let it go and settle into a deep faith, a trust in this moment, which allowed her to enjoy the challenge this unique moment offers.

And e) her confusion about the practice melted away, because she found the confidence to reveal her deepest doubts to her teacher, and, once these were resolved, she had the confidence to put her understanding into practice.

This step reached maturity when Susan realized that freedom from the hindrances is more rewarding than anything they have to offer. The unhindered mind, in its natural state, is joyful. Susan was now able to access this inner joy some of the time. Because of that inner joy, she could now clearly experience for herself that not having a sensual desire to fulfill is far more joyful than fulfilling it. She also saw clearly how awful wanting is, and that the reason fulfilling sensual desire feels so pleasurable is merely that the wanting vanishes for a little while. Not having the wanting to begin with is even more pleasurable. Since she could get rid of want at will, she could feel happy at will. Having so much more inner joy available, she could relax and let that joy draw her on without being internally divided.

She slowly worked through the other hindrances as well. In her particular case, the most confusing of these five was worry. She was deeply convinced that if one is not worried, one is not compassionate. She had previously felt that being worried about someone or some issue is proof that you care. This had been a primary reason for addictive behaviors in her life, since she craved a break from the constant worry that she felt an obligation to maintain. When she finally saw how faith is a greater source of compassion than worry, she escaped great pain, like going through the excruciating process of escaping an abusive relationship. And once she did, her face glowed and shone, from the inside, like a lamp.

Right around this point, Susan also started gaining a meaningful level of mastery over her emotions. For example, more than half the time, she found herself able to dissipate her anger the moment it arose. The Buddha had a profoundly beautiful analogy, he describes it as *like writing on water*: the moment it is written, it disappears.[2] This completely changed her relationships, as she no longer felt a need to argue with other people about whether they labeled food properly.

This was liberating and joyful, almost like magic. Better still, others went from fearing her and doing what she said despite resistance, to loving her and doing what she said due to admiration. One side benefit: the food now got labeled correctly.

Many meditators, upon reaching this step, feel that their lives have been profoundly changed in ways they did not even think were possible just a few months ago. Susan was no exception. She felt like Helena when she defeated all those pirate fleets and demons: invincible. But remember, this is only step three of ten. What could possibly go wrong?

Susan's Excellent Adventure, Part II: From Drudgery to Wisdom

Expectation

Exciting!

Reality

Tedious...

Guest artist: Natalie Tsang

Step 4: Assembling a meditative tool set to enable eventual mastery

Susan's practice had changed her life. And then, quite unexpectedly, her practice faced its first real test, which almost totally derailed it. It came from a surprisingly banal source: drudgery.

This step of her training required learning many methods of meditation, including compassion, scanning the body, awareness of the whole body, mental noting of various types of sense experiences, intense focus on specific phenomena, open awareness, inquiry into self, doing nothing, etc., etc. It is like a martial artist who must learn many techniques for various situations to gain eventual mastery. Unfortunately, this is generally not exciting, just a long path of drudgery.

You know how in movies about boxing, they show the exciting parts in full but hardly show the long hours of difficult training at all? The training montages are quick, usually only a few minutes, shorter even than the final fight and accompanied by exciting-sounding music. But in real life, the training takes orders of magnitude more time than the fight at the end, not to mention the injuries, illness, distractions, and lack of motivation that sometimes impede progress. Susan was now at this stage. Tedium. Drudgery. And then more tedium. With more drudgery.

Many people want to quit at this point. The life-changing results of the previous step have given them more than they had even hoped for. They are therefore satisfied to leave the tedious training to "do good in the world as a layperson" instead. Susan was no exception. She kept telling Soryu, "I'm really thinking about leaving," and then explained to him a compelling and inspiring idea for what she would do instead. It is hard to know what made her stay, and many do not, but there is a strength that comes from walking straight through a desert, and those with this strength can change the world. Susan had it in her. In staying, her heroic journey passed its first real test.

Happily, Susan's persistence paid off handsomely. She gradually gained experiential understanding of the Dharma. In particular, she directly encountered the seven factors of enlightenment.

She gained a) **mindfulness** that she could cultivate in all situations. That does not mean she could do it continuously, without a break, but she maintained enough mindfulness to allow her to gain all other factors of enlightenment.

Her mindfulness enabled her to b) **investigate each phenomenon**, knowing each directly and discerning its characteristics clearly.

To the extent that it was maintained without a gap, a new kind of c) **energy** emerged that drew her along the path. Her mindfulness and investigation allowed her to know what is skillful and what is not. After a while, she could often do it without spending mental energy. That enabled her to bring forth full energy to flow through her body, no longer breaking it by having to manage it with self-conscious thoughts.

With that, d) **exhilarating joy** naturally arose in her body.

This was so present that she stopped seeking elsewhere, and experienced e) **tranquility** and ease.

Since her body and mind were at ease, at times she glimpsed f) **samadhi**.

She allowed all things to come to her, no longer trying to fix everything by fighting against it, but tasting the subtle flavor of g) **equanimity** as a part of the path. Furthermore, mindfulness and investigation were applied to each of the factors, making each a chance to directly know the Dharma.

It was a long and confusing process, with much failure. She succeeded and then failed, gained and then lost the ability to know these states of mind. You should know about this because otherwise, if you walk the real path, this account of Susan may make you think you're failing. You should be clear that most of this path is just tens of thousands of hours of grueling hard work. So don't complain when it's your turn to do that work. Know that this is the first really heroic part.

Susan had not yet mastered the seven factors of enlightenment—that would come much later—but her mastery had begun to take root.

Step 5: Skillfully entering jhāna

Just like Helena acquiring her magic sword, Susan had now assembled the conditions required to gain a very powerful tool: samadhi. In both cases, acquiring the new tool was a massive game changer for an already high-ranking player.

As you have seen in the earlier pages of this book, samadhi makes perfect sense on paper. But in practice, parts of the process are beyond mental understanding, and therefore require you to step into the deep unknown. We set up samadhi using our effort and mental understanding, but as we make that effort, gradually something we do not understand takes over, and we know (and need to know) less and less. A new intelligence arises, and a new kind of effort already knows how to meditate. It is like sailing a boat. First, one must pull the boat down the beach to get it into the water. A boat isn't made to be dragged over dry land, but it is necessary at first. Then, once on the water, one can make use of the wind. If one knows how to use the wind, one can travel in a boat much faster than one could drag it over land, while using less effort. In the same way, one uses one's own mental understanding to make meditation happen. Then, once one actually enters jhāna, one can make use of a larger intelligence, and a larger energy, and therefore can make much faster progress. While it is true that most people aren't willing to do the hard work of the previous step, those who are willing to do this hard work face the next challenge: learning how that hard work becomes an energy beyond our control that naturally moves us along the path.

If this shift does not occur, we are still caught on thinking as a way to make jhāna happen. Jhāna must happen organically, without analysis or mental comprehension. We can later, once we exit jhāna, look back and see that what happened was what the texts describe. Nonetheless, while we are in these wonderful states, we let go of control and let it unfold mysteriously. That is the reason we know we can trust it. Mental control interferes with deep jhāna, so the only type of deep jhāna we can trust is the type that comes from letting go. It turns out this path is deeper than control.

What allows each of us to take a step into the mystery? It is unknown. In Susan's case, it was a chance encounter in the woods. She was wandering on the trails through the forest during a period of walking meditation, and suddenly found herself looking right at an owl. It was looking right at her. It was aware of her, present with her. She realized that she did not have any way to be aware of it, present with it. She was too lost in her own head. She realized that this was why she had been lonely her whole life. Even though a living thing was with her, she was so caught in the prison of her own ideas that she could not be with it. She could not see the owl; she could only see her idea of it and tell a story about that idea. She realized that if she did not do something, she would not only live her whole life lonely, she would die lonely. And worse still, everyone she met would die without having ever received her love. She was horrified. She dedicated her life to getting out of her head and meeting the world, at any cost.

We are all different and not all of us meet owls, but for all of us, this shift is basically a matter of trusting exactly what comes. In any case, once the skills and techniques are fulfilled, it's just a matter of time before each person makes the decision that will change everything: the decision to let go rather than hold on. Soryu says in a poignant way, "We make that decision, and later, when we look back, we see that it was the first real decision we ever made." We become willing to do whatever it takes to get out of our head, and abide in samadhi.

Susan gained the first jhāna and learned to master it. She knew for herself that the joy of the path is greater than anything the world has to offer. This is the end of one life and the beginning of another. We enter a new world, and it is alive.

Step 6: Samadhi deepens, and wisdom begins to blossom

Susan managed to avoid a surprisingly powerful trap here that catches a lot of people: not being competent enough to recognize their own incompetence.[3]

People are most vulnerable to this effect when they are competent enough to know a lot, but not yet competent enough to know there is still a huge amount they do not know.

A Buddhist practitioner is most vulnerable to this effect about the time they start gaining solid access to jhāna. Jhāna is such a powerful experience that many people, when they enter jhāna for the first time, mistakenly think they are enlightened. And if they cannot find a way forward from here, they decide (wrongly, of course) that they must have completed the path. All that is compounded by an emotional component: due to insecurity, some people have an attachment to being right, and so they get attached to the insights and samadhi they have gained. That is why they get stuck.

Susan did not get trapped here, however, because she had two resources. The first was a good teacher who knew she still had a long way to go and kept pushing her. Her second was, to put it facetiously, that she was granted the gift of humility. By now, she had many experiences where she mistakenly thought she was more advanced than she actually was, only to fall hard later, especially in the face of ethical struggles. Again and again she had thought, "I've almost finished the path!" only to agonize the very next day, "Have I even started?" It was painfully humbling, of course. She was lucky that she had a supportive community of fellow practitioners around her, some of whom were seniors more advanced on that path, so every time she fell hard, she received the "Yeah, I've been there too" type of support. Those friends gave her the loving container she needed to receive the gift of humility. Whenever you need to face the fact that you are wrong, if you can do that with equanimity, again and again, then you will not get stuck here.

Susan kept going and made her way deeper into the world of jhāna. She came to know its texture, its flavor, its rules. She saw, due to much instruction, that the basic rule is that you must keep going forward, and *forward is defined as the direction in which there is less. Forward* means "let go." Each next step of jhāna practice is losing the most important thing that supported you in the previous step. She learned how to see the remaining flaws in the new best experience, and to let go of even that in order to go beyond it. This means learning to cut through deep attachment to even the most wonderful things in the world.

Most important, she lost any sense that she knew how to do it. Soon enough, she didn't even know *who* was doing it. Who meditates? All the clever answers she had read in books were seen through. The sense that "I am the sort of person who has seen through the answers I read in books" was seen through. The sense that "I see through things" was seen through. "Things" was seen through. "I see" was seen through. It went on and on. Any idea you may have now as you read this is exactly what you will have to see through at this stage.

For most people, even most well-known teachers, "seeing through" remains imaginary. They merely learn from others what that is supposed to be like, and then subconsciously make that happen with mental fabrication. But for Susan, as this ripened, the path began to be real. In the same way that Helena began to cut down dragons and archdemons, Susan began to cut away some of the mightiest strands of ignorance. Her wisdom began to blossom.

(Soryu sheepishly admits that he loves meeting with those who are taking this and later steps. He can finally have an actual conversation with them. Usually, when people talk with each other, it's really just their patterns bumping into each other. There isn't a true connection at all. But once we take this step, those patterns are shed, and we can finally meet each experience—and each person—in true intimacy.)

Everything was going amazingly great for Susan. Pretty soon, though, everything would suddenly go very wrong.

Susan's Excellent Adventure, Part III: Breaking Unstoppable Resistance

Step 7: Wrestling with profound resistance

Like Helena finding that her most powerful enemy was an even mightier duplicate of herself, and that her only solution was to charge at it without any hesitation, Susan would soon find no way forward, except right through the person she thought she was. Doing this would give her great power, yet like Helena, the great challenge would be letting go of even that.

As we saw above, things were deepening and seemed to be going very nicely for Susan, but suddenly, seemingly out of nowhere, she faced a huge challenge: her mind wanted to revert. Despite her significant accomplishments on the path or, more accurately, precisely because of her significant accomplishments, grasping and identification became incredibly strong. She found herself in the midst of her oldest patterns, totally buying in. She made drama in the community to distract herself from her own path, yet saw herself as the victim. She refused to believe that anyone could care about her. She framed the fact that she had worked so hard but was not yet free as proof she couldn't ever get free. She watched herself use attachment to create suffering, and then she used that suffering to convince herself there is no way out of attachment. When given instruction on liberation from selfishness, she responded with statements such as, "What you just said was very hurtful." She thought up reasons for not letting go, and they became increasingly believable to her as she repeated them to herself and confided in people outside the training. Her ego used all the tricks in the book to regain control.

One of the most effective tricks the ego uses is getting attached to specific kinds of superb meditative states. Two of the most powerful states are non-dual awareness and nonconceptual awareness (which Susan entered later on, but they are worth discussing here). In the former, distinctions between inside and outside, right and wrong, existing and nonexisting are set aside. Without duality, there isn't a way to decide anything, so one cannot make a mistake, and the path opens without mistake. In the latter, the concepts we constantly impute are set aside. We no longer add on a story, an idea, to each phenomenon; we directly encounter experiences rather than our concepts about them. We become unable to delude ourselves about what is happening, so the path opens without mistake. Both of these states are excellent, and most people do not spend enough time in them. But there is a trick to making these medicines into poison: get attached to them. The most effective way to get attached to them is to think they are the final goal, that they are enlightenment. And it is possible to make this affliction even worse by adding an identity around it; for example, "I have had this non-dual or nonconceptual experience, so I am enlightened."

As powerful as non-dual and nonconceptual awareness are, they are *not* the final goal. They are *not* nirvana, *not* enlightenment, *not* awakening. Many people have been tricked into mistaking them for enlightenment. Some people have written books proclaiming their own "awakening," not knowing that the real goal is beyond. If you get attached, you will get stuck here. The way to use non-dual awareness to propel you toward nirvana is to completely let it go. It is akin to Helena completely letting go of Storm Maker by dropping it into the sea, due to the guidance of the goddess.

It may seem very hard to find and train under a good teacher, but it is important because a good teacher will not let us get stuck in these states. (Of course, if they themselves are stuck here, they will actually hinder us further.) Getting stuck here, caught in perception again, is tragic because one is so close to true insight. The price of working with a good teacher is worth it, since they help us to avoid this tragedy. In the end, we must come back to the path of letting go. It isn't about grasping to, or identifying with, a certain kind of experience. It is about letting go.

So the only question for Susan was whether she could reestablish her willingness to let go. This was difficult. It was difficult in the way that getting free of alcoholism is difficult, or the way that getting out of generations of poverty is difficult, or the way that fleeing from a militia across a continent without food is difficult. Please don't think these metaphors are mere poetic hyperbole. Letting go can be that difficult.

Why did this happen to Susan? It is actually a common occurrence for those who make real progress and then hesitate. It is like a trapeze artist who, while mid-flight from one trapeze to another, decides to grab hold of the previous trapeze instead. The important implication: this does not happen to those who do not hesitate (or those who did not make real progress to begin with).

Guest artist: Natalie Tsang

Over time, Susan found her way through the resistance and the pain she was creating. Two things got her through: her prior training in virtue, and being surrounded by good, trustworthy friends who understood the practice. Of course, this step can take place at any time, and can take place repeatedly.

It isn't really the seventh of ten steps, since it's always waiting for the moment we hesitate to strike.

Step 8: Clarity, and the abandoning of all hesitation

Eventually, in the midst of the suffering she herself was creating, right in the middle of distrust of others and herself, Susan realized there is no way out. This must be done, whoever we are, in whatever circumstances we find ourselves. Liberation is what we were born to do, which has nothing to do with how you see yourself, or how you see others, or what you want, or what you don't want.

She saw that no matter what, no one has control over impermanence. She saw that there is no safe place where she will not be destroyed, and that all her suffering was caused by her own ignorant mind. She saw that every action she takes, even the slightest thought, leads to happiness or sadness. She finally gave in to the understanding that we most try to avoid, the understanding that benefits us most deeply: she realized the totality of her vulnerability, and the totality of her power. She finally experienced the confidence of knowing that her own selfishness is the only problem in the world, that she never had any right to complain about anything, that she must break free of herself or die trying.

She came to know what the Buddha himself meant when he said that just before his enlightenment, his mindfulness became ceaseless and his effort became unrelenting.[4] The barriers that seemed insurmountable crumbled before her, opening the way. It was wonderful. All her previous achievements in life, such as getting into a romantic relationship, or succeeding at a job, or caring for a family member, were not one-tenth as fulfilling as *each day* of this adventure, this supreme adventure. She began to experience the most fun she had ever known. Also, the most urgency, the most joy, the most desperation, the most exhilaration, the most horror, the most peace, the most exhaustion, and the most energy. Why? Because she accepted what she had to do, and she did it without hesitation, without compromise, without reservation, without negotiation.

It was as if all eight parts of the Noble Eightfold Path were running in high gear, moving Susan along without mistake.

Step 9: The Dharma comes alive, at the unity of investigation and letting go

(Warning: you may not find everything in this step understandable. That is because it is the description of Susan's experiences, and the closer we get to nirvana, the less understandably they can be described.)

At this point, everything taught by the Buddha finally appeared to come together for Susan. Total urgency and total peace became one. Not one moment was wasted. Not one moment was grasped.

First, **craving was understood**.[5] While craving was still latent in Susan's mind, she no longer believed in any of its three forms: craving for sense pleasure, craving for existence, and craving for nonexistence.

   a) She had set aside the sense that she should get what she wants.

   b) She had set aside the sense that the most important thing, in the end, when your life is at risk, is to protect yourself.

   c) She had set aside the sense that the spiritual path is about destroying oneself.

With her life on the line, with total courage and without holding back, Susan was now able to enter and abide in deep samadhi during formal meditation. While abiding in that samadhi, she just forgot herself in each moment. She forgot everything she thought, everything she felt, everything she perceived. In this way she experienced all of it completely and honestly. This state is not easy to explain, but it is also very simple: *her mind was now like a mirror that accurately reflects everything because it does not hold on to anything*. Any grasping to body or mind is cut off as it arises. **Consciousness is free from grasping**: it is not caught on anything; it has no conflict with anything. Because of this, not only does it let go of things once they arise, it does not even grab onto them at the moment they arise. Therefore, it can be seen that all phenomena pass away the moment they arise, and there is nothing found to grasp onto at all.

This is experiencing everything so fully that nothing can be found. This is the beginning of understanding what the Buddha taught Bāhiya, and here

identity view begins to fall away.⁶ She settled into **unrelenting energy and ceaseless mindfulness**, so deeply that she couldn't be distracted or disturbed even if she tried.

During formal meditation, she entered formless realms in which perception attenuates, dwindles, and dissolves. In this state of samadhi, she found only vast emptiness and brilliance everywhere. She maintained **non-dual awareness** in which there was no distinction between self and other. She could not find suffering anywhere at any time, yet the path continued to open. She maintained **nonconceptual awareness** in which all things were known directly without the medium of mental constructions. She could not find delusion anywhere at any time, yet the path continued to open. This brought forth a new wisdom beyond her ideas of what could be possible.

That was important, but there was something else even more important: the non-grasping kept going whether she was in formal meditation or not. The quintessential aspect of this step is that endless energy and mindfulness continue all day long. She could mop the floor without grasping onto body or mind. She could see the mountains without grasping onto self or world. Again, this did not stop for one moment through the day. Not one thought about herself or her practice or her circumstances, not one moment of doing, not one moment of knowing. Both doing and knowing, both body and mind, were coming to rest, and the rest they were settling toward is true peace.

With the decline of interference by the activity of body and mind, Susan could now see things as they truly are, specifically, the **three marks of existence**.⁷ This is both horrifying and the most pleasant and wonderful experience of a person's life up to this point. She could see for herself what we usually just read about in books. How are things truly? 1) Things are impermanent. They do not remain, even for one moment. Therefore, if we hold on to them for even one moment, 2) they are dukkha ("suffering"). They are that which hurts us, if we try to do what cannot be done, namely, grasp them. And 3) they are revealed as nonself. While she hadn't completely realized this yet, it was nonetheless undeniable.

Everything her mind added on was cut off, and her mind had nothing to hold on to. It could not feed itself with its own conceptual imputation, and it could find no support for its views anywhere. The feedback loop between consciousness and name-and-form, the illusion most people call reality, was falling apart. She was seeing for herself the **functioning of dependent orig-ination**, especially its first four elements: ignorance, formations, conscious-ness, and name-and-form.

She saw that the support for her mind, the world, was made up by her mind, that this made-up thing called the world made up another made-up thing called her mind. She saw that this feedback loop between consciousness and name-and-form produces the illusion of existence, but neither existence nor nonexistence have inherent reality. The Buddha's profound teaching on the **emptiness of all five aggregates** became clear.[8] Therefore, without grasp-ing to any of them, and especially without grasping to constructions of mind, she could ask, "What is this?" And she did ask. She asked with everything she had, giving all of it to this one question. The enlightenment factor of investigation, settled by tranquility and fueled by urgency, came forth fully. For her, there were no things. There was no one perceiving things. All signs of all things were not acquired in any way. The Buddha calls this the signless liberation of mind.[9]

Her mind was unperturbed and unperturbable, constantly being corrected, in each moment, by the Dharma as it revealed itself. She gained mastery in mindfulness and equanimity, knowing for herself the import of the power-ful mind described in the passages on jhāna.[10] Every experience purified her mind, and moved her toward relinquishment, release, and liberation. Up until this point, effort was essential to the path. She had struggled for years to bring forth true effort and had just found it a few days ago, but as this ripened, even effort lost its meaning. Soryu says poetically, "There is only faith, the great energy of the whole universe coming to its end."

Step 10: The breakthrough

This breakthrough happened to take place during a talk on the classical teachings of the Buddha, just like the teachings you have learned in this book. It was unexpected, peaceful, unmistaken, and joyous. There is just no place anywhere for a self. Not inside, not outside, not in between. Not before, not after, not now. Everything is resolved. The bond broken, the obstacle obliter-ated, no conflict remains.

I asked Soryu to name it, and he says beautifully:

> What could we call this? This can't even be called peace and joy. It can't even be called perfection. It's better, incomparably better, than perfection. If there is anything at all, there is only the offering of love to all beings in all directions, without limit.
>
> The path does not end here. It leads on to further insights and deeper compassion. But this is a point of no return. May we all let go to this point and beyond, for the benefit of all living things.

Looking Forward to Your Own Excellent Adventure?

Guest artist: Natalie Tsang

Steps six through eight might jump out at you. Those steps best illustrate why it is important to work with a qualified teacher. This is a challenging path, and like all challenging paths, you are likely to meet unexpected roadblocks. A lot of times, those roadblocks are highly individualized, which means it is hard to learn about them in books, and oftentimes only a qualified teacher who knows your practice intimately can help you untangle yourself.

Another way to look at it is with a sports analogy. You cannot become an Olympian just by reading a book. A book can show you how to train and what the process looks like to become an Olympian, and it can even teach you all you need to know about exercise physiology and the science of peak performance, but to become an Olympian, you have no choice but to go through the training. In a training regime challenging enough to make you an Olympian, you really should be guided by a qualified coach. A good coach knows how best to optimize the training to specifically suit you; she knows what training you need when you hit a roadblock; and, perhaps most important, she knows how you can avoid training injuries and, if you do get injured, how best to recover.

That is not to say that you can never become an Olympian without a coach or reach enlightenment without a teacher. People have indeed done it. But having a good coach or a good teacher can help *a lot*.

You may be wondering how long it takes somebody to complete the entire training to stream-entry if they do it full-time. There is no way to predict for each individual, because you never know in advance where they will get stuck and how long it will take to unstuck them, but Susan walked the path you read about in under three years. Three years! That's even less time than it takes to earn a college degree. Yeah, I'm very impressed.

The reason we share Susan's story is to give you an informed idea of what the process may entail. More important, we want to demystify the enlightenment process. There is nothing mysterious about it; it is essentially letting go, and the intense training to learn how to let go. Even more important, we want to drive home the understanding that stream-entry is achievable within a single lifetime. Yes, it is hard work, and yes, it very likely requires some change in lifestyle, but it is achievable. Anybody committed enough, and with the right guidance, can do it. Yes, that means you. We hope this inspires you toward nirvana.

The Abbot's Commentary by Soryu Forall

Never give up!

CHAPTER THIRTEEN

Gods Just Want to Have Fun

How Buddhism Views Miracles and Gods

And That's Why Buddhist Monks Are Not Allowed to Levitate

In most religious traditions, miracles occupy a central place. In contrast, in early Buddhism, miracles are at best greeted with "meh." In fact, Buddhist monks are even explicitly banned from performing miracles in public.

The monastic code the Buddha prescribed to the monastics is codified in a volume called the Vinaya (literally: "discipline" or "training"), which contains more than two hundred rules for monks and nuns. The rules range from the essential to the seemingly trivial. The essential rules forbid killing a human being, stealing, having sex, and lying about one's own spiritual progress.[1] And then there are the trivial rules, for example, a monk shall not keep a spare bowl for more than ten days, a monk shall not tickle another monk or play in water, a monk shall not lie down on a bed scattered with flowers, a monk shall not polish his nails, and so on. Out of these hundreds of rules, there is one buried in the middle of the "Minor Matters" (*Khuddaka*) chapter that almost literally flies off the page: a monk shall not perform miracles in public. Say what?

One really nice thing about the Vinaya is it tells the story behind every monastic rule, so we know the story behind this one, and it's quite fascinating.[2] In the city of Rājagaha, a great merchant got his hands on a block of costly premium sandalwood. He had it carved into a bowl, tied a string around it, and suspended it high up at the end of a series of bamboo poles. And then he announced, "Whoever is perfectly enlightened and possesses the psychic power to fetch this bowl down, the bowl will be given to him." At that time, there were famous non-Buddhist teachers in India such as Pūraṇa Kassapa, Makkhali Gosāla, and others. They each went to the great merchant and said, "I am perfectly enlightened and possessing of psychic powers; give the bowl to me." And to each, the merchant gave the same reply, "If you can fetch down the bowl yourself, it is yours." None of them did.

One fine day, two great enlightened Buddhist monks, Piṇḍola Bhāradvāja and Moggallāna, entered the city for almsfood. As they walked near the bowl, Piṇḍola said to Moggallāna (presumably as a friendly tease), "Moggallāna, you are perfectly enlightened, you possess psychic powers, maybe you should get the bowl." Moggallāna replied, "Piṇḍola, you too are perfectly enlightened and you too possess psychic powers, maybe you should get the bowl." (It sounds like a joke, but that dialogue was actually documented in the Vinaya.) So Piṇḍola did. He levitated off the ground, flew all the way to the top of the cascade of bamboo poles, took the bowl, and, for good measure, "circled three times round Rājagaha." The people of Rājagaha witnessed it and made a huge commotion.

When the Buddha heard about it, he summoned Piṇḍola for what may be the most severe scolding ever given to an arahant by the Buddha. He compared Piṇḍola to a woman of negotiable modesty. He said to Piṇḍola, "Just like a woman exhibiting her privates for a miserable coin, you, Piṇḍola, exhibited your psychic powers for a miserable bowl." From then on, the Buddha banned all displays of psychic powers to householders.

Yeah, holy wow. That was my reaction too.

You may wonder what happened to Piṇḍola after that. Well, nothing. For a start, Piṇḍola was already a fully enlightened arahant; he didn't take the bowl because he was greedy, he almost certainly did it out of the purest of intentions: to inspire faith in the Dharma among the civilians, and surely the Buddha knew. In fact, despite the severe scolding, the Buddha didn't lose confidence in Piṇḍola.[3]

So why did the Buddha ban the display of miracles to the civilians? Because it distracts them from the Dharma. Essentially, psychic powers and enlightenment are totally separate matters. It is possible for one who is fully enlightened to not have any psychic powers at all. The Buddha's top disciple Sāriputta was the prime example; he was the wisest of all the Buddha's disciples but had zero psychic powers. On the other hand, it is possible to develop psychic powers in your meditation and still be evil. The Buddha's cousin Devadatta is the prime example.

If You See the Buddha on the Road, Please Don't Kill Him

Devadatta was a first cousin of the Buddha who became his disciple. He was a talented meditator who developed great psychic powers.[4] He used his powers to gain fame, power, and privilege. He appeared in front of Ajātasattu, who was then the crown prince of Magadha, and showed off his psychic powers. Ajātasattu was so impressed he took Devadatta as his teacher and showered him with a luxurious lifestyle. As Devadatta indulged in luxury and privilege, his psychic powers started to wane, but his ambition started to grow. Now he wanted to take over the entire Buddhist Sangha.

Alongside Devadatta's blind ambition was his lifelong jealousy against the Buddha, which went back to their childhood. When they were children, Siddhattha (the future Buddha) was the golden child, the future king, the nice, talented kid everybody loved, while Devadatta was "that other kid." Once, young Devadatta shot a bird, and young Siddhattha took it away to nurse it. They fought over the bird. Finally, they went to a guru for mediation, and the guru said, "Devadatta wants to take the bird's life, while Siddhattha wants to save its life. Therefore, the bird should belong to Siddhattha." Devadatta had resented Siddhattha since. After Siddhattha became the Buddha, Devadatta joined his order, learned to meditate, and developed psychic powers, but his jealousy of his better cousin never went away.

At a large gathering of monks where the king was also in attendance, Devadatta said to the Buddha, "You are now old, you should retire and live a life abiding in ease, and let me lead the Sangha." The Buddha replied with an unusually harsh rebuke, "I would not hand over the Sangha even to Sāriputta and Moggallāna. How then could I hand it over to you, a wretched one to spit out like spittle?" Devadatta bowed to him and left, but inside, he was so furious he started hatching murder plots.

When Devadatta returned to the palace, he incited Prince Ajātasattu to join him in a murder pact, "You kill your father so you would be king, and I kill the Buddha so I will be the new Buddha." Ajātasattu then attempted to assassinate his own father, the good king Bimbisāra. Ajātasattu failed, got caught, and was brought before the king. The good king asked, "Why do you want to kill me, my son?" "Because I want your kingdom." "Why didn't you just say so, I'd give it to you." With that, the good king Bimbisāra abdicated and gave Ajātasattu the throne. Ajātasattu became king, and then eventually murdered his father anyway.

Devadatta made three attempts to murder the Buddha. First, he had the now king Ajātasattu give him a squad of men to command. He ordered them to kill the Buddha. As they approached him sitting under a tree, they were so awed by him they greeted him, he spoke to them, and by the time he was done, they all became his lay followers. Next, the Buddha was taking a walk in the shade of Vulture Peak. Devadatta climbed to the top of Vulture Peak and hurled a large rock at him (I imagine he still had some psychic powers, and could still do that Jedi rock-moving thing). He missed and a fragment of the rock ended up hurting one of the Buddha's toes, drawing blood. The third murder attempt was a big deal because it was attempted in the city in broad daylight.

In the city of Rājagaha, there was a fierce war elephant called Nālāgiri who had been trained to kill people. The elephant was royal property, so Devadatta went to the mahouts to offer them a big reward and promotion by the king if they killed the Buddha. One day, while the Buddha was walking along the city's carriage road, the mahouts set Nālāgiri loose to charge at the Buddha. There must have been some distance between them, because people actually had time to react. The Buddha decided to stand still while the elephant charged at him. The townsfolk started climbing onto the roofs to watch the spectacle. As the elephant charged, the Buddha just stood there and infused it with loving-kindness. As the elephant got close, it stopped charging, sat down beside the Buddha, and let him stroke its forehead. Eventually, the elephant walked back to its own pen. The citizens of Rājagaha were beside themselves. There was a big brouhaha, and people around town sang:

> Some are tamed by stick, by goads and whips.
> The elephant was tamed by the great seer
> without a stick, without a weapon.

The people of Rājagaha eventually learned that Devadatta was behind this, so he became widely despised in the city, and he eventually lost his royal patronage. But he had one more trick up his sleeves: to break up the Sangha. With help from his coconspirator, the monk Kokālika Kaṭamorakatissaka, he caused a schism and attracted five hundred monks to his breakaway faction. Sāriputta and Moggallāna went to visit them. Devadatta thought they were there to join him, so he invited them to speak to the monks while he napped. When he woke up, he discovered that all of those monks except Kokālika had returned to the Buddha. He vomited blood. He was never heard from again.

If you wonder what happened to the new king Ajātasattu, he had a change of heart. Right after he gave the final order to execute his father, his own first son was born. Becoming a father, he experienced what it was like to love one's own son totally. He suddenly realized how his father must have felt for him. He immediately ordered a messenger to rush out to cancel his previous order to execute his father, but it was too late; his father was already dead. Ajātasattu was then wracked with profound remorse and, later, paranoia. Luckily for him, he eventually ended up going to the Buddha for instruction and became his follower.

The Greatest Miracle of All:
The Miracle of Instruction

The story of Devadatta illustrates how developing psychic powers in your meditation does not necessarily do anything to help you to attain enlightenment. Buddhism is primarily concerned with the cessation of suffering, and that can only come about through extinguishing the three fires of greed, hatred, and delusion. Psychic powers are a double-edged sword that can either help by deepening right samadhi, or hurt by flaming those fires even more. In Devadatta's case, the latter tragically happened. That is why the Buddha never encouraged nor discouraged the development of psychic powers among monastics. There is not a single discourse where he told anybody to develop those powers, but when good monks like Moggallāna and Anuruddha came upon those powers, he did not discourage them either. For civilians, however, those powers are generally considered an unskillful distraction, neither to be pursued nor promoted, and, therefore, monks are not to display those powers to them.

In modern times, I know a Zen teacher who told me in private that at one time, she accidentally acquired the ability to hear other people's thoughts. She found that very annoying because when she was not looking at somebody, she couldn't tell if that person was thinking something or saying it out loud, so she would sometimes answer to something somebody was merely thinking, and it got very awkward. That power eventually faded away on its own, and she was happy that it did.

The Buddha gave a discourse that illuminates the *meh*-ness of miracles in the Buddhist view, but with a slightly different framing. He was at that time staying at Nālanda. A man called Kevaddha came to ask him to perform miracles to show the local townsfolk so that "they would come to have even more faith in the Lord [Buddha]." The Buddha's reply was a fascinating menu of miracles the Buddha could perform, including:

- "Being one, he becomes many. Being many, he becomes one."

- Passing through walls, and "diving into and out of the earth as if it were water."

- Walking on water.

- Levitation.

- Traveling to the heavens.

- Telepathy.[5]

But for every menu item, the Buddha would say there was nothing impressive about it. Every single miracle on the list is a meh. After listing the menu, the Buddha talked about the most important miracle of all: **the miracle of instruction**. The miracle of instruction is when one is instructed in virtue, the jhānas, higher knowledge and vision, and finally, nirvana. Of all miracles, the miracle of instruction is the only one worthy of exhibition by an enlightened one. And that is why monks do not exhibit other miracles.

Oh, as a useful sidenote, in case this ever becomes relevant to you: yes, the Buddha did make an exception for saving lives. Buried somewhere in the monastic code in the chapter concerning stealing is a story where a superpowered monk named Pilindavaccha used his psychic powers to rescue two children kidnapped by criminals.[6] Some monks filed an ethics complaint to the Buddha accusing Pilindavaccha of breaking the rule disallowing the display of psychic powers in front of householders. The Buddha granted an exception for the saving of lives. So if you ever gain great power in your meditation, please feel free to discharge your great responsibility.

"I came all this way and what's his lesson? 'With great power comes great responsibility!'"

The Gods Are Merely Our Friends

The early Buddhist relationship with the gods is also very much unlike that in any religious tradition. Typically, a religion is built around the worship of one or more gods, and they almost always take the central and highest place in that religion. In early Buddhism, it is totally not the case; instead, the gods are merely friends.

In the volume of early Buddhist discourses called the Saṃyutta Nikāya, the first two chapters are devoted to the heavenly beings—the first one to the gods and the second to *devaputtas* (literally "god sons"), translated as "young gods." In almost all the discourses, the only role the gods play is to ask Dharma-related questions to the Buddha and receive answers. They would usually appear at night and be described as "a heavenly being of stunning beauty" who would illuminate the area, and they would bow to the Buddha and then ask questions. One such conversation, for example:

[The god asks:]
"What is good by not decaying?
What is good when made secure?
What is the precious gem of humans?
What cannot be stolen by thieves?"

[The Buddha answers:]
"Virtue is good by not decaying;
Faith is good when made secure;
Wisdom is the precious gem of humans;
Merit cannot be stolen by thieves."[7]

That's right, not much different from any conversation the Buddha would have with a typical human being, except for some reason, the conversations with the gods usually occur in verse (maybe because all good poets go to heaven). After each conversation, the god would be satisfied, bow to the Buddha, and then disappear.

There are a few exceptions to this pattern, but even in 100 percent of those cases, the gods play a subordinate role to the Buddha. For example, in one discourse, the young god Candimā was seized by a major demigod Rāhu; Candimā immediately took refuge in the Buddha, and Rāhu decided there was nothing he could do except to release him. When Rāhu was later asked why he had to release Candimā, he answered because he did not want his own head to be "split into seven parts."[8] (Yes, I thought it was funny too.)

Given this context, I was initially very surprised when reading the ancient discourses to come across one where the Buddha gave advice to "recollect the gods," until I read the fine print. This discourse was given to Mahānāma the Shakyan, the Buddha's cousin and Anuruddha's brother. Mahānāma did not become a monk. He did, however, attain stream-entry and he asked the Buddha what practice would support a stream-enterer's further growth. The Buddha prescribed to him the six recollections, which are:

1. Recollection of the Buddha

2. Recollection of the Dharma

3. Recollection of the Sangha

4. Recollection of your own virtue

5. Recollection of your generosity

6. Recollection of the gods[9]

For each recollection, the disciple gains wholesome joy and inspiration for deeper practice. That's not surprising to me, except the last one—I mean, what have the gods got to do with this? And then the Buddha explained: the disciple recollects thus, "The gods had the good fortune to be reborn as gods because of their previous virtue, faith, generosity, and wisdom, and I too have those same good qualities!" Thinking thus, the disciple gains wholesome joy and inspiration for deeper practice.

So even here, the gods are not the object of worship but inspiring equals. In the context of everything I know about early Buddhism, that makes perfect sense.

There is another fascinating story that illustrates the Buddhists/gods relationship from the perspective of early Buddhism.[10] This one involves Brahmā (literally: "supreme"), the highest of the gods. Our story begins with a monk with a profound question. This monk, while meditating, arrived at a question he could not answer: "Where do the four great elements cease without remainder?" Since the monk had attained psychic powers, he decided to go to the heavens to ask the gods.

First, he went to the lowest heaven, the Heaven of the Four Great Kings, to ask the gods there. They did not know the answer, so they suggested that he ask the Four Great Kings themselves. They are kings of those gods, surely they would know. Turns out, they did not know. They suggested he go upstairs to the next level of heaven, the Heaven of the Thirty-Three Gods. So he did. He asked those gods; they did not know the answer, so he asked their king, Sakka, and he did not know, so he suggested the monk go upstairs to the next higher heaven. And so on. And this went on all the way to the highest of heavens, the Heaven of Brahmā, the very seat of Great Brahmā himself.

Once again, our friend went around asking those gods, and they did not know the answer, so they suggested that he ask Great Brahmā. The monk approached Great Brahmā respectfully and asked the question, "Friend, where do the four elements cease without remainder?" Great Brahmā answered, "I am Brahmā, the Great Brahmā, the Undefeated, the Champion, the Universal Seer, the Wielder of Power, the Lord God, the Maker, the Author, the Best, the Begetter, the Controller, the Father of those who have been born and those yet to be born." The monk said, "Friend, I did not ask if you are Great Brahmā, my question is: Where do the four elements cease without remainder?" Great Brahmā repeated, "I am Brahmā, the Great Brahmā, the Undefeated, the Champion, . . . etc., etc. . . . , the Father of those who have been born and those yet to be born."

For the third time, the monk asked, "Friend, I did not ask if you are Great Brahmā. What I asked is: Where do the four elements cease without remainder?" This time, Great Brahmā did not answer. He grabbed the monk by the arm and took him to a quiet corner, and said to him, "All these gods think I know everything, but how would I know where the four great elements cease without remainder? This is all your fault. You are a disciple of the Buddha, go ask him yourself." And with that, the monk disappeared from that heaven and appeared in front of the Buddha. The Buddha made a gentle joke about his little adventure before giving him the answer in verse:

Consciousness unmanifest,
boundless, all-luminous:

Here water and earth,
fire and air find no footing;

Here long and short,
small and large, fair and foul;
Here name and form

are without remainder destroyed—
Here, with the cessation of consciousness,
This is all destroyed.[11]

Oh, and did you notice, the main character in this story, a mere unnamed Buddhist monk, addressed Great Brahmā as "friend" (*āvuso*), the same term monks use to address each other?[12] Whether you take the story literally or not, it illuminates the early Buddhist attitude toward the gods: that when it comes to the most important and most profound subjects, like nirvana, the gods do not necessarily know more than we do, and an enlightened human would know more about those topics than a typical god, up to and including Great Brahmā himself. And that is partly why, in early Buddhism, the total cumulative sum of worship of all gods is *zero*. Gods are just friends.

Wait, Didn't Brahmā Create the Universe or Something?

The religion Brahmanism predates the Buddha. The Buddha was born into a culture in which a certain group of priests, the Brahmans, believed in and worshipped Brahmā as the creator God, and they were in the process of spreading this doctrine to others. How does the Buddha account for their belief? The Buddha's explanation was one of the first things I read as a young man exploring Buddhism, and my jaw dropped.

First, the cosmology—Buddhist texts assume the existence of multiple realms (universes?) that exist alongside each other. Each realm has a life cycle: a realm comes into existence, and then it expands, and eventually it contracts, and then it no longer exists. Each heaven is a realm. This cosmology, or some version of it, almost certainly predates Buddhism.

Here, the Buddha was explaining why some teachers taught that Brahmā created everything in a famous long discourse called the Brahmajāla Sutta (Discourse on the Supreme Net), where the Buddha addresses sixty-two wrong views in one go. He tells a story that begins in the "realm of streaming radiance."[13] Beings with great virtue in their past lives are reborn there as gods. They are mind-made (i.e., they have no physical bodies), joyful, self-luminous, and glorious. As that realm expands, an empty "Palace of Brahmā" (presumably a subrealm) appears.

One particular being with amazing karma due to his many lifetimes of wonderful virtue passed away and became the first to be reborn in this subrealm of "Palace of Brahmā." He was Great Brahmā. There, he dwelled glorious for a long time, but he got lonely, and wished for other beings to exist. After a while, other beings with amazing virtue and past karma passed away and were reborn in Great Brahmā's realm. Great Brahmā thought to himself, "I wished for them to exist, and now they exist, I must have created them. I am Brahmā, the Great Brahmā, the Undefeated, the Champion, the Universal Seer, the Wielder of Power, the Lord God, the Maker, the Author, the Best, the Begetter, the Controller, the Father of those who have been born and those yet to be born." And all those new gods thought, "Wow, Great Brahmā wished for us to exist, and now we exist; he must have created us. He is Brahmā, the Great Brahmā, the Undefeated, the Champion, . . . etc., etc. . . . , the Father of those who have been born and those yet to be born."

After a long time, one of those gods passed away from Great Brahmā's realm and was reborn as a human being. He practiced meditation and became accomplished at it, but he could only remember one previous lifetime, and he remembered being in the presence of Great Brahmā and that Great Brahmā "created" him. Thus, he started teaching that Great Brahmā created everything, and this was how we ended up with those beliefs, even though they were based on misunderstanding.

Relating to that is a joke the Buddha made. The Buddha met a group of ascetics who believed in a creator God but also believed in clearing up their past bad karma by subjecting themselves to intense physical pain. The Buddha joked that, by their flawed argument, those ascetics giving themselves so much suffering must have been created by a "bad god," while fully enlightened ones who were always happy must have been created by an "excellent god."[14]

So Is Buddhism a Religion or Not?

"I pray that
we are not a
religion."

Is Buddhism a religion? Or is it, instead, a philosophy? First, let's see what the Buddha himself has to say. It turns out, he has an answer for that question. He says emphatically, "What I teach is suffering and the cessation of suffering."[15]

The Buddha was in Kosambi taking a walk with the monks in the forest. He held up a handful of leaves and asked the monks, "Which is more, the leaves in my hand or all the leaves on all the trees in this forest?" "The leaves on the trees, Venerable Sir." "In the same way, the leaves on the trees represent all that I have directly known, the leaves in my hand represent what I teach."[16] The Buddha then went on to say he only taught those teachings that lead to liberation from suffering, which is only a tiny subset of what he had directly known. That tiny subset is centered around the Four Noble Truths. This discourse is the reason the Buddha's teachings are sometimes poetically referred to as "a handful of leaves."

In that sense, Buddhism is not a religion. It is not even a philosophy. It is simply a collection of profound teachings and practices leading to liberation from suffering. More than that, as you have seen in this book, all the practices taught by the Buddha are extremely secular. In addition, if we define *religion* as "**the belief in and worship of one or more gods**," we can argue that there is no such thing as a religion where no god is worshipped.[17] I mean, it is kind of absurd, right? Which major religion do you know that has *zero* worship of any god *and* does not even give a damn about miracles? In that sense, Buddhism, at least early Buddhism, is not a religion.

But not so fast! Even if Buddhism is not a religious tradition, it is most definitely a spiritual tradition. It deals with essential spiritual matters such as death, the afterlife, and deathlessness (the transcending of death). At what point does such a spiritual tradition become a religion, or not a religion? There is no consensus on where to draw the line. Some people call Buddhism a "nontheistic religion," while some call it "spirituality, not religion."

But wait, there's more. As time went on, Buddhism took on the function and trappings of religion. In some cultures, it functions like a religion, especially in ceremonies involving, say, marriages, funerals, and coronations. Also, over time, a pantheon of gods started getting added to Buddhism. There is, for example, the character of Amitābha Buddha, whose name you can chant, and if you can recite his name in perfect mindfulness ten times as you are dying, you can be reborn in his "Pure Land."[18] There is the ever-popular Guan Yin, the Bodhisattva of Compassion; there is Maitreya, the upcoming Buddha; there is Manjusri, the Bodhisattva of Wisdom; and there is Brahmā, recast as the "Four-Faced Buddha." Each one is an inspiring symbol, and a useful aid for one's meditation practice. And, of course, in folk Buddhism, each one, plus the Buddha, also serves as a god that people can (and do) worship and ask divine favors from.

When I was growing up in Singapore, all the adults I knew went to the temple periodically to beg those "Buddhist gods" for winning lottery numbers, and lo and behold, in an awesome demonstration of their divine glory, the Buddhist gods actually granted winning numbers, at roughly a rate predicted by statistical probability. In that sense, yes, later Buddhism has definitely become a religion.

It is not just gods; miracles also started gaining a more prominent place in later Buddhism as well. Tibetan Buddhism, for example, is chock-full of stories about miracles. Tibetan Buddhism includes deeply scholastic traditions in which the systematic study and the extensive monastic curriculum in logic and epistemology can take decades to cover. At the same time, it also has an amazingly well-developed mystical side. Some of the most fascinating examples for me involve the Karmapas. The original Karmapa was a great Tibetan Buddhist master who lived from 1110 to 1193 CE. The Second Karmapa was the teacher of Kublai Khan, emperor of the Mongolian empire at its height and the most powerful man in the world. Kublai held a grudge against the Karmapa for a perceived snub, so after he became the emperor, he sent a small army to capture or kill the Karmapa, but the Karmapa got free every time, including at one time, freezing the entire army in place. Kublai was so impressed that he eventually asked the Karmapa to be his teacher. After the Second Karmapa, a few subsequent Karmapas were also teachers of emperors and were also known to possess psychic powers. The Sixteenth Karmapa passed away in 1981, so he was a modern-day lama with American students, some of whom I personally know, and they tell me they witnessed that Karmapa perform miracles. For example, one time, when the Karmapa was meditating with his students, his body became translucent. One Western student took a picture. I've seen the photo and I'm really not sure what to make of it (yes, his body did look translucent, as in you can see some of the things behind him). I'm quite fascinated, though.

You may wonder why there is a line of Karmapas. That is a unique feature of Tibetan Buddhism. The word *Karmapa* literally means "action doer," or one who performs actions (on behalf of the Buddha), so, unsurprisingly, the (original) Karmapa decided he wanted to continue staying in the world to serve all sentient beings even after he died. As he was passing away, he left a letter to his main disciple on how to find his upcoming reincarnation. His disciple did, and the little boy identified as his reincarnation was installed as the Second Karmapa. That tradition continues to this day: every time a Karmapa dies, his top disciples identify and install his supposed reincarnation as the next Karmapa. This is called the "tulku" system, a tulku being a reincarnate custodian of a lineage. This system has been applied to many other great Tibetan masters, most famously the Dalai Lama. (If you ask me, I think the tulku system has outlived its usefulness and it's time for it to be retired.)

The practices in Buddhism also became increasingly mystical and religious over time. In early Buddhism, the practices were extremely secular. In contrast, for example, in a later form of Buddhism called Pure Land Buddhism, the main practice (or sole practice, depending on which teacher you ask) involves having complete faith in a buddha known as Amitābha Buddha, and chanting his name frequently. That clearly crosses the boundary into "religion." One of the most important features of Pure Land Buddhism is you need to be able to chant Amitābha's name in perfect mindfulness as you lay dying, and in order to be able to do that, you need to train yourself to develop a very high degree of mindfulness and samadhi in your regular practice using devotion to Amitābha (or the sound of Amitābha's name, depending on the teacher) as the meditation object. So, clearly, this almost certainly started as a compassionate way to help the large uneducated lay populace of ancient times practice mindfulness and samadhi (remembering that very few people in ancient times had the opportunity to receive formal education), but it is also religious in its framing. That is not to say that Pure Land Buddhism isn't Dharma; of course it is still Dharma. Remember, Dharma is defined as "universal law pertaining to suffering and liberation from suffering." Wherever there is an understanding of suffering and liberation from suffering, there is Dharma. Pure Land Buddhism is Dharma delivered in a religious packaging for those inclined to practice it that way.

In Vajrayana Buddhism, which includes Tibetan Buddhism, practices got even more mystical and religious, involving energy, chakras, tantras, gods, tulkus, and secret teachings that can only be revealed by masters to a select few. In fact, Vajrayana Buddhism is so mystical its Chinese name is *mizong* (密宗), which literally means the "mystical tradition." This has, of course, come a long, long way from the original flavor of early Buddhism, where the Buddha said he did not have "the closed fist of a teacher," which means he had no secret teachings: everything he taught was in the open for all to clearly see.[19] Vajrayana Buddhism is still Dharma, no doubt, but the same wonderful medicine has now acquired a very different flavor. Early Buddhism is like clear miso soup, subtly tasteful and refreshing, while Vajrayana Buddhism is like spicy curry, packing a wallop of aroma and flavor. Both are delicious, in different ways. They can even be consumed together. I do that myself (for both soup and Dharma).

So is Buddhism a religion or not? I would say at its core, Buddhism is not a religion, it is a set of profound teachings and highly secular practices leading to liberation from suffering. However, Buddhism comes with an option that can be exercised to turn it into a religion, and societies and individuals are all free to exercise that option. Where and when that option is exercised, Buddhism becomes a religion.

Is a transformer a car or a fighter robot? It is either one that can be easily transformed into the other depending on whether you need to drive to college or defeat evil killer robots. In the same way, Buddhism can be a religion or a non-religion, and can be easily transformed from one to the other, depending on which one best serves the people. Just like transformers, Buddhism more than meets the eye.

I'm going to give Soryu the last word on this topic, because I think he says it best:

> The Buddha did not teach us that we must worship deities, but he also did not teach us that we must not worship deities. Because a Buddhist is not required to worship deities, Buddhism is secular. At the same time, because a Buddhist is allowed to worship deities, Buddhism may be religious. In any case, the core of Buddhism is our own path to liberation from suffering. This is a path of our own direct experience. We must walk this path ourselves. No one else can walk it for us. Not deities. Not even the Buddha.

The Passing of Sāriputta

I'd like to end this chapter with the story of Sāriputta's final days.[20]

Sāriputta was the Buddha's top disciple. He passed into final nirvana a few months before the Buddha. One day, during the final year of the Buddha's time on earth, Sāriputta saw that his own life force could only sustain him for one more week. What to do with your final week on this earth? Sāriputta thought of his mother, who was "one without faith." He decided his last deed would be to help his mom. The debt to one's parents is taken very seriously in Buddhism. The Buddha taught that even if one were to carry one's parents and care for them all day for a hundred years, it would not be enough to repay their kindness.[21] The only way to fully repay them is to help them walk the path to enlightenment.

Sāriputta tidied up his room and took one last look at it. He went to the Buddha, paid his respects, and told the Buddha that he would soon pass, and that he wanted to spend his last days with Mom. The Buddha approved, and told Sāriputta, "The monks will not see the likes of you again. Please give them one last discourse." Sāriputta did. At the end of the discourse, Sāriputta embraced the Buddha's legs and said, "I have fulfilled the ten perfections for countless aeons just so I could worship these feet. My wish has been fulfilled. I will now enter the City of Nirvana, the unaging, undying, peaceful, blissful, heat-assuaging, and secure, which has been entered by countless buddhas."

Sāriputta stood up and walked mindfully around the Buddha three times. He then saluted the Buddha and said, "This is my last sight of you; there will be no more." And he left.

By the time Sāriputta arrived at his home village of Nālaka, he had only one day left. At first, his mom was excited to hear that Sāriputta had returned, but she was disappointed to see he was still a monk. Sāriputta moved into the room he was born in, and then he became very, very sick. Even as Sāriputta lay rapidly dying, Mom barricaded herself in her room because she was still upset about Sāriputta becoming a monk.[22]

In the middle of the night, something happened. Mom noticed Sāriputta's room becoming very bright. She got curious and went to peek inside. To her astonishment, she saw a line of gods paying their final respects to Sāriputta. Sāriputta had the same conversation with every one of them. He would ask, "Who are you?" They would identify themselves, "I am the god so-and-so." Sāriputta would then ask, "Why are you here?" "I came to take care of you." "I already have an attendant, you may go."

Every god that came to pay his last respect, Sāriputta would dismiss. Mom's jaw dropped. She realized for the first time that her son was no ordinary monk.

After all the gods had been dismissed, Mom sat down next to Sāriputta and asked who all those gods were. Sāriputta gave her the list, the first four were the four great heavenly kings, and then there was Sakka the king of the Heaven of the Thirty-Three Gods, and that last one was Great Brahmā. Mom asked, "The Great Brahmā that I worship came to bow to *you*?" "Yes, that Great Brahmā, your lord and master," Sāriputta said. When Mom heard this, faith in the Buddha arose in her, and consequently, rapture and joy arose in her, suffusing her entire body and mind.

Seeing that Mom was now finally ready to hear the Dharma, Sāriputta gave her a discourse. By the end of the discourse, Mom understood the Dharma and gained stream-entry. Sāriputta's final debt had been repaid by offering the greatest gift to his mother, the gift of Dharma. Early the next morning, he passed.

The Abbot's Commentary
by Soryu Forall

There is no one anywhere who has control over the world. Many people feel that one or more gods are in charge, but none of them are. Many others feel that humans are, or should be, in charge, but we aren't either, and never will be.

This world is created by natural law and the choices each of us makes within that law. That law is cause and effect, which in Buddhism is called the law of karma. In the same way that physical laws function whether we understand them or not, ethical laws function whether we understand them or not. Each of us is creating the world together. No one is in charge, because all of us matter. Every living thing creates the world in every moment, together.

To grasp onto being in charge is suffering. To relinquish that grasping is peace. To not even grasp onto peace is compassion. The Buddha, for example, was not attached to the peace he had found, and was willing to be troubled by getting involved in the turmoil of the world, just to help all sentient beings. Compassion saves the world without being in charge of anything at all.

CHAPTER FOURTEEN

Buddhism and Modern Science Sitting Together

The Surprisingly Intimate Relationship
Between Buddhism and Science

The Dalai Lama Is Half a Scientist, He Says

The first time I saw the 14th Dalai Lama share a stage with scientists was in 2009, at Stanford University, and it was not what I expected. He sat occupying center stage surrounded by prominent scientists. I saw the way he engaged with the scientists, and I was in awe. About thirty minutes in, one began to suspect that this laughing bald man in robes, who spent most of his time whispering with his interpreter, was the smartest person onstage.

The most amazing moment came when the Dalai Lama was responding to a presentation about the neuroscience of compassion and suffering. Professor William Mobley, founding director of the Wu Tsai Neurosciences Institute at Stanford, made a presentation showing that similar parts of the brain light up when a subject experiences pain versus when he empathizes with somebody else in pain. The Dalai Lama raised a major issue that nobody else had considered. Interrupting his interpreter, he explained in his broken English that there are two types of compassion: one for people close to oneself, which he calls "limited compassion," and one for total strangers, which he calls "genuine compassion." Both are qualitatively different experiences and therefore must have different neural correlates. He added, if the brain patterns for both are the same, "then I feel the brain is very foolish." Everybody laughed. The Dalai Lama had just uncovered a major limitation of the study: it turns out all the subjects were watching videos of their loved ones in pain, therefore this study only captured the brain activation for "limited compassion," not for "genuine compassion." Professor Mobley was so impressed he commented, "This is one of those experiences where you really understand how that incisive thinking completely defines a twenty-year research program."

That was when I realized, the Dalai Lama is not just the "humble Buddhist monk" he claims to be; he also has serious scientific chops.

Back in Chapter 1, we quoted the Dalai Lama making a declaration that might have seemed blasphemous if spoken by the highest leader of some other religions: "If scientific analysis were conclusively to demonstrate certain claims in Buddhism to be false, then we must accept the findings of science and abandon those claims."

He has demonstrated his willingness to walk his talk. According to sacred Tibetan Buddhist texts, the earth is flat and Mount Meru is the center of the earth. After the Dalai Lama learned that science had already conclusively proven that the earth is round, he declared that the teaching about Mount Meru is to be abandoned. I've heard him joke to an audience that the Mount Meru teaching is "embarrassing" before letting out a big laugh. But you have to ask, when one of the highest of all living Buddhist masters openly and officially abandons traditional Buddhist teachings recorded in sacred texts in favor of science, does that shake people's faith in Buddhism? The Dalai

Lama says no, and, as usual, he puts it in an amusing way: "The purpose of the Buddha coming to this world was not to measure the circumference of the world and the distance between the earth and the moon, but rather to teach the Dharma, to liberate sentient beings, to relieve sentient beings of their sufferings."[1] Yes, I approve.

Actually, the Dalai Lama went even further than that: he got in cahoots with the scientists. He has had a lifelong fascination with how mechanical things work. Since he was young, he would take watches and other mechanical things apart and put them back together again. He once said that if he wasn't a monk, he would have been an engineer. To satisfy his curiosity in how everything works, he invited some top scientists to visit him so he could learn from them, and they did, because it is kind of cool to hang out with the Dalai Lama. This eventually inspired the founding of the Mind & Life Institute, which organizes annual conferences attended by the Dalai Lama and leading scientists. The themes of these conferences range from neuroscience to psychology to education to quantum physics and philosophy.

Out of these conferences come some very important research projects. For example, two of the top scientists in their own respective fields, Paul Ekman and Richard Davidson, were given access to study some top Tibetan meditation masters, and they published some important pioneering scientific findings. For example, they found that master-level meditators can do things with their brains previously thought impossible, such as voluntarily not startle in reaction to a sudden loud sound (called the "startle reflex," previously thought to be impossible to suppress because it is a "reflex"). Those masters were also found to be able to volitionally, in a matter of seconds, bring the mind to a state of extreme joy. They also have healthier genes: the part of a cell called telomeres that protects chromosomes from damage is more robust in advanced meditators.

These studies are all fascinating, and they are only possible because those meditation masters allow themselves to be subjects of those studies. It is actually not easy to get any Buddhist master to participate in any study, mostly because they spend a lot of time in retreat, and when they are not in retreat, they usually have overwhelming teaching schedules. Compared to everything else they need to do, plus the fact that most masters do not see the value of scientific validation of their meditation, it is very challenging to convince any master to spend time in a lab. The only reason the scientific community has access to so many top Tibetan Buddhist masters is that the Dalai Lama invited them, and if you are a Tibetan monk, you kind of don't say no to the Dalai Lama. The Dalai Lama's example also encourages the participation by Buddhist masters of other schools of Buddhism in scientific research. In that sense, the Dalai Lama has been instrumental in advancing of the fields of science relating to advanced training of the mind. That means that Buddhism has contributed more to brain science than any religion has contributed to any field of science.

Hence, in modern times, Buddhism is not just fully compatible with science, we are in active cahoots.

How deeply are we in cahoots? At one public conference, the Dalai Lama openly declared that he is "half scientist, half Buddhist monk."[2] Everybody cheered, Buddhist monastics, lay Buddhists, and scientists alike. Remember back in Chapter 13, we mention that Tibetan Buddhism is, by far, the most mystical of all schools of Buddhism? When the paramount leader of the most mystical school of Buddhism calls himself a half scientist in a public setting, and all the Buddhists cheer, *that* shows how deeply comfortable Buddhism is with science. If you are someone accustomed to thinking that science and religion are necessarily in conflict, I hope this is a pleasant surprise for you.

You might be wondering, is this a recent thing? Maybe this friendliness with science is a modern phenomenon thanks to the 14th Dalai Lama. Actually, no. This attitude can be traced all the way back to the Buddha himself!

Don't Believe What the Buddha Says

The spirit of inquiry is one of the most important aspects of Buddhist practice. We have seen in Chapter 7 that "investigation of phenomena" (*dhamma vicaya*) is one of the seven factors of enlightenment. I'm going to say it again in case you missed the significance: the spirit of inquiry is so important in Buddhism that it is a factor of enlightenment.

This spirit of inquiry expands to all things, even toward the Buddha himself. There is a very famous discourse that illustrates this. It is officially titled the *Kesamutta Sutta* (Discourse Spoken in Kesamutta), after the town it was delivered in, but it is very popularly known as the Kālāma Sutta, after the people it was delivered to.[3]

Once the Buddha was in a town called Kesamutta, populated by a people called the Kālāmas. They knew the Buddha by reputation, so when they heard the Buddha was in town, they gathered to see him. This town got visited by many famous teachers, so they asked the Buddha, "Every teacher who visits us promotes his own doctrine and then disparages and badmouths the doctrines of all other teachers. How do we know who to believe?" Being the Buddha, he could have just said, "You believe me, duh."[4] Instead, he delivered a discourse on how to apply the spirit of inquiry to any teaching, including his own. He listed ten criteria that are *not sufficient* for accepting any spiritual teaching:

1. oral transmission

2. lineage of teaching

3. hearsay/rumor

4. holy scriptures

5. logical reasoning

6. inferential reasoning

7. reasoned contemplation

8. acceptance of a view after pondering it

9. the seeming competence of the speaker

10. the fact that the speaker is one's own teacher

The Buddha then spoke of the criterion to accept a spiritual teaching: after examining a teaching for yourself, you know it is wholesome and leads to benefit and happiness for oneself and others.

But how do you know that? Here, the Buddha suggested examining this question deeply for yourself: Are greed, hatred, and delusion causes of suffering or causes of happiness? If they are causes of suffering, then use that as the yardstick for measuring any teaching by asking yourself: Does this teaching increase or decrease greed, hatred, or delusion? With that, you will know the answer to whether or not to accept a teaching.

In other words, do not accept any teaching solely because it comes from your teacher (including the Buddha), or sacred scripture, or any of the above ten criteria. Instead, investigate it yourself, with its effect on greed, hatred, and delusion as the most useful yardstick, and then decide for yourself.

There is a teaching in Tibetan Buddhism that frames the same thing in a way I find very understandable: just as a goldsmith would test his gold by burning, cutting, and rubbing it, so you must examine the Buddha's words, not merely accept them out of faith.[5]

In a separate discourse called the *Vīmaṁsaka Sutta* (Inquirer Discourse), the Buddha made it explicit that his disciples should investigate him.[6] He did not say "you should investigate your teachers" and implicitly include himself; no, instead he explicitly said (referring to himself in third person as the Tathāgata), "A monk who is an inquirer, who is unable to read minds, should investigate the Tathāgata to find out if he is really enlightened." And then he spent the rest of the discourse explaining how they can do that. The steps include:

- Examine the Teacher with your eyes and ears to see if his daily actions are compatible with one of a pure heart.

- See whether fame and renown cause any danger to the Teacher.

- Find out if he is without greed and lust, and whether he indulges in sensual pleasure.

- See if he despises anyone (a buddha doesn't).

- Ask him if he needs to restrain his behavior out of fear, or if he doesn't have to because he is already without lust.

- Don't be shy to ask him point-blank whether his heart is pure.

The Buddha concludes, "When anyone's faith has been planted, rooted, and established in the Tathāgata through investigating him thoroughly, his faith is said to be supported by reasons, rooted in vision, firm. That is how an investigation of the Tathāgata is in accordance with the Dharma."

I'm fascinated. Rarely have I come across any religious or spiritual leader who actively teaches that any faith you have in him must come from an investigation of him. It is no wonder that any religious or spiritual tradition founded by such a man should have the spirit of inquiry deeply embedded in.

And it is no wonder that more than two thousand years later, the Dalai Lama is so comfortable with scientific inquiry.

"They are here to conduct the double-blind experiment."

Why Buddhist Monks Did Not Invent Telescopes

You may ask, if Buddhism was so comfortable with science, why didn't they develop the fields of physics or chemistry or biology, and why didn't they invent telescopes?

Buddhism could have been the tradition that gave us modern science. The most important thing that gave birth to modern science is what historians call the "Discovery of Ignorance." Buddhism was possibly the earliest major tradition in the world to discard dogma and place observation and investigation at its center, so you would think that Buddhism would be the natural pioneer in the Discovery of Ignorance. Why then did modern science not emerge from a Buddhist civilization?

The main reason is that other things were also needed for modern science to emerge. In the book *Sapiens*, historian Yuval Noah Harari identified three essential things that led to the rise of modern science:

1. The willingness to admit ignorance. Modern science is based on the Latin injunction *ignoramus*—"we do not know." It assumes that we don't know everything. Even more critically, it accepts that the things that we think we know could be proven wrong as we gain more knowledge. No concept, idea, or theory is sacred and beyond challenge.

2. The centrality of observation and mathematics. Having admitted ignorance, modern science aims to obtain new knowledge. It does so by gathering observations and then using mathematical tools to connect these observations into comprehensive theories.

3. The acquisition of new powers. Modern science is not content with creating theories. It uses these theories in order to acquire new powers, and in particular to develop new technologies.[7]

Of these three, 1) sounds exactly like Buddhism, but while observation is central to Buddhism, mathematics is not, and therefore, Buddhism only has half of 2). Needless to say, Buddhism has no interest in 3). Therefore, of these three things, Buddhism only has one and a half, and that is probably why modern science did not emerge from a Buddhist civilization.

In addition, Buddhism is totally uninterested in metaphysics. In the "handful of leaves" simile from Chapter 13, the Buddha makes clear that he only teaches a tiny subset of everything he knows, and that tiny subset is those teachings that lead to liberation from suffering. Metaphysical questions fall well outside of that subset. In fact, the Buddha was asked those questions, and he famously refused to answer. This is known in Buddhism as "noble silence."

There was a monk by the name of Mālunkyāputta. He had a list of ten metaphysical questions:

1. Is the world eternal?

2. ... or not?

3. Is the world finite?

4. ... or infinite?

5. Is the soul the same as the body?

6. ... or different?

7. After the Buddha dies, does he exist?

8. ... or not exist?

9. ... or both?

10. ... or neither?[8]

He presented this list of ten questions to the Buddha and said if the Buddha did not answer them, he would leave the monastic order. The Buddha refused to answer them. Why? Because those questions do not lead to "disenchantment, dispassion, cessation, peace, direct knowledge, enlightenment, nirvana." That was why the Buddha left them undeclared. The only things he would declare are things that lead to nirvana, which are the Four Noble Truths.

To reinforce the point, the Buddha gave the famous simile of the man struck by a poison arrow. Suppose a man was wounded by a poison arrow, and his friends brought a surgeon to treat him. The man would say: "I will not let the surgeon treat me until I know whether the man who wounded me is a noble or a brahmin or a merchant or a worker, and his name and clan, how tall he is, his skin tone, whether he lives in a village or town, etc., etc., etc." By the time this man found out all the answers, he would be dead. His highest priority should have been to let the surgeon treat him first. In the same way, a monk should learn and practice the Dharma first, instead of being distracted by metaphysical speculations.

"Before you treat the patient, please fill out this questionnaire."

This is probably why Buddhist monks never invented telescopes. Buddhism is unconcerned about metaphysics and, by extension, generally unconcerned about how things work in the physical world. Their application of the scientific method is entirely internal, aimed only at looking at the mind to gain insights into suffering and liberation from suffering. Anything else is a distraction.

Mālunkyāputta was satisfied with the Buddha's explanation. He stayed. In case you wonder what happened to him later, in the ancient texts he was scolded by the Buddha at least twice (including for threatening to leave the order if the Buddha didn't answer his metaphysical questions). Finally, when he was an old man, he went to the Buddha again for more teachings. The Buddha gave him a surprisingly short and basic teaching: "Four things give rise to craving in a monk: food, clothing, lodging, and rebirth in this or that state. A monk who gives up that craving completely makes an end to suffering." Mālunkyāputta meditated on those instructions and achieved full enlightenment.[9]

Buddhism Is the Science of the Mind

While Buddhist civilizations did not give birth to modern science, Buddhism can justifiably be called the "Science of the Mind," as the Dalai Lama has done. That is because the entirety of one's Buddhist training can be thought of as repeated applications of the scientific method.

The application of the scientific method begins with a question and a hypothesis, and then the construction of an experiment that can test the hypothesis, running the experiment to collect data, and analyzing the data to see if the hypothesis is verified, and if not (or not fully so), a new question emerges and the cycle continues.

Let's say the question is: Does gravity apply to everything equally? One hypothesis that can arise from this question is: earth's gravity applies equal acceleration to all objects falling to earth. To test the hypothesis, you can try dropping two spheres of unequal weight from the top of the Leaning Tower of Pisa. The data you'd need to collect is the time it takes for each sphere to land.

If the time for both spheres to land is the same, you can say the hypothesis is verified. If you later drop a wooden ball and a feather, you will find the new data not supporting the supposedly verified hypothesis. That may lead to a new hypothesis: that air resistance causes the feather to fall at a much lower speed than predicted by gravity, and therefore, if you drop it in a vacuum, it will fall at the same rate as a wooden ball. That new hypothesis can lead to a new experiment, and so on.

Essentially, using the scientific method, all questions are answered by collecting data from empirical observation. This is true for physics, and it is also true for Buddhism. If you are working with a teacher, for example, she might start by assigning you a hypothesis and experimental method. For example, the hypothesis is as you settle attention on the breath, your mind becomes alert and relaxed, and the experimental method is to relax your body and repeatedly bring a wondering attention to the breath. If you become alert and relaxed after a while, then the hypothesis is verified. So you try that out, and then you may come back to the teacher and say, "When I do that, I don't become alert and relaxed, I fall asleep instead, so that hypothesis appears to be falsified." The teacher might then suggest a new parameter: maybe you're falling asleep because you are sleep-deprived, so do the same experiment again about fifteen minutes after you get a full night's sleep, and then see if the hypothesis holds. And so on. The Buddhist path includes a series of insights concerning the mind gained by repeatedly applying the scientific method to yourself.

There is one essential attitude in Buddhism that also forms the foundation of the scientific method: not holding tightly to any view. We saw in Chapter 6 that right view is an extremely important part of the Noble Eightfold Path. In the Buddha's default formulation, it is the first part that guides the other seven, while in the highly popular Dhammadinnā formulation, right view is the cumulation of the other seven. Either way, it is of central importance. And even for something as vitally important as right view, the Buddha's instruction is: don't hold on tightly to.

The teaching most illustrative of the Buddha's attitude toward views is his simile of the raft.[10] Suppose a man were to cross from one shore to another on a raft. He would be foolish to think, "This raft has been helpful to me for getting to this shore, therefore, I should hoist it on my back and take it wherever I go." A wise person would instead leave the raft where it is. Similarly, the Dharma is only a tool to get from here to nirvana, and once you have arrived, you should be free to let it go. Yes, even the Dharma itself is to be let go of. The Buddha gave numerous discourses collected in the book called Sutta Nipāta that reinforce that point. For example, an enlightened one does not grasp anything as supreme,[11] he does not grasp onto any view,[12] and he is not a "pursuer of views."[13]

Why is this important? Because Buddhism is essentially an insight tradition, and insights cannot be gained if you hold tightly to preexisting views. For example, let's say the Dalai Lama read as a young person in the holy scriptures that the earth is flat and Mount Meru is the center of the earth, and let's say he held tightly to it because it came directly from holy scriptures. And then later he learned about conclusive scientific evidence that the earth is actually round. If he had held tightly to the preexisting view, he would not have been able to gain the insight that the earth is round. For that reason, to gain insight all views must always be held lightly (including this one, of course). That means:

1. Knowing my views can always be wrong.

2. Holding all my existing views as tentative, based only on currently available evidence.

3. When I get new evidence, my views may change.

4. Even when it is absolutely clear my views are correct, they may still be wrong.

The most spectacular example of (4), to me, is quantum physics versus Newtonian physics. If you look at the laws of Newtonian physics before quantum physics was known, you can be absolutely sure of the correctness of Newtonian physics. I mean, look, it perfectly predicts the motions of apples, planets, and entire galaxies; how could it possibly be wrong in any way? And then it turns out, the laws of physics function differently at the subatomic level. If we had held on to Newtonian physics as the absolute truth, given how conclusive and unmistakable all the evidence was, we would never have gained quantum physics.

Buddhism is about gaining insights that lead to freedom from suffering.

Only by holding views very lightly at every stage can that happen. If you do that, you may find yourself first becoming a skeptic, because you realize all views may be wrong. A skeptic who is sufficiently thirsty for knowledge becomes an empiricist, because the only kind of knowledge that is satisfactory to a skeptic is the type backed by evidence. And that is precisely what the Buddha encourages, starting with encouraging skepticism about himself, and then, over time, based on investigation of phenomena (which is, again, the second factor of enlightenment), building a portfolio of evidence-based knowledge to get from here to nirvana. For a skeptical empiricist gaining knowledge, the most natural method is the scientific method, and that is why the scientific method comes so naturally to Buddhism.

Dharma always beats dogma.

The Abbot's Commentary by Soryu Forall

I see Buddhism and science as two ways of approaching wisdom. Buddhism studies suffering and the end of suffering. I would say that any aspect of science that studies this is also Buddhism. In general, however, science studies issues that the Buddha warned are irrelevant. Whether that is an astrophysics textbook claiming that space is curved or an arcane Tibetan text claiming the world is flat, it is an unfortunate diversion of Buddhist methods.

Buddhism is the part of science that matters. Science is the part of Buddhism that doesn't matter. Why would I be so strong in my language? Because science gives us enormous power, without giving us the wisdom or love to use that power skillfully. Instead, we generally use the power we gain with science to serve our craving. Craving is the source of suffering. For this reason, science is the source of technologies that endanger life on earth.

Use the part of science that matters. Use Buddhism to resolve the only issue that matters: how to resolve suffering.

CHAPTER FIFTEEN

How Early Buddhism Was Preserved
A Tale of Heroism by the Buddha's Disciples

The Buddha's Passing

Siddhattha became the Buddha at the age of thirty-five. He taught for the next forty-five years or so until he was eighty. At the ripe old age of eighty, he passed away, or, more accurately, he entered final nirvana. His last days were documented in an unusually long discourse in the canon called the Great Discourse on the Final Nirvana (Mahāparinibbāna Sutta).[1] This discourse is also unusually heavy with mystical elements that you seldom see in the rest of the early canonical texts.

By this time, the Buddha was very old and his physical body was falling apart and causing great pain. It's useful to remember that for most of history, eighty was a rare old age. In the absence of modern medicine, it is not surprising for anybody at the age of eighty to feel his body is falling apart. That, plus the six years the pre–Buddha Siddhattha spent torturing his own body probably did not help. The Buddha commented, perhaps half-jokingly, that his body was "like an old cart that can keep going only because it is held together by straps."

At this point, the Buddha must have felt confident that the Dharma would continue after him. We know that because in one of the mystical parts of this discourse, Mara went to the Buddha and said to him, "You previously said that you would not take final nirvana until you have established communities of male and female monastic disciples, and male and female lay disciples, who are accomplished, trained, skilled, learned, knowers of the Dharma, who will pass on what they have gained from their Teacher, who can teach it skillfully, and who can refute false teachings that have arisen. Well, you did all that. It's now time for you to go."[2] The Buddha told Mara, "Relax, Evil One, you don't have to wait long, the Realized One will pass into final nirvana in three months." After Mara left, the Buddha sat mindful and fully aware, and surrendered his life force. The earth shook and thunder cracked the sky. The Buddha spoke joyfully in verse:

> Weighing up the incomparable against an extension of life,
> the sage surrendered the life force.
> Happy inside, serene,
> he burst out of this self-made chain like a suit of armor.[3]

The Buddha's last meal is a subject of endless debate. He accepted a meal from a man called Cunda Kammāraputta (also commonly known as Cunda the smith). Cunda offered the Buddha a dish called "pig's delight." Historians and scholars have debated endlessly whether that was a pork dish, or a mushroom dish, or something else (for example, soft boiled rice with meat). In any case, it is possible that the food was accidentally tainted (perhaps somebody picked a poisonous mushroom by mistake, perhaps the pork wasn't properly cooked) and that maybe the Buddha knew because he made the unusual request to Cunda to serve that dish only to himself, and not to any others.

After that meal, the Buddha became severely ill with bloody dysentery and dreadful pains, all of which he experienced mindfully, free from mental suffering. He wanted to make sure that Cunda did not feel bad about serving him his last meal, so he told Ānanda to tell Cunda, "You are very fortunate, friend Cunda, to serve the Exalted One his last meal. I have heard from the Exalted One's own lips that two meal offerings lead to equal great merits: the meal which, after eating, the Exalted One gained full enlightenment, and the meal just before his final nirvana. You are so lucky!"

At this point, the Buddha was in the town of Kusinārā. As it became increasingly clear that the Buddha's passing was very imminent, Ānanda started crying. The Buddha chided him gently, "Ānanda, do not cry. Have I not already taught you that all things that are pleasant and delightful are impermanent and subject to separation? So how could it be, Ānanda, that whatever is born should not pass away?"

As the Buddha lay dying, he said to Ānanda and all the monks present, "After I pass, you may think, 'We have no teacher!' It should not be like this. After my passing, the Dharma and the discipline (*Dhamma-vinaya*) I taught you shall be your teacher."

Finally, the Buddha spoke his last words.

> Now, monks, I declare to you:
> "all conditioned things are of a nature to decay—
>   strive on untiringly."[4]

> *handa dāni, bhikkhave, āmantayāmi vo,*
>   *"vayadhammā saṅkhārā appamādena sampādethāti."*

Having said his last words, the Buddha moved through the jhānas one last time. He entered the first jhāna, and then went into the second jhāna, and then made his way up the successively subtler jhānas all the way to the base of neither-perception-nor-non-perception. After that, he made his way back down all the way to the first jhāna. And then he made his way back up again to the fourth jhāna. From there, he passed into final nirvana.

And with that, my teacher passed.

Ānanda and Mahā Kassapa's Excellent Adventures

"Excellent!"

The Buddha taught for about forty-five years. He left a body of teachings so voluminous it can take somebody reciting it full-time many months to do it. Just an initial detailed study of the entire collection took me sixteen months and Soryu twelve months (and we are still learning more every time we look).

How did the teachings get preserved? It took two remarkable individuals to do that: Ānanda and Mahā Kassapa, each a fascinating character in his own right. Here are their stories.[5]

Ānanda was a first cousin of the Buddha (their fathers were brothers) and brother of Anuruddha (the arahant with the "divine eye" from Chapter 5). He joined the monastic order the same day as Anuruddha, which was about a year or so after the Buddha's enlightenment, but he stayed out of the limelight for a long time. About nineteen years later, as the Buddha was getting old, he told the monastic community that he would like a permanent attendant. Everybody volunteered, except Ānanda. It turns out Ānanda was precisely the person the Buddha wanted, so the Buddha went to ask him. Ānanda said he would do it, but only if the Buddha agreed to eight conditions:

1. If the Buddha received a gift of robes, he was not to pass one to Ānanda.

2. The Buddha was not to give Ānanda any food that he received.

3. If the Buddha received a gift of a dwelling place, he was not to give it to Ānanda.

4. If the Buddha received a personal invitation, he was not to include Ānanda.

5. If Ānanda was invited to a meal, he had the right to transfer that invitation to the Buddha.

6. If people came from outlying areas to see the Buddha, Ānanda had the privilege to lead them to him.

7. If Ānanda had any question regarding the Dharma, he could ask the Buddha at any time.

8. If the Buddha gave a discourse and Ānanda was not there to hear it, Ānanda had the right to ask the Buddha to repeat the entire discourse back to him verbatim.

Ānanda explained that the first four conditions were to ensure that he would not benefit from this position materially in any way, and the last four conditions were so that he could do this job while constantly mindful of his progress on the spiritual path. So right off the bat, you get a hint of how self-less and ethical a person Ānanda was, and why everybody loved him. More remarkably, Ānanda did not gain full enlightenment during the lifetime of the Buddha, so this wonderful, purehearted, selfless, ethical, loving person was pre-arahant Ānanda! Oh, yes, the Buddha agreed to all those conditions, and thus began their very close twenty-five-year relationship.

Ānanda had many wonderful qualities. The first was that he treated everybody with selfless generosity and loving-kindness. Consequently, everybody loved him. According to the Buddha, people felt uplifted just seeing Ānanda or hearing him speak.[6] Remember that he was effectively the Buddha's executive assistant, and executive assistants have a lot of power over who gets to see the boss and when. To do that job and still have everybody love you says something. Another of Ānanda's wonderful qualities was his amazing memory. He was said to be able to memorize verbatim everything he heard from the Buddha. This was why he was sometimes tasked to deliver lectures on the Buddha's behalf, and he would do so by repeating what the Buddha said before. In that sense, Ānanda was the Buddha's personal podcast. In fact, Ānanda wasn't just a podcast, he was a skilled teacher of Dharma, even though he was not fully enlightened. The Buddha praised Ānanda, saying that, "Ānanda is still a trainee, yet it is not easy to find one who equals him in wisdom."[7]

Mahā Kassapa had a very different personality from Ānanda. *Mahā* means "great," so *Mahā Kassapa* means "the Great Kassapa," mostly to distinguish him from many others also named Kassapa, but there is a good reason why people tagged the *Mahā* onto him. While Ānanda was the brother everybody loved, Kassapa was the no-nonsense wise elder brother everybody looked up to. Kassapa was the perfect model of the disciplined and austere life devoted to Dharma. In fact, Kassapa is such an important figure in Buddhism that the Zen tradition traces its lineage back to him.

Kassapa was born to a very rich family. His father owned sixteen villages and he was the only child, yet somehow he always wanted to be an ascetic. Out of duty to his parents, he agreed to take a wife, a beautiful young woman from another rich family called Bhaddā Kapilānī. Fascinatingly, Bhaddā shared the same aspiration; she too wanted to be an ascetic and only married out of duty to her parents. When they both found out that they shared the same aspiration, they both decided to remain celibate, even while living as a married couple and sharing a bed. They continued doing that until both of Kassapa's parents passed away. Shortly after that, the couple gave away all their property, set free all their serfs, shaved each other's heads, donned ascetics' robes, and wandered off in different directions. It was said that the day they parted, the power of their virtue shook the earth.

As the story goes, the Buddha felt the earth shaking and knew an outstanding disciple was coming his way, so he walked alone to where he knew Kassapa would wander to and sat under a tree. When Kassapa arrived at the spot, he saw a man sitting there with the full splendor of a buddha and he immediately knew, "This must be the master for whose sake I have gone forth." He fell to the Buddha's feet and asked to be his disciple. The Buddha ordained him on the spot. Seven days after that, Kassapa gained full enlightenment.

Kassapa chose to practice the "austere practices," including wearing only robes made by stitching together discarded pieces of cloth, subsisting only on almsfood given outside the door (not accepting any invitation to enter anybody's house), and living only in the forest (not living in a monastery in town). He lived it to perfection. Kassapa was praised by the Buddha as the monk "foremost in austere practices."[8] The Buddha once asked Kassapa why he did that, and he replied, "I do it for two reasons. First, it's for my own happiness here and now, and second, it is out of compassion to future generations so that they have an example to follow."[9] The Buddha praised his wisdom.

In case you were worried about Bhaddā Kapilānī, she also eventually found her way to the Buddha, also achieved full enlightenment, and was praised by the Buddha as the nun "foremost in recalling past lives."[10] So things went well for both of them.

These two characters, Ānanda and Mahā Kassapa, became the people most responsible for preserving the teachings. What happened?

How to Preserve a Buddha's Teachings

Seven days after the Buddha passed, the news reached Mahā Kassapa. He was at that time with a community of five hundred monks not far from Kusinārā. They quickly headed toward Kusinārā. According to the text, the townsfolk of Kusinārā could not light the Buddha's funeral pyre, so they asked Anuruddha what was happening (remember, Anuruddha possessed the "divine eye"). Anuruddha told them, "Because the gods have a different plan." "What do the gods want?" they asked. "The gods want to wait for Mahā Kassapa." "If that is what the gods want, let's honor their wishes," the townsfolk of Kusinārā decided. So they waited. Finally, Mahā Kassapa arrived to pay his respects to the Buddha's body. When he was done, the funeral pyre lit on its own.

Whether you interpret that story literally or metaphorically, it gives you an indication of the importance of Mahā Kassapa at this point. Both of the Buddha's two chief disciples, Sāriputta and Moggallāna, passed into final nirvana months before the Buddha. The Buddha did not name a successor, instead telling Ānanda and the other monks that, "the Dharma and discipline shall be your teacher." Of all the Buddha's surviving disciples, Mahā Kassapa was the most revered. Hence, Mahā Kassapa became the informal godfather of the entire monastic community and its de facto leader. With the Teacher now gone, everybody now looked to Mahā Kassapa for what to do next. What Mahā Kassapa did next should inspire immense gratitude from every Buddhist in the world for all time.

Remember how when the news about the Buddha's passing reached Mahā Kassapa, he was with a community of five hundred monks? As usual, in that community, there were enlightened monks and there were unenlightened monks. When the unenlightened monks in the community heard the news, they all started weeping and wailing loudly. Except for one monk, Subhadda; he was happy. He told the other monks, "Why are you crying? You should be happy. The Buddha was always telling us we must do this, and we cannot do that. Now that he is gone, we can do whatever we want!" When Mahā Kassapa heard that, he realized that monks like this would put the teachings in future danger, hence he resolved to consolidate the teachings so they would not be lost to future generations. With the conclusion of the Buddha's funeral, he correctly decided that this was the most important task at hand.

Mahā Kassapa's plan was to convene a gathering of arahants to consolidate, solidify, and preserve what the Buddha taught. Remember, the Buddha called his main training system *Dhamma-vinaya*, where *Dhamma* (or *Dharma*) refers to "the teachings" and *vinaya* refers to "the discipline." The gathering would preserve both parts. This gathering would be known in history as the First Buddhist Council. It would be attended by roughly five hundred arahants, and presided over by Mahā Kassapa. It would be held at the Sattapani cave at Rajgriha, under the patronage of King Ajātasattu.

The central character in preserving the teachings would be Ānanda because he had, by far, the most familiarity with all the discourses taught by the Buddha. The plan was for Ānanda to tell the gathering what he remembered, and if everybody agreed that what he remembered was correct, they would all commit it to memory in a systematic way.

There was only one problem: Ānanda was not fully enlightened. Imagine a gathering of five hundred fully enlightened people and only the main speaker was not. Ānanda didn't think it was an optimal situation either. Even worse, his own brother Anuruddha suggested strongly that Ānanda not be allowed in if he hadn't achieved full enlightenment by then. Hence, Ānanda resolved to attain full enlightenment before the council. He practiced hard day and night, but still did not reach it.

The night before Ānanda was scheduled to testify, he practiced extra hard, but he still could not reach full enlightenment. Finally, when it got really late, Ānanda gave up and decided to lie down. As his body relaxed, right in that funny position while transitioning between sitting and lying down, he suddenly gained full enlightenment.

The next morning, according to popular lore, Ānanda flew into the council while sitting cross-legged.[11] If that was true, it would make Ānanda the first person in history to fly in for a business meeting.

This meeting was mostly a conversation between Mahā Kassapa presiding, and Ānanda giving personal testimony. Mahā Kassapa would ask about a discourse, and Ānanda would usually say, "This is what I heard," and then proceed on with the content of the discourse. This is why many discourses in Buddhism begin with "Thus I have heard" (*Evaṃ me suttaṃ*).

Soryu and I both think we are very lucky to have the combined personalities of Ānanda and Mahā Kassapa. Essentially, the discourses passed down to us are the discourses as recollected and recited by Ānanda. Even though Ānanda was supposed to be merely repeating what the Buddha said, still, it was Ānanda's personal testimony, so very likely his kind, gentle, and loving personality gave the recorded teachings a bias toward those lovely qualities. However, if it was just Ānanda alone, we might have ended up with recorded teachings that were too far biased toward loving-gentleness, so it's a good thing we also have the strict, no-nonsense personality of

Mahā Kassapa to balance out Ānanda's loving-gentleness. In fact, this even played out in real life. Ānanda was sometimes too gentle with his disciples, so some of them became lazy and undisciplined, Mahā Kassapa saw that happening and chided Ānanda, telling him his laxity with his disciples was a disservice to them, for which Ānanda apologized. I think that perfect combination of personalities gave the recorded teachings the right amount of loving-gentleness without compromising its necessary strict rigor. We are so lucky.

The central character in preserving the discipline was a highly prominent monk called Upāli, who testified to the monastic code. In fact, Upāli's testimony came before Ānanda's.

Upāli was born into the Sudra caste, a low caste whose members were destined for menial work. When he grew up, he became a barber, and he was so good at his job he ended up cutting the hair of the Shakyan princes. When the Buddha first visited his hometown as the Buddha, a group of six Shakyan princes, including Anuruddha and Ānanda, decided to become Buddhist monks. They decided to head to where the Buddha was staying, and they brought along their favorite barber, Upāli. When the princes got near, they had Upāli shave off their hair and beard, and they gave him all their jewelry in gratitude for his years of service. As they bid farewell to Upāli, he told them, "Wait, I can't go back home now. I came here with you princes carrying my blade. If I return without you but with all your jewelry, people will think I murdered and robbed all of you, and those fierce Shakyans may kill me. So I would rather go with you."[12] So they left all their jewelry there and headed toward the Buddha.

When they saw the Buddha, the princes asked him to ordain Upāli first, because Upāli came from a humble background and the princes wanted to do this to humble their own Shakyan pride. The Buddha agreed. That was how Upāli was ordained before Anuruddha and Ānanda, and how he became their senior in the monastic community.

Upāli gained full enlightenment and became a respected expert on monastic discipline and the monastic code, so he did for the monastic code at the First Council what Ānanda did for the teachings. And with that, the First Council had both parts of *Dhamma-vinaya*.

Baskets and the Early Buddhist Canon

Compilation of discourses

With Ānanda and Upāli giving testimony, and the gathering of five hundred arahants verifying the correctness of their testimonies, the early Buddhist canon was thus established. The compilation offered up by Ānanda was so large it was divided into five collections. They are:

1. Dīgha Nikāya, the collection of long discourses

2. Majjhima Nikāya, the collection of middle-length discourses

3. Saṃyutta Nikāya, the collection of discourses organized by topics

4. Aṅguttara Nikāya, the "increase by one" collection (see below)

5. Khuddaka Nikāya, the minor collection

The Pali word *nikāya* means "collection."[13] Since the names of all five collections ends with the word *nikāya*, this entire compilation is commonly known in English as **"the Nikāyas."** Each discourse is called a *sutta* (literally: "thread"). For that reason, the Nikāyas are also often known colloquially as "the *suttas*."

The "increase by one" collection contains eleven books, each named after an increasing number. It starts with the "Book of Ones," followed by the "Book of Twos," and so on. The Book of Ones contains discourses where the Buddha says the equivalent of "there is one of . . ." For example, this discourse:

> Monks, I do not see even one other thing that when developed leads to such great good as the mind. A developed mind leads to great good.[14]

The Book of Fours includes, for example, a discourse on four kinds of verbal misconduct, the Book of Five includes discourses on the five powers of a trainee, and the Book of Sevens includes a discourse on the seven underlying tendencies, and so on. Unsurprisingly, the length of the discourses in this collection varies very wildly. The Book of Ones has many discourses that are only one or two sentences long (the example above is actually an entire discourse), while the Book of Elevens has very long discourses. So if you are a Buddhist teacher and you commit your students to reading one sutta a day before they can play, know that there's a loophole to be exploited somewhere.

The Khuddaka Nikāya ("Minor Collection") is really the "miscellaneous bin" containing all the books that do not fit nicely into the four main nikāyas. Included, for example, are two books containing the inspired utterances of monks and nuns after they reached nirvana, and a very popular book called the Dhammapada that contains 423 short verses spoken by the Buddha.

Compilation of monastic rules

The compilation of monastic rules put together with the leadership of Upāli is unimaginatively called the Vinaya. Today, there is some variation between the Vinayas of different schools of Buddhism, but if you take the conservative Theravada school as an example, the Theravadin Vinaya contains 227 rules for monks and 311 for nuns. The Vinayas from other schools contain a comparable number of rules. The rules range from the essential (for example, a monk shall not take life) to the trivial (for example, a monk shall not tickle another). The best thing about the Vinaya, for me, is the stories. It contains stories explaining how each rule came into being, including that jaw-dropping account of the flying monk we talked about in Chapter 13. It also contains the account of how the First Council was put together that this chapter is based on.[15]

Compilation of higher teachings

A third compilation, called the Abhidhamma ("Higher Teachings"), was formulated that takes scholastic deep dives into Buddhist topics. Tradition claims that this was composed by the Buddha himself in heaven, where he went regularly to teach his mother, Mahāmāyā. When he came back to earth, he reported it to Sāriputta, who then systematized it. Historians claim that it was composed by anonymous monks some years after the First Council.

Together, the Nikāyas, the Vinaya, and the Abhidhamma form what is known as the **Tipiṭaka**, which literally means the "Three Baskets." The

Nikāyas are known as the Sutta Piṭaka ("Basket of Discourses"), and the other two are known as the Vinaya Piṭaka and Abhidhamma Piṭaka (the meaning of which is an exercise left to the reader).

Crate&Bodhi
500 BCE collection

The version of the Tipiṭaka that we have today was preserved by the Theravada school of Buddhism in a language known as Pali. Pali is an ancient Indian dialect related to Sanskrit, and the Buddha probably spoke a number of northeastern Indian dialects related to Pali. This version is known as the **Pali Canon**. It is the most complete early Buddhist canon in existence today.

Throughout this book, Soryu and I quote extensively from the Pali Canon, which is why we use a lot of Pali words, except in cases where the Sanskrit equivalents are already co-opted into English and listed in at least one major English dictionary, in which case, we use the English equivalents. For example, we use the Sanskrit/English *dharma* and *nirvana* instead of the Pali *dhamma* and *nibbana*.

It Took a Little While to Write It All Down, Like Three Hundred Years

Even though the Nikāyas were formulated at the First Council only months after the Buddha passed, the Pali Canon was actually written down much later, like three hundred years later.[16] Why did it take so long? For starters, in ancient India, writing was known but almost never used. People then trusted human memory as a means of preserving information far more than they trusted written materials. I think a lot of it has to do with technology and climate. Ancient Indians wrote by scratching on dried palm leaves either with a stylus or fingernail before applying ink. Those palm leaves were vulnerable to decay, insects, and flaking. The hot, humid, and monsoon-ridden climate certainty did not help one bit.

Not being able to rely on writing, ancient Indians devised an ingenious solution that we modern people don't give enough credit for: they perfected memorization into an art form. The Vedic texts, for example, have been known to be transmitted orally with extreme accuracy for over two thousand years.[17] Part of it is in the use of repetition as a mnemonic tool, which is why you see a lot, like *a lot*, of repetition in the early Buddhist texts.

In any case, for the reasons stated above, the Buddhist teachings were committed to memory and learned by heart instead of being written down.[18] To enhance the fidelity of storage and transmission, there was a tradition of monastics reciting the teachings together regularly. That went on for a long time.

In 268 BCE, Ashoka became king in India. Ashoka would be remembered in history as Ashoka the Great. Circa 263 BCE, he witnessed the large numbers of dead bodies that were the direct result of his wars of conquest. Shocked and remorseful, he renounced war and converted to Buddhism. One of Ashoka's great cultural contributions to the world was the erection of the Pillars of Ashoka, thirty-three stone pillars dispersed around his empire carved with inscriptions that provide vital historical information about Buddhism. Another was the Buddhist mission sent to Sri Lanka, led by Ashoka's own son, Mahinda. Mahinda was later joined by his sister, Sanghamitta.[19] Mahinda and Sanghamitta were so successful that Sri Lanka has been an important bastion of Buddhism ever since.

In the first century BCE, there was famine and war in Sri Lanka that took the lives of many monks. Dying sucks, of course, but it also created another danger: the monks held the Buddhist canon in their heads, and if they got wiped out, the canon would die off with them. Fortunately, the Fourth Council was convened in Sri Lanka in 25 BCE, and for the first time, the Pali Canon was committed to writing, on palm leaves.

How Do I Know the Nikāyas Are Authentic?

As a skeptic, the very first question I'd ask is: How do I know if the Nikāyas are an authentic representation of what the Buddha taught, especially since they were written down so long after the First Council?

First, I think we really need to eat humble pie and admit that knowing anything with certainty from more than two thousand years ago is very hard. In fact, we don't even have sufficient data to gain certainty on a fundamental question: In which year was the Buddha born? Tradition holds that he was born in 623 BCE, but Buddhist scholars generally put it around 500–480 BCE. That is why I never know how many candles to buy for the Buddha's birthday.

Fortunately, however, we are blessed with a stroke of uncanny good luck: the early Buddhist teachings turn out to have a second, independent preservation that survived to this day! Separately from the Nikāyas, which was transmitted to Sri Lanka and preserved in Pali, those teachings were also transmitted to China and preserved in Chinese. The key difference is while the collections in the Pali corpus all came from a single school, the Theravada school, the Chinese corpus apparently derived from different schools of Buddhism, which means that the Chinese corpus represents multiple lines of transmission. This Chinese edition is commonly known as the **Āgamas** (literally: "that which has come [to us]" or "tradition").[20] Since both corpuses were separately and independently preserved, we can compare them, and if they compare well, we can gain a high level of confidence in them. So how do they compare?

First, the Āgamas only have four collections, corresponding to the four main Nikāyas (minus the "minor" collection of miscellaneous books). Each Āgama has Sanskrit and Chinese names that correspond closely to its Pali counterpart. Here are their corresponding Pali, Sanskrit, and Chinese names (with my translation of the Chinese in parenthesis):

1. Dīgha Nikāya, Dīrgha Āgama, 长阿含经 ("Long Āgama")

2. Majjhima Nikāya, Madhyama Āgama, 中阿含经 ("Middle Āgama")

3. Saṃyutta Nikāya, Saṃyukta Āgama, 杂阿含经 ("Varied Āgama")

4. Aṅguttara Nikāya, Ekottara Āgama, 增一阿含经 ("Increase-by-One Āgama")

The books in the Pali Khuddaka Nikāya ("Minor Collection") are represented in the Chinese canon, except they exist as separate books rather than as gathered in a single collection.

In terms of content, there appears to be no difference at all in any of the major doctrinal points such as the Four Noble Truths, the Noble Eightfold Path, the five aggregates, the five hindrances, the four establishments of mindfulness, the seven factors of enlightenment, the four jhānas, and all. Yay! That makes me so happy!

Even though the Nikāyas and Āgamas are essentially identical on all major doctrinal points, things are not entirely free from real-life messiness. For example, there are discourses that appear to be added later. Fortunately, the late additions are very easy to spot, according to Buddhist scholar monks Bhikkhu Sujato and Bhikkhu Brahmali, partly because the style is distinctly different from the older texts, and whoever inserted those discourses did not even try to disguise it.[21] There are also some differences in detail, though many appear to be fairly minor. For example, in the discourse where Moggallāna was nodding off in meditation and the Buddha was giving him advice, the Āgama version[22] includes the advice to wash his face and body with cold water, while the Nikāya version[23] does not.

In any case, I think the most important point is that despite all the messiness and thousands of miles of separation and more than two thousand years of separate transmission, there is an uncanny agreement between the Nikāyas and Āgamas on all major doctrinal points and the vast majority of the text, and that is great news. In addition, there are two other reasons to have confidence in the early Buddhist texts.

First, the agreement on all major doctrinal points is not just between the two separately preserved corpuses of the early Buddhist texts, but also among all major schools of Buddhism. There is, for example, no Fifth Noble Truth in any school of Buddhism. At minimum, we can say the early Buddhist texts are congruent with the common doctrine shared by all major schools of Buddhism, but I'd even go further and claim that the most likely reason all major schools share that same common doctrine is because of the early Buddhist texts. The teachings represented in early Buddhist texts were the underlying foundation upon which every major school of Buddhism was built, and their high-fidelity transmission ensured the common core among all major schools of Buddhism even to this day. Soryu adds that the agreement may be due to the actual realization of the Dharma by masters throughout the centuries. They had direct access to the truth, and then could check their realization with the suttas, creating a positive feedback loop of correcting errors.

The second additional reason to have confidence in the early Buddhist texts is that there is a lot of evidence supporting their fidelity. There is so much evidence that Buddhist scholar monks Sujato and Brahmali wrote an entire book on it titled *The Authenticity of the Early Buddhist Texts*.[24] They conclude that:

> Most academic scholars of Early Buddhism cautiously affirm that it is possible that the EBTs [(Early Buddhist Texts)] contain some authentic sayings of the Buddha. We contend that this drastically understates the evidence. A sympathetic assessment of relevant evidence shows that it is *very likely* that the bulk of the sayings in the EBTs that are attributed to the Buddha were actually spoken by him. It is *very unlikely* that most of these sayings are inauthentic.[25] [*Emphasis by original author.*]

I'm not going to be able to summarize an entire book here, but I can share some points that stood out for me. "EBTs" refers to the Nikāyas, Āgamas, and the core part of the Vinaya called the Pāṭimokkha, known to be its oldest part. Some points are:

- The keepers of the EBTs left the parts that contradict their own positions untouched. For example, the Theravada school is the keeper of the Nikāyas, and according to their own text, the Kathāvatthu ("Points of Contention"), there are passages in the EBTs that contradict their own teachings. Yet, the Theravadin school left those passages intact.

- Oddities are not normalized. The EBTs narrate awkward episodes that reflect the messiness of real life that could easily have been edited out if it was meant to be propaganda material for glorifying the Buddha and his teachings. The fact that they were not edited out indicates that the attitude toward preserving the EBTs was very conservative. For example:

- The Buddha's attendant at that time, Meghiya, rudely refused to obey his instructions.[26]

- The Buddha went to visit a group of monks; the groundskeeper did not recognize him and asked him to leave.[27]

- The Buddha gave a talk, but the monks were not happy with it.[28]

- The Buddha was disparaged, called names, verbally abused.[29]

- Monk Bhaddāli told the Buddha he was unable to keep the monastic rule about not eating after midday.[30]

- The Buddha complained of a bad back and had to lie down in the middle of giving a talk.[31]

- The Buddha was more comfortable being alone when responding to the calls of nature.[32]

- King Pasenadi became fat and the Buddha got him to lose weight.[33]

- Monk Purāṇa (who was not at the First Council, presumably not invited) declined to recite the Dharma as it was recited at the First Council, instead reciting it according to what he himself had remembered; this was recorded despite its implications for the diminished authority of the Council.[34]

• There are early manuscripts. For example, ancient Buddhist manuscripts dating back to the first century CE were found preserved in modern-day Afghanistan that contain both EBTs and texts from later Buddhism, and the EBTs found correspond closely to the Pali EBTs.

• There is evidence from comparative textual analysis. For example, the Pali Abhidhamma refers frequently to the suttas, but the suttas never refer to the Abhidhamma, which indicates that the suttas predate the Abhidhamma. There is also evidence coming from analysis of comparative styles, phrasing, and vocabulary.

- With respect to Brahmanism (a religion that predates the Buddha and continues today as a major aspect of Hinduism), the EBTs refer only to three Vedas, not the four that became standard in later years, and they are unaware of the Mahābhārata and the Rāmāyana. This and other such data points relating to other religions help us date the EBTs.

- The political geography of Northern India changed drastically and rapidly after the period described in the EBTs. Within a few decades, the diverse kingdoms had been unified under the Nanda Dynasty. Yet there is no trace of this later situation anywhere in the EBTs, not even as a prophecy or anecdote. That means the EBTs must belong to a period of history at least several decades prior to the reign of the Nandas. This locates them at or very near the historical Buddha.

Given the sheer weight of the evidence, I have to agree with Sujato and Brahmali that "it is *very likely* that the bulk of the sayings in the EBTs that are attributed to the Buddha were actually spoken by him."

"Yes, there are a lot of Buddhist texts to read, but don't worry, I've downloaded all of them for you."

The Abbot's Commentary by Soryu Forall

The greatest achievement of the Buddha was the founding of the Sangha. It might seem that becoming a buddha was his greatest achievement. But fully realizing the Dharma was what made him a buddha, so realizing the Dharma was more important than the mere label *Buddha*. Then isn't realizing the Dharma his greatest achievement? No, because he needed to do something else, even more difficult, which was the creation of a group of people who had realized the Dharma for themselves. To do this, he created systems. The most fundamental system is called Dhamma-vinaya, where *Dhamma* (or *Dharma*) means "the teachings that represent the truth," and vinaya means "the way to live in accord with that truth." Both Dhamma and *vinaya* represent the goal and the way. Dhamma is right view, and explanations for how to understand the path that leads to the realization of right view. Vinaya is a description of how one lives once one has realized right view, and also instructions for how to live in a way that leads to the realization of right view.

But more impressive than any of this, and the true reason the founding of the Sangha was the greatest achievement of the Buddha, is that the Sangha has kept the Dharma alive. They did this partially by repeating the words of the Buddha, but far more significant, they did this by realizing the Dharma directly. It was this realization that allowed them to remain true to his original intent, and it was this realization that gave meaning to the words passed down. If the words do not lead to this realization, they have no value. In the original meaning of the word *Sangha* it is this realization, not ordination, that makes one a member of the Sangha.

Therefore, realize the meaning, the true significance, of the words of the Buddha. Give them life.

CHAPTER SIXTEEN

Having Sects in Buddhism
Understanding the Shocking Diversity Within Buddhism

Like Separated Children of One Mother

In May 1998, in New York City, there was a historic dialogue between two highly revered masters from two different sects of Buddhism. One was the Dalai Lama, the leader of Tibetan Buddhism, the other was the Chinese Zen master Sheng Yen. They were sharing a stage for the first time.

The topics discussed were fascinating. The way the discussion played out was equally eye-opening. As expected, each master often started with positions congruent with their sectarian party lines, but they also quickly arrived at an agreement. One major topic, for example, was whether enlightenment is "sudden" or "gradual." Both sects have opposing traditional positions, but both the Dalai Lama and Sheng Yen made clear, each in his own way, that there is no real contradiction between the sudden and gradual approaches.

Even when there were genuine differences, there was no tension. For example, Sheng Yen said that in Zen, the step-by-step development of *dhyana* (Sanskrit for jhāna) is not emphasized; instead, the emphasis is placed on the direct experience of emptiness, whereas the Dalai Lama said that Tibetan

Buddhism can be viewed as a "sophisticated development of dhyana practice." Both masters noddingly accepted the other sect's approach as different but equally valid.

Even more instructive was the warmth and mutual respect between the two masters. Sheng Yen started his speech by saying these two sects of Buddhism are "really like the separated children of one mother," and then praising the "rich explication of Dharma and detailed elaboration of doctrine" in Tibetan Buddhism. Similarly, the Dalai Lama praised Sheng Yen's work and acknowledged the contribution of Chinese Zen to Tibetan Buddhism in its early stage of development.

Even more impressive is how the two masters behaved together. Though they had only met a few times before, they looked at each other as if they were beloved old friends. They also made gentle fun of themselves and each other. The older Sheng Yen joked that even though he admired the Dalai Lama's teachings, he himself was too old to be a good student. When Sheng Yen was speaking, the Dalai Lama interrupted him, asking, "Can I ask a question?" Sheng Yen said, "You can ask when I'm finished." And the Dalai Lama replied with a huge grin, "If I wait until you're finished, I'm going to forget my question." Everybody laughed out loud. Sheng Yen let the Dalai Lama ask his question. At the end of the talk, they walked off the stage holding hands.[1]

Wow.

Despite how friendly true Buddhist masters are to each other, we still have to wonder: How did we go from unified early Buddhism to sectarian Buddhism in the first place? And more important, what is a good Buddhist to do about sects? That is the topic of this chapter.

If you take only one thing away from this chapter, it is that as fascinatingly diverse as the different Buddhist sects appear to be, they all share the common core teachings that are contained in this book. If you take a second thing from this chapter, it is that despite all our apparent differences, we are really one big family.

One Thing Led to Another, and Then We Had Sects

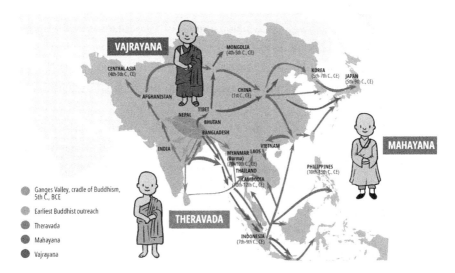

There are now three major sects of Buddhism: Theravada, Mahayana, and Vajrayana.[2] Here is a short historical account of how that came to be.

Back in Chapter 15, we talked about how two of King Ashoka's children, Mahinda and Sanghamitta, were sent to Sri Lanka as Buddhist missionaries. This line of transmission resulted in what we know today as the Theravada ("Teachings of the Elders") sect.

The Theravada sect is the holder of the Pali Canon. They put the Pali Canon front and center, and for that reason, of all the branches of Buddhism in existence today, they are the most respectful of the primacy of the early Buddhist texts. I find this aspect extremely attractive. As you can probably tell by now, I'm a huge megafan of early Buddhism and early Buddhists texts.

One of the main epicenters of this line of transmission was an important monastery in Sri Lanka called Mahāvihāra. The Theravada we know today is, to a large degree, the Buddhism as passed down by the monks at Mahāvihāra. From Sri Lanka, it eventually spread to Burma, Thailand, and beyond.[3]

The modern-day "Vipassana movement" pioneered by S. N. Goenka origi-
nates from this lineage.

In that sense, the Theravada lineage comes from the southward transmis-
sion of Buddhism from India. In Chinese, the Theravada sect is known as
Nanchuan Fojiao (南传佛教), which literally means "Buddhism of Southern
Transmission." The other direction of transmission went north, and it took
on a very different flavor. That transmission became what we know today as
Mahayana ("Great Vehicle") Buddhism.

The origin of Mahayana as a major branch of Buddhism is really quite
muddled. Modern scholars do not agree whether Mahayana started as a lay
movement or an elite "hard-core" monastic movement, a separate school (or
collection of schools), or a "spiritual vocation" pursued by some within existing schools.

There is, however, an important known milestone in the history of Buddhism's northward transmission. As Buddhism spread north, Kashmir became an important bastion of Buddhism. This happened a few centuries after
the establishment of Buddhism in Sri Lanka.

Mahinda and Sanghamitta established Buddhism in Sri Lanka during the
lifetime of Ashoka (304–232 BCE). While Ashoka also sent missionaries to
Kashmir who were successful in spreading Buddhism there, it only really
became big more than four hundred years later during the reign of King Kanishka of the Kushan Empire, centered in Kashmir, which started either in 78
CE or 127 CE—maybe (nobody today knows for sure, the historical docu-
mentation is not ideal).

Kanishka was a devout Buddhist who became an important patron of Buddhism. One of his biggest contributions was the convening of the Fourth Buddhist Council to safeguard the teachings of the Sarvāstivāda ("Everything Is
Said to Exist") school. What came out of that council was an Abhidharma
text in the form of a huge book titled *Abhidharma Mahāvibhāṣa Śāstra*. How
huge is it? The great Tang Dynasty Buddhist master Xuanzang translated it
to Chinese; you can today download a pdf version of it on the Internet, and
that pdf is more than thirteen hundred pages.[4] Kanishka had it engraved on
copper plates in the Sanskrit language. Today, only the Chinese translation
of that text survives.

It was said that this council marked the ascendancy of Sanskrit as the
language for propagating Buddhism.[5] It also marked the ascendancy of the

Sarvāstivāda sect, which exerted tremendous impact, directly or indirectly, on the subsequent development of Indian Buddhism.[6] As the Sarvāstivāda evolved over centuries, and was eventually overtaken by Mahayana schools such as the Yogācāra and the Madhyamaka, Sanskrit remained the dominant language of this northern version of Buddhism. The Pali language still distinguishes the southern version of Buddhism. As the Mahayana spread, it took elements from other forms, including the Sarvāstivāda, and made them into even more complex and sophisticated teachings. This included using the stories of the Buddha's past births (before his enlightenment twenty-five hundred years ago) as a way to inspire all of us to fully practice the path so that we also might attain the full and complete enlightenment of a buddha.

Mahayana Buddhism eventually spread through India, and to countries including China, Japan, and Korea.

You might be asking me, "Wait a minute, didn't you say in Chapter 15 that the Fourth Council was held in Sri Lanka? Are you lying? Even more than usual?" My friends, may I present to you Exhibit A on the tyranny of geography in the ancient world. The folks in Sri Lanka held the Fourth Council in the first century BCE, and then the folks in Kashmir held it between one to two hundred years later, and neither side appeared to know what the other was doing. This was, to me, an indication of how completely these two bastions of Buddhism had grown apart thanks to the distance and challenging terrain between them. During ancient times, the world was a very big place, distances were very large, and nobody could get any news from the Internet.

The establishment of Vajrayana ("Diamond Vehicle") Buddhism in Tibet came much later. While the seventh-century CE Tibetan king Songtsän Gampo was famously a Buddhist, Buddhism was only really established in Tibet in the eighth-century CE, when the great Indian monk Śāntarakṣita was invited by the Tibetan king Trisong Detsen to help do so.

Śāntarakṣita came from the Buddhist university known as Nālanda. Nālanda was a big deal in Buddhism. How big? When the Tang Dynasty Buddhist master Xuanzang traveled (mostly walked) the arduous journey all the way from China to India to study Buddhism, his destination was Nālanda. Nālanda was established in the fifth century CE, making it the oldest university in the world. At its height, it was said to have ten thousand students and two thousand staff.[7]

Śāntarakṣita is a huge figure in Tibet, and his story is revered and retold there in the monasteries and villages alike. It is said that he founded the Samye Monastery in Tibet, and basically imported Buddhism wholesale. He estab lished the monastic code, oversaw the translation of Buddhist texts into Tibetan, and attracted a number of talented Buddhist scholars to Tibet. At some point, Śāntarakṣita was said to be joined by the great Buddhist Vajra master from India, Padmasambhava ("Lotus-born"), also known as Guru Rinpoche ("Precious Guru"). Padmasambhava is revered as the most important figure in Tibetan Buddhism.

It is due to this intimate link to Nālanda that the Dalai Lama frequently refers to Tibetan Buddhism as "true Nālanda tradition."[8]

This is history for you, my friends. A little dry, I know. Fear not, you drama-loving ones, the popular narrative is a bit more salacious, and it involves a painful schism.

Fifty Shades of Saffron

"Master, when you were young, did you also have sects?"

According to the popular narrative, sectarian Buddhism started with a schism at the Second Buddhist Council due a disagreement over monastic rules.

Remember that the Buddha passed without naming a successor? The good news is that it left the Sangha (the monastic community) somewhat of a democracy without a formal power hierarchy, which means everything was decided by discussion and consensus among senior monks. The bad news is consensus is vulnerable to bad actors, and the bigger the community, and the further away in time from the Buddha's passing, the more likely it was for bad actors to create real problems.

Roughly a century after the First Council, there was a problem with a number of monks who broke the monastic code but refused to admit fault. Since there was no formal monastic hierarchy and everything had to be decided by consensus, there was nothing the community could do except to call a major meeting and deal with these issues. That meeting was the Second Buddhist Council.

During the Second Council, a major disagreement emerged between a small group of elders (*Sthavira*, "sect of elders") and everybody else (*Mahāsāṃghika*, "majority community"). The elders wanted to add more rules to the Vinaya, while the majority resisted. Accusations flew in both directions, and matters became unresolvable. Eventually, there was a schism where those two groups broke off. The group of elders eventually became what we know today as the Theravada, and the majority community eventually became what we know today as the Mahayana. Eventually, the Mahayana branch in Tibet became a distinct branch and called itself the Vajrayana.

That is the popular narrative. I think this narrative is, at best, "based on a true story." What actually happened? The answer is: nobody today knows for certain. The account of the schism is recorded by four separate schools of Buddhism, but they do not match up.

First, the dates are different, the different accounts put the schism either before, during, or after Ashoka. There is also a difference in the account of the cause of the schism, whether it was due to disagreement over the Vinaya or doctrinal matters. And then there is this character of Mahādeva, who is mentioned in one account as a thoroughly evil man who caused the schism, but modern scholars agree that the historical Mahādeva is very likely an entirely different person with no connection at all to the schism (in fact, he was probably born centuries later).

What is one to make of all this? Buddhist scholar monk Bhikkhu Sujato puts forth a hypothesis in his book *Sects and Sectarianism* that is a radical departure from the popular narrative, which, upon reflection, I suspect is the correct hypothesis.[9] Sujato's hypothesis is that there was no schism per se. Yes, there were disagreements, there was tension, there were real problems to be resolved at the Second Council, and there may even have been heated exchanges, but it was not enough to cause a schism. No one dramatic event caused one group to say, "That's it, I'm so done with you, I'm out," and break away. Of the four accounts of the schism, Sujato says none stands up to scrutiny, and that, "The sectarian accounts in which these ideas are found are mythic texts whose prime purpose is to authenticate the schools." Instead, he thinks sectarian Buddhism was a natural outcome of large numbers of monastic communities spread over a large area whose geography makes communication between the communities challenging.

When I first read that, I was a bit shocked because it is such a departure from conventional wisdom, i.e. what we all thought we knew. But as I reflected further on the evidence Sujato provides, I remembered a story that puts things in perspective for me. During the Tang Dynasty in China, there was a famous Zen master called Mazu Daoyi (马祖道一, 709–788 CE). He was successful at attracting and training good disciples, who then also had good disciples. So in just his lineage alone, two major schools emerged not long after him: his disciple's disciple founded the Guiyang school (沩仰宗), while another one of his disciple's disciples' disciples founded the Linji school (临济宗), which later spread to Japan as the Rinzai school. So just in one localized geography, from a single lineage, two major schools emerged in a short time, due entirely to the emergence of great masters. There was no painful schism here; the only reason these schools emerged was because of the super-outsize influence projected by exceptional masters.

A similar process probably happened that brought us from unified early Buddhism to sectarian Buddhism, except the conditions guiding the process were much more fertile, being multiplied by greater distances, less forgiving geography, and, due to closeness to the time, place, and language of the Buddha, probably a much more frequent emergence of exceptional masters than we can reasonably expect. Given all those conditions, the emergence of different schools of Buddhism was probably inevitable, hence sectarian Buddhism is a natural and expected outcome. Schism is sold separately, but not required.

This idea is reinforced for me by archaeological finds. The region known as Gandhara, in present-day Afghanistan and Pakistan, was a great bastion of Buddhism. Buddhists texts have been unearthed there dating back to the first century CE, and the texts that have been found are usually the early Buddhists texts together with what we think of today as the texts from later Buddhism. This suggests that people in that region were familiar with both forms of Buddhism and probably practiced them in tandem. It is even likely that monks training together in the same monasteries were practicing with these different approaches. This isn't schism; it is harmony in diversity. It is probably like my meditation room, where I have the entire collection of the Nikāyas and also the main texts from later Buddhism. It suggests to me that there was no painful schism; schools emerged over time because of all those great masters, each of whom has his or her own personality and different way of teaching. Compound that over many generations of masters and their personalities and, over time, you will end up with a proliferation of schools with very different flavors.

It feels like one of those family dramas where a bunch of cousins, while cordial, had always had an awkward relationship because their late fathers (who were brothers) had a painful falling out. And then it turns out that there never actually was a falling out at all, they just kind of drifted apart over the years after they moved to different cities and adopted different political views. And then it turns out the falling-out stories were myths perpetuated by stepmothers on both sides, and the cousins only figured it out when they discovered the stepmothers' stories didn't match and the letters they found from their late fathers to each other were friendly. I think we may be like that.

Even today, there is a cordial but still awkward relationship between different branches of Buddhism, due partly to the discomfort around the supposed original schism. But what if it turns out the schism never actually happened? Then all that awkwardness around having sects was for nothing.

We Are One Big Family

"Say samadhi!"

My own experience as a Buddhist was cross-sectarian. I consider my "home base" to be Zen. Zen was my first real encounter with Buddhism, as a teenager, and even though I did not understand it at the time, it made an indelible impression on me, and I kept going back to it as an adult. My first real Dharma teacher was Vajrayana, and my first real meditation teacher was Theravadin. I learned Pure Land Buddhism (another branch of Mahayana) as a young adult, and I still practice it alongside my meditation. So all three major sects are represented in my own growth. All that, plus I am a huge fanboy of the early Buddhist texts, which is itself cross-sectarian.

Since I'm not a member of any sect in particular, whenever anybody asks me which sect of Buddhism I belong to, I answer, "Hahayana."

As usual, Soryu does better than me on all counts. His experience of Buddhism contains far more breadth and depth than my own. When Soryu was in his late teens, he flew to Japan in order to train in a Buddhist monastery. But he did not know anything about the different sects and practices available to him. In fact, he had never read a single book on Buddhism. He did not care about any of that. He only wanted to find a true master.

He found one: Shodo Harada Roshi of the Rinzai school of Zen. This master resolved the deep questions he had been asking since he was a child, and gave him deep faith in the Dharma. For this reason, not due to any preferences about style of teaching or practice, he trained under him for several years. Due to great kindness, Harada Roshi allowed him to train in other traditions as well. That was how Soryu ended up also living and training full-time in monasteries of other Buddhist sects around the world. All that, plus he is familiar with the major Mahayana texts, and the Nikāyas. Plus, his training is deep enough to qualify him as an abbot. Wow. Somebody get this guy a beer. (Actually, don't.)

Given the breadth and depth of Soryu's exposure to Buddhism, he appears to be a great person to ask about sectarian Buddhism. I mean, in ancient times, it was easy for different branches of Buddhism to grow apart due to distance. Imagine needing to walk or ride a horse for thousands of miles to have a conversation with a monk who teaches a style of practice you do not understand. But nowadays, you can get on a plane, sit in a cushioned chair for the length of time it takes to read a book, and when you walk off that plane, you're on the other side of the world. So why are there still differences between sects of Buddhism? Well, Soryu actually did get on a plane, sit in a cushioned chair, read a book, and end up on the other side of the world to study Buddhism. So I asked him.

Soryu's first answer shocked me, in a way that made me laugh. In the modern world, people appreciate Soryu's firsthand knowledge of different forms of Buddhism. They feel that a person who has such breadth of knowledge must be an "expert." But he told me that in a traditional Buddhist setting, a person who has trained in many sects is considered a "quitter." This may seem funny, but there is truth to this claim. It just takes a long time to gain deep understanding of any tradition. That also means there are few people who can really discuss more than one tradition, and any attempts to do so by those without the expertise of decades of training will be limited in their clarity. This is why communications between different sects is still problematic to this day, even when we have airplanes and cell phones.

A more important reason Buddhism has so much diversity is that it tries to serve all people, and different people respond best to different methods of practice. One example, already mentioned in Chapter 13, is that for a practitioner who takes naturally to devotional faith, Pure Land Buddhism can do wonders on all three parts of the threefold training: virtue, samadhi, and wisdom. Whereas for somebody resistant to any form of devotional faith (yes, I'm an engineer, I understand), the more secularized forms of practice commonly found in Theravada Buddhism can do wonders. Therefore, in order to best serve these two populations, at least these two very different forms of Buddhism need to exist.

Soryu gave examples regarding other parameters too. Some monastic traditions run monasteries like benevolent dictatorships, where the teacher's every instruction is obeyed immediately. Some monastic traditions train so rigorously the monastics do not even lie down to sleep. They sleep upright in sitting meditation posture, to ensure that they practice even when sleeping. But other monastic traditions are far more relaxed about everything. Again, these variations exist because some people do very well with some training parameters, and very badly with others.

Having said all that, Soryu tells me I am missing the most important point. He says having sects is actually a good thing, not a bad thing. The reason we have so many sects and subsects is that there is so much creativity in Buddhism. Everyone is different, and different styles are needed to fit each person. To help everybody, masters got creative. All that creativity breeds the enormous diversity you see in Buddhism today. In other words, sectarian Buddhism is what it is today because Buddhism values creativity, and disregards fixed views and attachment to rituals. That is a very good thing.

Of course, there is a downside: diversity begets disagreements, and disagreements beget conflicts. The most important thing is not to have no disagreements, but to be able to disagree without conflict. Zen master Sheng Yen and the Dalai Lama provide an example of how great masters can openly disagree without any conflict whatsoever.

In real life, this actually happens very commonly at all levels of Buddhism. Soryu experienced a lot of that himself. When he was traveling from monastery to monastery, wherever he went, the resident monks welcomed him warmly, knowing full well that he came from a different sect of Buddhism. Not only did they welcome him warmly, but they treated him like a brother, and let him train with them as if he were one of them. The difference in sectarian origin did not matter even one bit.

I experienced some version of that myself. In any Buddhist training class, it is not uncommon to have students from all branches of Buddhism. For example, I attended a meditation retreat where the instructors were a Theravadin monk and a lay teacher, and the students included monastics from a variety of Buddhist sects. Similarly, in a public talk by a prominent monastic from any school of Buddhism (for example the Dalai Lama or the late Thich Nhat Hanh), you will see monastics from a variety of Buddhist schools in attendance, usually given the same preferential seating.

Every true Buddhist practitioner knows: we are all one big family.

Common Core, Common Realization

"Look, Master, I'm focusing on the core!"

With all that diversity within Buddhism, and all that potential for nasty conflicts, how is it that we are so frequently able to treat each other like we are from the same family? There are at least two things that tie all Buddhist sects together: common core and common realization.

Buddhism is, first and foremost, concerned primarily (or solely) with liberation from suffering. This is the first thing that ties all of us together. We all also accept the Buddha as the Teacher. In Theravada, he is more commonly referred to as Gotama Buddha (after his family name), or simply as the Buddha. In Mahayana and Vajrayana, he is more commonly referred to as Śākyamuni Buddha (*Śākyamuni* meaning "Sage of the Sakyans").

In addition, the core teachings are identical in all three types of Buddhism. They include:

- The Four Noble Truths

- The Noble Eightfold Path

- Dependent origination

- The Dharma seals of impermanence, dukkha, nonself, and nirvana

- The threefold training of virtue, samadhi, and wisdom

- Karma and rebirth

- Taking refuge in Buddha, Dharma, and Sangha

- Rejection of the idea of a supreme being who created and governs this world[10]

(Yes, the same core teachings you find in this book. You're welcome.)

The second thing that ties all of us Buddhists together, which is perhaps even more important, is that the experience of nirvana is exactly the same for everyone. The Buddha famously says:

> Just as the great ocean has one taste, the taste of salt, this Dhamma-vinaya has one taste, the taste of liberation.[11]

It does not matter which sect of Buddhism you trained in, the taste of liberation is exactly the same. That is why a master from one tradition can recognize a master from another tradition as having tasted the exact same liberation and, therefore, know that all their "differences" are superficial. In addition, a true master, having tasted liberation, is also free from fixed views and free from self-ness, and they can recognize that in other masters as well.

This common core and common realization bring all Buddhists together, in a beautiful way.

Just Because It's Not Historical Doesn't Mean It's Not Dharma

Soryu often points out one type of debate that modern Buddhists tend to get into, a new type of argument: disagreements about whether certain Buddhist texts are historical. Modern people often think that if something is not historical, it cannot be true Dharma. They also think that if it is true Dharma, then it must be historical.

This debate comes up often in reference to Mahayana texts. The vast majority of Mahayana texts are almost certainly later in composition, historically speaking, than the vast majority of the early Buddhist texts. They are more like a historical drama about the Buddha's teachings, whereas the early texts are more like a documentary. That is easy to see. One illustration of this is in extreme embellishment. Here is, for example, the typical opening of a discourse in an early Buddhist text:

> Thus have I heard. On one occasion the Exalted One was living at Sāvatthī in Jeta's Grove, Anāthapiṇḍika's Park. There he addressed the monks thus: . . .

In contrast, here is the opening of a Mahayana text, the Maha Prajñāpāramitā Sūtra (well, actually, just a small fraction of it):

> Thus have I heard. At one time the Exalted One dwelt at Rājagṛha, on the Vulture Peak, together with a large gathering of monks, with one thousand two hundred and fifty monks, all of them Arhats [Sanskrit for "arahants"]—their outflows dried up, undefiled, fully controlled, quite freed in their hearts, well freed and wise, thoroughbreds, great Nāgas, their work done, their task accomplished, their burden laid down, their own weal accomplished, with the fetters that bound them to becoming extinguished, their hearts well freed by right understanding, in perfect control of their whole minds—with five hundred nuns, laymen, and laywomen, all of them liberated in this present life—and with hundreds of thousands of millions of Bodhisattvas. . . . etc. . . .
>
> Thereupon the Exalted One on that occasion put out his tongue. With it he covered the great trichiliocosm and many hundreds of thousands of millions of rays issued from it. From each one of these rays there arose lotuses, made of the finest precious stones, of golden color, and with thousands of petals; and on those lotuses there were, seated and standing, Buddha-frames demonstrating Dharma, i.e., this very demonstration of Dharma associated with the six perfections. They went in all the ten directions to countless world systems in each direction, and demonstrated Dharma to beings, i.e., this very demonstration of Dharma associated with the six perfections. And the beings who heard this demonstration of Dharma, they became fixed on the utmost, right and perfect enlightenment . . . etc. . . .
>
> Thereupon the Exalted One exhibited his own natural body in this

great trichiliocosm. The gods of the world of sense desire and of the world of form, in this great trichiliocosm, saw that glorified body of the Tathagata. They took celestial flowers, incense, perfume, garlands, ointments, powders, robes, parasols, flags, banners, and streamers; they took celestial lotuses—blue lotuses, night lotuses, water lilies, white lotuses—they took Kesara flowers and Tamala leaves; and they approached with them the glorified body of the Tathagata. Likewise the human beings in this great trichiliocosm took land and water flowers and approached the Tathagata's glorified body. Both gods and men then strewed these flowers, etc., over the body of the Tathagata. By the sustaining power of the Buddha all these flowers, etc., formed high in the firmament one single pointed tower, which had the dimensions of the great trichiliocosm . . . etc. . . . .

Yeah. Wow.

The main reason masters teach from those texts is that they contain immensely valuable wisdom that either clarifies or expands on the teachings in the Nikāyas. For example, the Nikāyas teach nonself and compassion, but do not address a question faced by a practitioner who is becoming very advanced at both practices: Can we harmonize nonself-ness with great compassion, and if so, how? The Diamond Sūtra, one of the most important of all Mahayana texts, shows the Buddha in conversation with his disciple Subhūti, addressing it head-on:

[To cultivate a mind that harmonizes nonself and compassion, one should abide thus:] "However many living beings there are . . . I should bring all of them to final Nirvana . . . But after I have brought immeasurable living beings to final Nirvana in this way, no living being whatsoever has been brought to Nirvana." What is the reason for that? If, Subhūti, the idea of a living being occurs to a bodhisattva, he should not be called a bodhisattva. Why is that? Subhūti, anybody to whom the idea of a living being occurs, or the idea of a soul or the idea of a person occurs, should not be called a bodhisattva.[12]

This passage offers an important teaching, that a bodhisattva (the model of an ideal practitioner) must aspire to have the type of infinite compassion to save all beings, while at the same time, fully knowing that all beings are without self. It also alludes to another important teaching, that the total letting go of selfness is exactly where great compassion arises from. Immensely valuable stuff.

As you can get a sense from the above example, the Mahayana texts have a tendency to address issues that come up for highly advanced practitioners, so the more advanced your practice, the more valuable you will find them. That is their main upside, and it is a huge one. The main downside is that for the vast majority of people, especially those without a deep foundation in samadhi, those texts are mostly incomprehensible.

The wisdom contained in those texts is equally applicable to an advanced practitioner regardless of whether the texts are historical. That is why the true masters do not fight over their historicity.

What Is a Good Modern Buddhist to Do About Sects?

It has been said that there exists in the world at least thirty-one flavors of ice cream (I aspire to someday verify that claim empirically myself).[13] The many schools of Buddhism are like all those different flavors of ice cream: they all taste different, but they are all ice cream. In the same way, all the schools of Buddhism appear different, but they all lead to the same thing: liberation.

If you are new to Buddhism, and you are confronted with this large variety of schools, each with its own colored robes and ceremonies, and sometimes appearing to have contradictory teachings with other schools, what do you do? It is like being confronted with thirty-one flavors of ice cream all at once, and your friends have different opinions about which flavor you should have if you want to be seen as one of the cool kids. What to do?

The first thing you can do is to learn the core teachings of Buddhism. Once you finish reading this book, you have done that. Yay, you!

The next thing you can do is to get exposure to core Buddhist meditation practices, such as mindfulness meditation. You can find instructions on Buddhism.net. Alternatively, you can learn it from a good Buddhist teacher. We have a list of recommendations on Buddhism.net that you may find useful.

With that, you can go exploring. See, the most important thing to be aware of is there is no one school of Buddhism that is perfect for everybody. Every system has its upsides and downsides. Therefore, the school of Buddhism you are looking for is one that most suits *you*.

As to how to do the exploration, Soryu and I have complementary suggestions.

I suggest starting with a breadth-first approach of learning widely from a variety of teachers representing a diversity of schools, and then once you get a good idea of what works for you, choose one approach. From there, keep building depth in that one approach until you see nirvana directly for yourself.

Soryu suggests that after we have examined different schools and have chosen to take up one style of practice, we should do it until we are so grateful for it that we would do our best to protect it if it were to come under attack. This is a commitment that Soryu made for every style of practice he began. He would keep with it until it gave him something so valuable that out of gratitude, he would honor and protect the entire tradition. He says if we are willing to seriously study in a certain tradition, whichever that may be, we should do that practice carefully and correctly, without mixing in other practices, until it gives us something we will appreciate forever.

Whatever style you choose, whichever school you end up in, what is of the utmost importance is that we all practice together in harmony. We can, at this time when all forms of Buddhism can speak with each other easily and frequently, support each other while keeping our own lineages clear. If we can do that, then we can do something even more important: bring great benefit to all sentient beings, together.

The Abbot's Teacher's Commentary, *Not* by Soryu Forall

We usually end each chapter with an Abbot's Commentary, but for this chapter, we have a special treat for you. We invited the abbot's first meditation teacher, Sumi Loundon, to share her commentary on the different schools that she and Soryu learned from. Sumi was a college sophomore teaching meditation to her fellow students. One of her students was a freshman called Teal Scott (yes, he had a last name for a first name, and a first name for a last name). The most inspiring part of the story for me is that Teal grew up to become Soryu Forall. Soryu is still grateful that she was willing to offer him the Dharma, and bows in her general direction each day.

Here is her commentary.

During my first year teaching meditation in college, a new student who was one year junior to me began coming regularly. One morning, as I bowed upon entering the room, Teal asked, "Why do you bow so much?" His tone was slightly mocking.

As I came up from the bow, I looked at him. His challenging way of asking questions irritated me greatly. Teal was a very smart guy, but so smart that it got in the way of his learning.

"To show respect, to humble myself," I replied.

"Why do you wear nice clothes to meditation?" he asked. I didn't consider my clothes nice, but they were definitely a step up from his stained sweatpants and T-shirt.

"To show respect, to signal to others that this practice is noble and important."

"Your bowing and clothes seem superficial to me," he said. "What matters is what is inside."

"You're right," I said, "but these outward forms are expressive of an inner attitude, and vice versa." He didn't seem satisfied with my answer.

The next year Teal went to Japan to study and, while there, he began learning Rinzai Zen at a monastery that welcomed Westerners. When he came back to the States, he said to me, "Now I know why bowing is so important. In fact, bowing is the essence of practice. Everything can be accomplished in a bow." He now wore simple clothes, but they were tidy and clean.

A year later, he dropped out of college and returned to the monastery, where he was ordained as a monk. When he re-enrolled, after I graduated, I once visited him. His room was completely empty except a desk, a laptop, and his robe, which he was carefully smoothing out on the floor. I have never understood how the koan form of Zen leads to enlightenment, because I have never tried it for myself, and I have long felt intimidated by its muscular expression. But after I saw how Teal had transformed into Soryu, his ordained name, from tough intellectual to a compassionate and thoughtful monk, I realized that it was just as effective a form of practice as any other in Buddhism. I learned from him that it's not what we practice but that we practice.

CHAPTER SEVENTEEN

You Don't Have to Be a Buddhist to Be a Buddhist

The Amazing Inclusiveness of Buddhism

Come, See

When it comes to spreading the Dharma, the Buddhist attitude can be summarized in a single Pali word: *ehipassiko*, which literally means "come, see." Buddhism is not a faith tradition; it is an evidence-centric insight tradition. For that reason, the Buddha does not invite you to believe; he invites you to come and see it for yourself, and then decide what you want to do with it.

Soryu and I hope this book helps you see Buddhism for yourself. I think of my job as that of a door opener. The Dharma is like the precious treasure of a generous king who is giving everything away. This Dharma treasure is free for all to take, no strings attached, but not many people know where the door to the treasure house is. My job is to show you where the door is and to open it for you. I invite you to come see the treasure for yourself, and to take whatever you like, or nothing at all, whatever suits you. My job is not to tell you how much treasure to take, it is simply to open that door. That door to the teachings is popularly known in Buddhism as a Dharma Door.

Allow us to end this book with three stories.

Don't Be Like a Buddhist, Be Like a Buddha

"I don't think that is what the Master meant when he said, 'Be like a buddha.'"

The first story is a conversion story.

During the Buddha's time, there was a famous lay follower of the Jain religion called Upāli. (This is not the same Upāli as the barber in Chapter 15. I know, right? People should really have unique names like Soryu Forall or Chade-Meng Tan.) Upāli engaged the Buddha in a debate, and at the end of it, he was so impressed with the Buddha that he asked to be the Buddha's lay disciple, "From this day forth, may the Buddha remember me as a lay follower who has gone for refuge for life."

What did the Buddha do? He gently declined. He said to Upāli, "A well-known person like you should act after careful consideration." Now Upāli was really impressed. He said, "If any other master were to gain me as a disciple, they'd carry a banner all over Nālanda saying: 'The householder Upāli has become our disciple!' But you tell me to consider carefully first. Now I'm even more delighted and satisfied with you." And then he asked again to be his disciple.

This time, the Buddha laid down a condition, "For a long time, your family has been a supporter of the Jains. If you become my disciple, please continue to give to them."

Now Upāli was even more impressed. He said, "If it were any other master, he would have told me to give only to his own people, and not to the others, but you tell me to continue giving to the Jains. Now I'm even more delighted and satisfied with you." He accepted the condition and, for a third time, asked to be the Buddha's disciple. This time, the Buddha accepted him.[1]

I am fascinated by the Upāli story. What it says is we do not care about adding more people who mark the box next to "Buddhism" on census forms; what we really want to do is help everybody in the best way for them, and if that best way is for them not to identify as "Buddhist," we should encourage it. This coming from any religious leader would earn my approval, but coming from the founder of the religion itself, that inspires awe in me. This is also why many Buddhist teachers do not mind if somebody considers themselves Buddhists while they are simultaneously followers of another religion.

To be clear, it is not that us Buddhists do not care about sharing Buddhism widely; we do, but we do so with open arms, open hearts, and open minds.[2]

Adding to that attitude is the definition of a "Buddhist." A Buddhist is usually defined as a person who takes refuge in the Triple Gem (Buddha, Dharma, and Sangha).[3] Taking refuge simply means finding shelter, as in taking refuge at the closest hotel lobby when a storm gets really heavy. If you want, there is actually a ceremony you can partake in where you formally take refuge in the Triple Gem and declare yourself a Buddhist. Being raised in the tropics, I also joke that I take refuge in air-conditioning. Hence, I take four refuges. I brand myself as "taking 33 percent more refuges."

One of the best things about this definition of a Buddhist is it does not exclude a Buddhist from simultaneously holding any other religion, as long as that other religion is OK with you taking refuge in the Triple Gem. If there appears to be any disagreement between Buddhist teachings and the doctrine of the other tradition, then we are invited to investigate to discover the truth, whether that turns out to be one, the other, both, or neither. Buddhism is like a country that permits multiple citizenships.

Another definition of a Buddhist is one who understands the Four Noble

Truths and actively practices the Noble Eightfold Path. I find this definition of Buddhist to be more useful and practical. Once again, this definition does not exclude a Buddhist from simultaneously practicing another religion.

I heard a modern-day story of an American who became a Buddhist, but since she came from a conservative Christian family, her family became upset with her, so every family gathering was filled with tension. After a while, she decided that when she was with her family, she would not try to be a Buddhist, she would instead try to be a buddha. And that worked. She realized that her family didn't like her being a Buddhist, but liked her when she tried to be like a buddha.

So the lesson, my friends, is don't try to be a Buddhist, try to be a buddha. And if you do want to identify as Buddhist anyway, it is not a bad idea to continue to seek the truth in your original religious faith, if you have one. A number of my Christian friends have told me that learning and practicing Buddhism has helped them become better Christians. Theologian Paul Knitter even wrote an entire book expressing this sentiment, beautifully titled *Without Buddha I Could Not Be a Christian.*[4]

Soryu had an experience while living in Asia that surprised and deeply moved him. See, he grew up as a Christian boy in America, where he learned that being Christian involves two things: 1) identifying yourself as Christian and, 2) holding on to a certain set of prescribed beliefs. When he encountered the Buddhist practitioners in Asia who he found most inspiring, he found that they did the exact opposite. First, they were too humble to identify themselves as "Buddhist" because, to them, being a "Buddhist" signifies embodying a deep practice and upholding high ethical standards, and even though they appeared like that to Soryu, they humbly did not claim anything. Second, to those people, what matters most is not your beliefs. Instead, what matters most is practice and virtuous behavior.

Soryu was very moved. He realized then that identity and beliefs are not the point. The real point is the practice. Their example inspired him then, and has continued to inspire him since. That is why as an abbot today, he frequently reminds his students that being a Buddhist is not about having an identity label, it is about practice.

The Dalai Lama himself frequently says he does not wish to encourage people to convert to Buddhism. When asked what his religion was, he once said, "My true religion is kindness."[5]

Yeah, Like Whatever, Mr. Buddha

The second story occurred not long after the Buddha's enlightenment. He had no disciples at this time, and he was walking to where he knew his five former companions were so that he could teach them the Dharma. On his way, he met his first potential disciple, and that did not go well.

On the road between Uruvela and Benares, the Buddha met a man called Upaka. Upaka was immediately impressed, so he stopped the Buddha to ask him, "Friend, your features are serene, your complexion is pure and bright. Who is your teacher and what is his Dharma?" The Buddha answered, "I have no teacher, I alone am fully enlightened." Upaka said sarcastically, "If that is the case, you must be the Universal Victor (*anantajina*, a 'spiritually perfect one')." The Buddha said, "Yes, I am." Upaka said, "So you are."

Upaka shook his head. They both continued walking in different directions.[6]

The most striking part of this story is, true to the spirit of *ehipassiko* ("come, see"), the Buddha did not try to convince Upaka of anything; he just let him continue walking away. Oh, don't worry about Upaka; he eventually figured it out and became a disciple of the Buddha.

There is a similar modern story from another source told in this way.

> Soon after his enlightenment the Buddha passed a man on the road
> who was struck by the Buddha's extraordinary radiance and peaceful
> presence. The man stopped and asked,

"My friend, what are you? Are you a celestial being or a god?"

"No."

"Are you some sort of a magician or a wizard?"

"No."

"Are you a man?"

"No."

"Well, my friend, then what are you?"

And the Buddha replied, "I am awake."[7]

Little Dust in Their Eyes

The final story tells us that the Buddha actually had to make up his mind whether or not to teach the Dharma.

After his enlightenment, the Buddha spent a few weeks dwelling in solitude abiding in the bliss of nirvana. While sitting under a tree in Uruvela, the Buddha reflected, this Dharma he had discovered is profound and hard to understand. Just understanding it is hard enough, much less trying to explain it. Moreover, people are mired in greed and hatred; their minds are obscured by ignorance. Hence, if he were to teach the Dharma, people might not understand it, and it would just be "tiresome and troublesome" for him. As the Buddha so reflected, his mind inclined to not teaching the Dharma.

Brahmā Sahampati knew what the Buddha was thinking, and was alarmed.[8] He thought, "The world will be lost if the fully enlightened Buddha does not teach the Dharma." Brahmā Sahampati vanished from the Brahmā realm and reappeared in front of the Buddha. He arranged his robe over one shoulder, knelt with his right knee on the ground, raised his joined palms toward the Buddha, and said, "Venerable Sir, please teach the Dharma. There are beings with little dust in their eyes. They will understand the teachings!" He added, "You are now free of sorrow, like one standing high on a rocky mountain, but look at all these people, still overwhelmed with sorrow, oppressed by rebirth and old age. So please teach the Dharma! There will be those who understand."

And then the Buddha, having understood Brahmā's request, out of compassion for all sentient beings, surveyed the world with the "Eye of the Buddha." He saw that there are sentient beings with much dust in their eyes, and there are those with little dust in their eyes. Having seen that, he decided he would teach the Dharma. He declared his intention to Brahmā in verse:

Flung open are the doors to the deathless!
Let those with ears to hear decide their faith.

Then Brahmā Sahampati, knowing that his request for the Buddha to teach the Dharma had been granted, bowed and respectfully circled the Buddha, keeping him on his right, and then he vanished.[9]

Soryu and I hope there are billions of people in the world with little dust in their eyes, including you, friend—and we hope our work has been helpful to you.

My friend, may you soon have no more dust in your eyes.

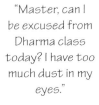

"Master, can I be excused from Dharma class today? I have too much dust in my eyes."

EPILOGUES

Meng's Epilogue:
It Is So Pleasant to Be in Your Shadow

Siddhattha left home to seek enlightenment shortly after his son, Rāhula, was born. After six years of intense struggle, Siddhattha gained full enlightenment and became the Buddha. When he came home to visit his family a year later, Rāhula was already seven years old.

As the Buddha approached the palace, Rāhula's mother, Princess Yasodharā, pointed to the Buddha in the distance and instructed her son, "That man is your father, go to him and ask for your inheritance."

Rāhula ran toward the Buddha and then walked alongside him. It was presumably a hot day and Rāhula kept himself shaded in the Buddha's shadow.

After a while, little Rāhula looked up to the Buddha with a smile and said, "It is so pleasant to be in your shadow."

That last sentence resonated with me to my core. It felt like the perfect metaphor for me. All I really want is to be in the shadow of the Buddha.

To the Buddha, I want to say, "Thank you for your shadow, beloved old man."

Soryu's Epilogue: We Must Cast Our Own Shadow

When I was about the age Rāhula was when he finally got to walk in his father's shadow, I realized I didn't have anyone's shadow to walk in.

It was clear then, in the early 1980s, that humans were killing life on this planet. Furthermore, the rate at which our greed and hatred were destroying living beings was increasing. In fact, that had been clear for decades, but it was so obvious then that even a child could understand it.

I realized that no one was dealing with this issue, and in fact no one had ever dealt with it. Somebody had to do something. I had to. It haunted me for many years.

As I considered how to deal with these humans who were destroying the planet, I never thought I would study Buddhism, and certainly never thought that I would teach it. I assumed I would create a big nonprofit. Or, if not that, then I would be an entrepreneur who would invent a technology that would solve the problems of the world. Or, if not that, then I'd be a politician who would create the policies that would finally save the world and make people happy. But I realized that those professions don't solve the actual problem.

I looked for those who have done good work in this area. I found that the person who did the most to prevent humans from making ourselves miserable and destroying the world was the Buddha, and that the tradition that has done the best work in this area is Buddhism. The Buddha discovered the most important information: how to resolve suffering and make people trustworthy. So I set out to learn his teachings and practice his methods, and shift history from increasing destruction of life on earth to flourishing of life on earth. We thank him for doing so much good for so many living beings. Yet even he didn't solve our problems. Here we are, thousands of years later, facing existential crisis. The Buddha can show the way, but we must walk it. That is a matter of working with our own minds. We have to work with our minds because the major crises today are all caused by the human mind.

The Buddha said that our minds are the most harmful thing in the world. The next thing he said was that our minds are the most beneficial thing in the world.[1] If our minds are trapped in greed, hatred, and insanity, then they are the most harmful thing in the world. They will literally kill everyone. If our minds are well trained, having learned how to make ethical choices, enter spiritual wonder and bliss, and gain insight beyond birth and death, then they are the most beneficial, the most wonderful, the most magnificent, the most beautiful, the most good, the most true thing in the world. They will literally save everyone.

The problems we have created in the world are now so big, so serious, and so intractable that those who solve them must be the greatest people who ever lived. That can be us. It's time for all of us to become the greatest people who ever lived.

May we walk the path the Buddha set forth. May we walk it fully, and when we come to the end, may we take a further step. May we do this for the benefit of all living things.

ACKNOWLEDGMENTS

Meng

First and foremost, Soryu and I would like to thank **the Buddha**, the most important person in our lives and possibly the most important person in history. He gave us the most valuable gift of all: the gift of Dharma. And in his great genius, he gave us the Dharma in a form that is understandable, accessible, and practicable for all of us.

All that is good in me, I owe to the Buddha. The Buddha is my most beloved father and teacher. He has always been, and he will always be. There is not a single day where I'm not immensely grateful to the Buddha. I aspire for this gratitude to grow, from something I experience every day to something I experience every living moment. Thank you, beloved old man.

I vow to dedicate my life in service to Buddha and Dharma. I hope that coauthoring this book constitutes a partial fulfillment of my vow. I also hope that this work will benefit many millions. When I die, I hope that I may finally feel worthy of being in the shadow of the Buddha.

Soryu and I are grateful to the countless generations of masters who passed down the teaching and the discipline taught by the Buddha, most notably **the Venerables Mahā Kassapa**, **Ānanda**, and **Upāli**.

We are very grateful to and very touched by **His Holiness the 14th Dalai Lama** for giving his personal blessing to us and to this book. More than anybody alive today, His Holiness is an inspiration who shows me what it is like to be a good practicing Buddhist in service to the world. Even more impactful for me are his love and hugs. Mere words cannot express how much his personal blessing means to the both of us.

I want to express my personal gratitude to **Shodo Harada Roshi**. I haven't met him, but he is Soryu's main teacher, and without Harada Roshi, there would be no Soryu, and without Soryu, there would be no book. Of course, it goes without saying, I'm enormously grateful to my teacher, brother, and friend, **Soryu Forall**. Without him, I would never have been able to write this book.

In the actual authoring of this book, the most important person we need to thank is **Venerable Bhikkhu Bodhi**. He is one of the greatest scholars of early Buddhism of our time, and the author of the most carefully researched and the most authoritative translation of the Nikāyas into English. We are immensely grateful that he took the time and trouble to review the manuscript. We knew how busy he was, and that he was not necessarily in the best of physical health, and still, he did this for us. After two rounds of review, Bhikkhu Bodhi told us, "I thought you did a good job in representing the teachings of early Buddhism." Whoa. I was gleefully excited to hear that. I felt like I was back in college, having a professor who was world-renowned but who was so strict that merely getting a passing grade from him would be a significant achievement, and then finding that he gave me an A. Happiness.

We are also grateful to other Buddhist teachers who reviewed the early manuscript, and who pointed out places where changes were needed and/ or gave us early encouragement when the work seemed unbearably daunting. Among them are: **Venerables Sujato, Anālayo**, and **Buddharakkhita**; **Lamas Tenzin Choesang, Barry Kerzin**, and **Thubten Damcho**; **Roshi Joan Halifax** and **Misan Sunim**; and **Jack Kornfield** and **Trudy Goodman**.

We are grateful to the team for helping us author and publish this book. At the top of that list is our editorial consultant **Koh Kai Xin**. To put it simply, Soryu and I could not have done the work this well without her. We are also grateful to our wonderfully talented main illustrator **Colin Goh**, guest illustrators **Natalie Tsang** and **Angeleen Tan**, and our publishing team, especially **Lisa Zuniga, Ralph Fowler, Tanya Fox, Bianca Pahl, Rebecca Lown, Hal Clifford**, and **Mark Chait**.

Many friends reviewed the early manuscript (some multiple times) and gave us a lot of helpful advice and early encouragement. They include **Tom Duterme, HueAnh Nguyen, Rich Hua, Navin Amarasuriya, Kimiko Bokura, You Jungeun, Moses Mohan, Ng Yi Xian, Dawn Engle, Kate Cumbo, Brandi Brown, Chang Jieun, Angela Ho**, and **Stephanie Tade**.

We are grateful to all our friends who are public figures who took the time to read the manuscript and generously gave us their endorsements. Their names are listed in the endorsements section, but there are two I'd like to specifically point out—**Yaacob Ibrahim** and **Father Laurence Freeman**—because I have a story to share. Yaacob was a prominent Muslim leader in Singapore. In fact, he was the Minister-in-Charge of Muslim Affairs. Yaacob and I are dear friends. When he wanted to seriously learn meditation, he reached out to me. I was, however, based in the United States, so I suggested to him a meditation teacher whom I love and trust and who visited Singapore more often than I did, and that was Father Laurence Freeman. They both said yes to that arrangement. I later reflected on it and realized how big of a deal it actually was. A prominent Muslim leader asked a prominent Buddhist for spiritual advice, and that prominent Buddhist recommended a prominent Christian leader, and all three of them treated it as if it was the most natural thing in the world. This, my friends, is the power of the practice. It brings peace and harmony to the world. If global religious harmony ever happens in my lifetime, and I get the honor to write about it, this will be the opening story.

Finally, I'd like to give thanks to my family. **My parents** have done so much for me that even if I carry them on my back for one hundred years, I cannot fully repay them for their kindness. My only hope of ever repaying them is with the gift of Dharma, and I hope this book serves as an adequate downpayment. I'm also grateful to my wife, **Cindy**, and daughter, **Angel**, for continuing to keep this useless old man at home. I don't know why they still do; it must be because of my stunning good looks.

To all of you whom I owe a debt of gratitude, let me repay you partially with this poem, mostly because it costs me nothing, and also because I did it in all my other books and nobody complained.

Let's go, *vamanos.*
Beyond the limited mind.
Everybody let's go.
Welcome to enlightenment!

(In original Sanskrit: *Gate, gate. Paragate. Parasamgate. Bodhi svaha!*)

Soryu

We pay homage to **the Buddha** with reverence and gratitude. Reverence because he found the way to enlightenment beyond form, preference, information, intelligence, and consciousness. Gratitude because he taught that way right within form, preference, information, intelligence, and consciousness.

We pay homage to **the Dharma** with reverence and gratitude. Reverence because it is not restricted to space and time. Gratitude because it is everywhere, always relevant to this place and this moment, so we can offer our lives to it.

We pay homage to **the Sangha** of the enlightened ones, with reverence and gratitude. Reverence because they have kept the light of the Buddha Dharma alive and clear day after day, despite the hindrances and obstacles of the world. Gratitude because we can strive to join them in their exalted work as the incomparable field of blessings for the world.

Thank you to my teachers, first and foremost **Taigen Shodo Harada Roshi**, who allowed me to believe in the truth. And **Bhante Bodhidhamma**, who allowed me to believe in myself. And **Doryu Zenji, Thierry Bonnabesse, Jake Agna, Jim Bruchac, Tom Cross**, and **Sumi Loundon**. And **Peace Pilgrim**, who had passed away before I heard of her, but who allowed me to believe that I could walk a different path. And **Miss Grace**, my guidance counselor, who encouraged me to be more than I could see.

Thank you to **all those I have trained with** over the years. It is good to walk a real path with real people in real circumstances. Relationships are where this gets real. Each relationship is sacred.

Thank you to my friend and brother **Meng**, whose dedication to the Dharma has been even more important for this book than his writing of most of this book. Thank you for helping me to better express my training with your brilliant words. And most important, thank you for being a true friend throughout.

As Meng said, we are grateful to **His Holiness the 14th Dalai Lama** for giving his personal blessing to us and to this book. This was the moment I knew we had done what we set out to do when we first envisioned this way of offering the Dharma to the world.

And finally, thank you to **my parents**, who taught me to care, to sacrifice for what's right, to maintain integrity no matter what my mind or anyone else's might be saying, to do what must be done even if it's not perfect, and to give my life to the world.

Thank you for this breath.

WHAT IS NEXT?

Friends, we hope you enjoyed this book. If you are interested to learn basic meditation instructions, visit our website at Buddhism.net. If you are looking for a teacher to learn from and/or a community to practice with, we have a list of teachers and communities around the world at Buddhism.net. If you are hoping to read more about Buddhism, we have a recommended reading list for you at (drumroll . . .) Buddhism.net.

See you there.

NOTES

Every effort has been made to provide publication data for titles referenced below, but sometimes original sources proved a little vague as to the whereabouts of their publishing house, so to speak.

Introduction

1. Noah Shachtman, "In Silicon Valley, Meditation Is No Fad. It Could Make Your Career." *Wired*, https://www.wired.com/2013/06/meditation-mindfulness-silicon-valley/2013.

2. In this book, when we refer to the Dalai Lama, we always mean the 14th Dalai Lama, unless otherwise stated.

Chapter One

1. The Dalai Lama, *The Universe in a Single Atom* (New York: Harmony Publishing, 2006).

2. "Buddhism Is a Science of the Mind," November 6, 2006, https://www.dalailama.com/news/2006/buddhism-is-a-science-of-the-mind-dalai-lama.

3. Majjhima Nikāya 7. The exact words are: "visible here and now, immediately effective, inviting inspection, relevant, the wise can experience it for themselves."

4. See Chapter 14.

5. Majjhima Nikāya 22.

6. Dzogchen Ponlop Rinpoche's argument is at: https://www.lionsroar.com/is-buddhism-a-religion-november-2013/.

7. Ajahn Brahmavaṃso Mahāthera, "Buddhism, the Only Real Science," *Lanka Daily News* (Colombo), March 28, 2007.

8. Robin Sacredfire, *The Ultimate Book of Powerful Quotations: 510 Quotes about Wisdom, Love and Success* (New York: 22 Lions Bookstore, 2018).

9. Walpola Rahula, *What the Buddha Taught* (New York: Grove Press, 1974).

10. Shravasti Dhammika, *Praised by the Wise* (Singapore: Buddhist Research Society, 1987).

11. Dhammapada 1.

Chapter Two

1. The authoritative traditional source of the biography of the Buddha is the commentary known as the Nidānakathā, composed in the fifth century CE based on earlier sources. We base our telling on it, along with a modern authoritative source: Nārada Mahāthera's *The Buddha and His Teachings*, Fourth Edition (Kuala Lumpur, Malaysia: Buddhist Missionary Society, 1988).

2. *Siddhattha* in Pali; *Siddhārtha* in Sanskrit.

3. Nalaka Sutta (Sutta Nipāta 3.11).

4. *Gotama* in Pali; *Gautama* in Sanskrit.

5. Dhammacakkappavattana Sutta (Saṃyutta Nikāya 56.11).

6. Sukhamala Sutta (Aṅguttara Nikāya 3.39).

7. Jataka 75. Slightly different versions of this story abound. For example, one version said Siddhattha saw all four sights in one day, and another said he saw them over multiple days. Another version said that the king tried hard, but ultimately unsuccessfully, to prevent Siddhattha from witnessing suffering in the streets. In all versions of the story, though, the four sights exposed Siddhattha to fundamental suffering and caused him to decide to be an ascetic.

8. Majjhima Nikāya 26.

9. Majjhima Nikāya 26. The Buddha calls this the "ignoble search."

10. The story of the Siddhattha training under his two teachers is documented in Majjhima Nikāya 26.

11. Majjhima Nikāya 26.

12. Majjhima Nikāya 26.

13. Majjhima Nikāya 36. The story of Siddhattha's experiment with severe austerity and his enlightenment (including all the quotes) is taken from Majjhima Nikāya 36, except for the mythical version of the enlightenment story involving Mara.

14. Majjhima Nikāya 12.

15. A nice coincidence: Soryu and I did not know when we wrote this, but we found out later that in the mythical account recorded in the medieval Nidānakathā, Siddhattha lost his "thirty-two marks of a great man" when he started torturing himself, and suddenly regained them here.

16. There is a stupa built to commemorate Sujata near the Mahabodhi Temple, and this stupa is dated to the second century BCE, which means it predates even the earliest written scriptures. See: David Geary, Matthew R. Sayers, and Abhishek Singh Amar, *Cross-disciplinary Perspectives on a Contested Buddhist Site: Bodh Gaya Jataka* (New York: Routledge, 2012).

17. According to Henepola Gunaratana in "The Jhanas in Theravada Buddhist Meditation," *Access to Insight (BCBS Edition)*, November 30, 2013, http://www.accesstoinsight.org/lib/authors/gunaratana/wheel351.html; "Whereas serenity meditation is recognized as common to both Buddhist and non-Buddhist contemplative disciplines, insight meditation is held to be the unique discovery of the Buddha and an unparalleled feature of his path." Rahula, in *What the Buddha Taught*, makes a similar assertion, that the Buddha discovered insight meditation, calling it the "essentially Buddhist meditation."

18. Bhikkhu Bodhi, "On Translating 'Buddha,'" *Journal of the Oxford Centre for Buddhist Studies* 19 (2020): 52–78.

19. It is not found in canonical Pali texts, but in the Nidānakathā.

20. The ten perfections are perfection in generosity, virtue, renunciation, wisdom, energy, patience, truthfulness, determination, loving-kindness, and equanimity.

21. These are the traditional ten epithets of the Buddha.

22. The full story of Buddha's first seven weeks of Enlightenment can be found in the Theravadin Vinaya Khandhaka 1.

23. Saṃyutta Nikāya 6.1; also Majjhima Nikāya 26.

24. Dhammacakkappavattana Sutta (Saṃyutta Nikāya 56.11).

Chapter Three

1. Chinese writer and historian Zhang Hongjie (张宏杰) has a fascinating twenty-three-part lecture series on the life of Qianlong, titled《百家讲坛》

成败论乾隆. Available on YouTube, https://www.youtube.com/watch?
v=34OilrHUEPM.

2. This is a common explanation, appearing, for example, in Bhikkhu
Anālayo, *Satipatthana: The Direct Path to Realization* (Cambridge, England:
Windhorse Publications, 2003). *Du* means "difficulty" or "badness," and
akkha means "axle of a wheel." Bhikkhu Bodhi clarifies that it is actually a
playful etymology found in the Visuddhimagga, not a literal meaning.

3. http://www.leighb.com/bummer.htm.

4. The Pali term for "five aggregates subject to clinging" is
pañcupādānakkhandhā.

5. In Pali, the five are: *rūpa, vedanā, saññā, saṅkhāra,* and *viññāṇa,*
respectively. The Pali word for "aggregate" is *khanda.*

6. To be more technical: form is physical matter and, in general, we
identify with that part of form that is our body.

7. Saṃyutta Nikāya 22.79.

8. Saṃyutta Nikāya 22.79.

9. Ajahn Brahm on the five aggregates: https://www.youtube.com/watch?
v=5VTzlXna8I0.

10. Majjhima Nikāya 43.

11. Saṃyutta Nikāya 22.60.

12. Saṃyutta Nikāya 22.85.

Chapter Four

1. I think "thirst" is a far superior translation for *taṇhā,* not just because it
is literal, but because it also denotes a certain desperation, compulsion, and
sense of suffering that the word *craving* does not. However, since "craving"
is the most common English translation, I will use it (<grumble, grumble,
grumble . . .>).

2. Majjhima Nikāya 126.

3. In Pali: *kama-taṇhā, bhava-taṇhā,* and *vibhava-taṇhā,* respectively.

4. Majjhima Nikāya 75.

5. Saṃyutta Nikāya 35.243. Also relevant is Saṃyutta Nikāya 35.232.

6. Based on my book *Search Inside Yourself* (San Francisco: HarperOne,
2012).

7. "The Thirty-One Planes of Existence," edited by Access to Insight, BCBS Edition, November 30, 2013, http://www.accesstoinsight.org/ptf/dhamma/sagga/loka.html. Of those thirty-one realms (or planes of existence), twenty-six are heavenly realms.

8. "The Thirty-One Planes of Existence." That is one way to look at it, but the texts also describe various types of hell with different names, so you can look at it either as one hell realm with different parts, or different hell realms. In any case, that distinction is not important in the context of Buddhist practice.

9. For example, in Dīgha Nikāya 1, the Buddha talks about the contraction of one realm, the expansion of another, and the appearance of a third.

10. Not in the canonical texts, but an illustrative lore, nonetheless.

11. Thanissaro Bhikkhu, *Samsara*. Access to Insight, BCBS Edition, 2010, http://www.accesstoinsight.org/lib/authors/thanissaro/samsara.html.

12. Jeff Wilson, *Saṃsāra and Rebirth* (Oxford Bibliographies, 2021). DOI: 10.1093/OBO/9780195393521-0141.

13. Majjhima Nikāya 22.

14. Itivuttaka 2.22.

15. Pheṇapiṇḍūpama Sutta (Saṃyutta Nikāya 22.95).

16. Anatta-lakkhana Sutta (Saṃyutta Nikāya 22.59).

17. More formally, "that [material] substratum by means of which an active process is kept alive or going." See *The Pali Text Society's Pali-English Dictionary* (Chipstead, Surrey, United Kingdom: Pali Text Society, 1921–1925).

18. Richard Gombrich, *How Buddhism Began* (New York: Routledge, 2011).

19. Dīgha Nikāya 29, and many other places.

20. Aṅguttara Nikāya 1.49.

21. A hint of this frame of reference comes from early Chinese Buddhist masters' decision to translate *aggregate* (*khandha*) as *yùn* (蘊), which literally means "accumulation."

22. Ben Johnson, *The Great Horse Manure Crisis of 1894*, Historic UK, https://www.historic-uk.com/HistoryUK/HistoryofBritain/Great-Horse-Manure-Crisis-of-1894/.

Chapter Five

1 This story was first told by nineteenth-century British Buddhist monk Silacara Bhikkhu. Recorded in *The Buddha and His Teachings*, by Nārada Mahāthera.

2. Dhammacakkappavattana Sutta (Saṃyutta Nikāya 56.11).

3. Or *nibbana* in the Pali language.

4. Majjhima Nikāya 26.

5. Stephen Hawking, *A Brief History of Time* (New York: Bantam Books, 1998).

6. Nyanatiloka Bhikkhu, *Buddhist Dictionary, fourth edition* (Kandy, Sri Lanka: Buddhist Publication Society, 1980).

7. In many places, the destruction of craving is listed as a synonym for *nirvana*. Examples are Majjhima Nikāya 64, Aṅguttara Nikāya 3.32, and Saṃyutta Nikāya 43.14–43.

8. Aṅguttara Nikāya 3.55.

9. Saṃyutta Nikāya 35.28.

10. Fun fact: the original *Guinness Book of Records* was published by the Guinness Brewery as a promotional item, before quickly becoming its own thing. For reference, see: Laurie L. Dove, "Ridiculous History: How an Irish Beer Became an Authority on World Records," https://history.how stuffworks.com/history-vs-myth/are-guinness-book-world-records-beer -company-related.htm.

11. Saṃyutta Nikāya 35.29 is one example.

12. Majjhima Nikāya 22.

13. Aggivacchagotta Sutta (Majjhima Nikāya 72).

14. Saṃyutta Nikāya 12.15.

15. Thich Nhat Hanh, *The Heart of the Buddha's Teachings* (New York: Harmony, 1999).

16. Nārada Mahāthera, *The Buddha and His Teachings*. Soryu provided the Pali translations in this list for *parāyana, tāna, kevala,* and *amata,* the rest are by Nārada.

17. Udāna 8.3.

18. Udāna 8.1.

19. Itivuttaka 2.16.

20. Majjhima Nikāya 64.

21. Aṅguttara Nikāya 6.46.
22. Majjhima Nikāya 75.
23. Aṅguttara Nikāya 10.13.
24. Bhikkhu Bodhi's translation.
25. In Pali: *suddhāvāsa*.
26. Majjhima Nikāya 11, and other places.
27. Anuruddha's stories here are taken from Nyanaponika and Hellmuth Hecker's *Great Disciples of the Buddha* (Somersville, Massachusetts: Wisdom Publications, 2003).
28. Majjhima Nikāya 32.
29. Aṅguttara Nikāya 3.130.
30. Saṃyutta Nikāya 55.5.

Chapter Six

1. Dhammapada 183, translated by Nārada Mahāthera. This is one of the most quoted sayings of the Buddha, and deservedly so.
2. The Buddha's exact words were, "Now this, monks, is the noble truth of the way leading to the cessation of suffering: it is this Noble Eightfold Path; that is, right view, right intention, . . . right samadhi" (Saṃyutta Nikāya 56.11).
3. In his first discourse, the Buddha gave only the headlines without going into detail, but expanded on them in a large number of later discourses, my favorite of which is the *Magga-Vibhaṅga Sutta* (Saṃyutta Nikāya 45.8), where the Buddha's expansion of each part is concise enough to be easily understood and remembered, yet detailed enough to be useful and practicable. It heavily informs this chapter.
4. Majjhima Nikāya 117.
5. Saṃyutta Nikāya 45.8.
6. Sammā-diṭṭhi Sutta (Majjhima Nikāya 9).
7. Brahmajāla Sutta (Dīgha Nikāya 1).
8. Saṃyutta Nikāya 45.8.
9. Dvedhāvitakka Sutta (Majjhima Nikāya 19).
10. Soryu's framing of the "Buddhist Dream" is grounded in the etymology of the word *saṅkappa*, since *saṅkappa* closely relates to the word *kappeti*, which means "to create, to build."

11. Saṃyutta Nikāya 45.8.

12. Majjhima Nikāya 58.

13. Saṃyutta Nikāya 45.8.

14. Pali: *pañcasīla*.

15. Dhammika Sutta (Sutta Nipāta 2.14).

16. Aṅguttara Nikāya 8.39.

17. Barbara O'Brien, "Thich Nhat Hanh's Five Mindfulness Trainings," *Learn Religions*, updated February 10, 2019, https://www.learnreligions.com/thich-nhat-hanhs-five-mindfulness-trainings-449601.

18. Aṅguttara Nikāya 5.213.

19. Aṅguttara Nikāya 5.171.

20. This is Ajahn Munindo's rendering of Dhammapada 290, which reads, "If by renouncing a lesser happiness one may realize a greater happiness, let the wise man renounce the lesser, having regard for the greater."

21. Aṅguttara Nikāya 5.177.

22. Dīgha Nikāya 2.

23. Saṃyutta Nikāya 45.8.

24. Aṅguttara Nikāya 2.19.

25. Dīgha Nikāya 16 and Dīgha Nikāya 29.

26. In Pali: *bodhipakkhiyā dhamma*. They are: four establishments of mindfulness, four right efforts, four bases of mental power, five spiritual faculties, five spiritual powers, seven factors of enlightenment, and the Noble Eightfold Path. Phew.

27. Effort is not one of the headline items in the four establishments of mindfulness, but the Buddha explicitly and repeatedly says to practice each establishment with ardency.

28. Saṃyutta Nikāya 47.20.

29. Ākaṅkha Sutta (Aṅguttara Nikāya 10.71).

30. Samatha Sutta (Aṅguttara Nikāya 10.54).

31. Aṅguttara Nikāya 4.93.

32. Saṃyutta Nikāya 45.8.

33. Saṃyutta Nikāya 45.8.

Chapter Seven

1. Saṃyutta Nikāya 46.53.
2. Bhikkhu Bodhi, "What Does Mindfulness Really Mean? A Canonical Perspective," *Contemporary Buddhism* 12 (2011): 19–39, DOI: 10.1080/14639947.2011.564813, p. 22. This entire section is heavily informed by Bhikkhu Bodhi's very comprehensive paper.
3. For example, in Saṃyutta Nikāya 48.9, where *mindfulness* is defined both as "alertness" and as "the ability to remember what was said and done long ago."
4. Bhikkhu Bodhi, *The Middle Length Discourses of the Buddha* (Somersville, Massachusetts: Wisdom Publications, 1995).
5. Bodhi, "What Does Mindfulness Really Mean?," p. 22.
6. Bodhi, "What Does Mindfulness Really Mean?," p. 21.
7. *The Pali Text Society's Pali-English Dictionary* (Chipstead, Surrey, United Kingdom: Pali Text Society, 1921–1925).
8. In Saṃyutta Nikāya 54.13, the Buddha taught that by *anupassanā*-ing body, sensations, mind, and dharmas, one "develops and fulfills the enlightenment factor of mindfulness."
9. Stated in Paṭisambhidāmagga 1.1, "mindfulness is to be directly known as *upaṭṭhāna*."
10. Majjhima Nikāya 117.
11. Bhikkhu Bodhi makes this point very skillfully in "What Does Mindfulness Really Mean?"
12. Satipaṭṭhāna Sutta (Majjhima Nikāya 10). It is also recorded in the Great Discourse on the Establishment of Mindfulness (Mahasatipaṭṭhāna Sutta, Dīgha Nikāya 22). The "great" edition is identical to the standard edition, except the Buddha talked a bit more about the Four Noble Truths.
13. In Pali: *ātāpī*, *sampajañña*, and *vineyya abhijjhādomanassa*, respectively.
14. Saṃyutta Nikāya 16.2.
15. Saṃyutta Nikāya 47.35.
16. In Bhikkhu Ñāṇamoli's translation of Majjhima Nikāya 10.
17. In Bhikkhu Sujato's translation of Majjhima Nikāya 10.
18. Dalai Lama and Thubten Chodron, *Following in the Buddha's Footsteps* (Somersville, Massachusetts: Wisdom Publications, 2019).

19. Ajahn Brahm makes this same point in *Mindfulness, Bliss and Beyond* (Somersville, Massachusetts: Wisdom Publications, 2006).

20. For example, Bhante Gunaratana in *Mindfulness in Plain English* (Somersville, Massachusetts: Wisdom Publications, 2011).

21. Aṅguttara Nikāya 1.575.

22. Ānāpānassati Sutta (Majjhima Nikāya 118).

23. Dhammapada 147. The story comes not from the canonical texts, but from Buddhaghosa's fifth-century commentary on the Dhammapada.

24. Majjhima Nikāya 137.

25. Saṃyutta Nikāya 36.3. Also see Saṃyutta Nikāya 36.5.

26. Saṃyutta Nikāya 36.5.

27. There is a list of sixteen mental states, but there is no consensus among modern teachers on what most of them mean. The sixteen are: 1–2) affected or unaffected by lust, 3–4) affected or unaffected by hate, 5–6) affected or unaffected by delusion, 7) contracted, 8) distracted, 9) exalted, 10) unexalted, 11) surpassed, 12) unsurpassed, 13) concentrated, 14) unconcentrated, 15) liberated, 16) unliberated.

28. Aṅguttara Nikāya 10.51.

29. Specifically, the *mano*, which is the aspect of the mind related to thinking.

30. Saṃyutta Nikāya 46.5.

31. Anālayo, *Satipatthana: The Direct Path to Realization* (Cambridge, England: Windhorse Publications, 2004).

32. This chain of directly experiencing impermanence (*aniccānupassī*) → lust fading away (*virāgānupassī*) → cessation (*nirodhānupassī*) → "letting go" (*paṭinissaggānupassī*) is very important and appears in multiple places in the early texts.

33. In Pali: *kāmacchanda*, *vyāpāda* (also spelled *byāpāda*), *thīna-middha*, *uddhacca-kukkucca*, and *vicikicchā*, respectively.

34. Ajahn Brahm, *The Five Hindrances*, Buddhist Society of Western Australia newsletter, April 1999, https://www.budsas.org/ebud/ebmed051.htm.

35. Bhikkhu Bodhi, *Comprehensive Manual of Abhidhamma* (Kandy, Sri Lanka: Buddhist Publication Society, 1993).

36. Bodhi, *Comprehensive Manual of Abhidhamma*.

37. Itivuttaka 42.

38. Soryu's favorite translation of *hiri* and *ottappa* are "moral shame" and "moral dread" (i.e., "fear of wrongdoing"). These provocative but accurate translations wake people up to the fact that they almost never experience shame and dread as positives. In truth, shame and dread can be used to propel you on the path.

39. Aṅguttara Nikāya 10.76.

40. See Triple Gem in Chapter 9.

41. Bodhi, *Comprehensive Manual of Abhidhamma.*

42. Brahm, *The Five Hindrances.*

43. This point is made in the medieval Buddhist commentary called the Sāratthappakāsinī.

44. Saṃyutta Nikāya 46.39.

45. Dīgha Nikāya 2. The original text gives five similes for the five hindrances, but does not explicitly link each simile to a hindrance. The explicit link is made in the later medieval commentaries.

46. Aṅguttara Nikāya 10.103.

47. Majjhima Nikāya 117.

48. See Chapter 6.

Chapter Eight

1. Quoted from Yuval Harari's *Sapiens: A Brief History of Humankind* (New York: Random House, 2015). A more complete story of Antonie van Leeuwenhoek can be found at: https://www.famousscientists.org/antonie-van-leeuwenhoek/.

2. Pañcaṅgika Sutta (Aṅguttara Nikāya 5.28).

3. Majjhima Nikāya 139.

4. Udāna 7.9.

5. Majjhima Nikāya 78.

6. Majjhima Nikāya 25.

7. Saṃyutta Nikāya 9.39.

8. Aṅguttara Nikāya 4.36.

9. The version of this simile in the Pali Nikāyas does not mention the bath, but one in the Chinese Āgamas does.

10. Majjhima Nikāya 79.

11. Majjhima Nikāya 139.

12. Dhammacetiya Sutta (Majjhima Nikāya 89).

13. Kandaraka Sutta (Majjhima Nikāya 51).

14. See Chapter 6.

15. Anālayo, *Mindfulness of Breathing* (Cambridge, England: Windhorse Publications, 2019).

16. Aṅguttara Nikāya 9.34.

17. Pāsādika Sutta (Dīgha Nikāya 29).

18. On fetters, see Chapter 5.

19. Majjhima Nikāya 138.

20. Aṅguttara Nikāya 4.169.

21. Aṭṭhakanāgara Sutta (Majjhima Nikāya 52).

22. Aṅguttara Nikāya 6.60.

Chapter Nine

1. Dhammacakkappavattana Sutta (Saṃyutta Nikāya 56.11).

2. Mahā Cattārīsaka Sutta (Majjhima Nikāya 117).

3. In Pali: *sīla*, *samādhi*, and *paññā*, respectively.

4. In Pali: *tisikkhā*.

5. Mahāparinibbāna Sutta (Dīgha Nikāya 16).

6. Majjhima Nikāya 44.

7. Aṅguttara Nikāya 5.35.

8. Upanisa Sutta (Saṃyutta Nikāya 12.23).

9. The Flower Garland Discourse (Chinese: 华严经, Sanskrit: *Avataṃsaka Sūtra*). Specifically, this is in Chapter 26, Part 2 (which is confusingly in Scroll 35), on the Ten Stages (十地品).

10. Aṅguttara Nikāya 5.47.

11. A few other examples are Aṅguttara Nikāya 4.55, 5.40, 5.63, 5.64, and 8.25.

12. In Aṅguttara Nikāya 4.61, the Buddha lists "delighting in relinquishment" and "devotion to charity" as two of the features of "accomplishment in generosity."

13. In Pali and Sanskrit: *paramita*.

14. The teaching on the perfections arose after the Buddha. The Theravadin version contains these ten perfections, while the main

Mahayana version contains six: generosity, virtue, patience, energy, *dhyāna*, and wisdom. In all versions, generosity is the first perfection.

15. Aṅguttara Nikāya 3.95, 3.124, and other places.

16. In Pali: *saṅgahavatthu*, sometimes beautifully translated as "four ways of embracing others."

17. Aṅguttara Nikāya 4.32. Also see Aṅguttara Nikāya 8.24.

18. See Chapter 16 for a discussion on the different schools of Buddhism.

19. Saṃyutta Nikāya 45.2.

20. Saṃyutta Nikāya 45.49 and 45.56.

21. Aṅguttara Nikāya 9.1.

22. Majjhima Nikāya 110. I summarized "has faith, shame, and fear of wrongdoing" into "virtuous."

23. Of course, a good friend is "never gonna give you up, never gonna let you down, never gonna turn around and desert you."

24. Aṅguttara Nikāya 7.36 and 7.37. The Buddha lists fourteen qualities of a good friend in these two discourses; I curated them here for brevity.

25. Aṅguttara Nikāya 9.3.

26. Aṅguttara Nikāya 4.95.

27. In Pali: *appamaññā*. One place this reference was made was in Dīgha Nikāya 33.

28. In Pali, the four are: *mettā*, *karuṇā*, *muditā*, and *upekkhā*, respectively.

29. Majjhima Nikāya 52.

30. Saṃyutta Nikāya 47.19.

31. Majjhima Nikāya 117.

32. In Sutta Nipata 2.4, the Buddha says that to support one's parents is one of the greatest blessings.

Chapter Ten

1. In Pali: *yathābhūta*. Also relevant is the Pali word *ñāṇadassana*, which means "knowledge and insight."

2. Saṃyutta Nikāya 46.55.

3. Saṃyutta Nikāya 46.55.

4. Aṅguttara Nikāya 10.61.

5. Saṃyutta Nikāya 22.126. Also see Saṃyutta Nikāya 22.17.

6. Dhammapada 277–79.

7. One place this can be found is in Scroll 46 of《瑜伽师地论》
(Sanskrit; *Yogācārabhūmi-Śāstra*), mentioned as 四种法嗢拖南 (four
Dharma Udānas). In Chinese, they are: 一切诸行皆是无常, 一切诸行皆悉是苦,
一切诸法皆无有我, and 涅槃寂静.

8. Saṃyutta Nikāya 45.165.

9. The Pali terms are *dukkha-dukkhatā*, *saṅkhāra-dukkhatā*, and
viparinama-dukkhatā, respectively.

10. Bhikkhu Bodhi, *Anicca Vata Sankhara*, Access to Insight, BCBS
Edition, June 16, 2011, https://www.accesstoinsight.org/lib/authors/bodhi/
bps-essay_43.html.

11. I have a lot of sympathy for that preference, partly because early
Chinese Buddhist masters decided to translate it as *xíng* (行), which most
commonly means "to move," but sometimes means "elements" (as in the
"five elements" as understood by the ancient Chinese: metal, wood, water,
fire, and earth), so it appears that ancient Chinese masters also wanted to
emphasize the aspect of *saṅkhāra* as a process. Nevertheless, "formations"
is the most common translation and that is why we are using it.

12. Visuddhimagga, XVI 34–35.

13. Saṃyutta Nikāya 36.6.

14. Dalai Lama, *The Four Noble Truths* (London: Thorsons Publishers,
1998).

15. See Chapter 3.

16. This story is from the Theravada Vinaya Khandhaka 1.23.

17. Soryu's translation.

18. Aṅguttara Nikāya 6.63.

19. Majjhima Nikāya 135.

20. Aṅguttara Nikāya 3.100.

21. Majjhima Nikāya 135.

22. Majjhima Nikāya 136.

23. Aṅguttara Nikāya 4.77.

24. The teachings of all these teachers are mentioned in Dīgha Nikāya 2.

25. Milindapañha 8.

26. Milindapañha 3.2.1, translated by T. W. Rhys Davids. I made minor
edits for clarity.

27. Majjhima Nikāya 115, Bhikkhu Bodhi's translation.

28. The Buddha gave very useful short definitions for each chain on the link in Saṃyutta Nikāya 12.2, used in this section.

29. Majjhima Nikāya 38.

30. For example, in Dīgha Nikāya 15, the Buddha says that name-and-form conditions consciousness, while in Majjhima Nikāya 109, he says that consciousness conditions name-and-form.

31. Saṃyutta Nikāya 12.2.

32. An engineer would more accurately call it a directed graph with cycles.

33. For example, in Aṅguttara Nikāya 10.61 and 10.62, where the Buddha calls the five hindrances "nutriment for ignorance."

34. As an example, in Saṃyutta Nikāya 12.43, even though multiple links of dependent origination are mentioned, the "remainderless fading away and cessation of craving" is identified as the first step in ending suffering.

35. Sutta Nipata 3.12.

36. Saṃyutta Nikāya 36.1. Bhikkhu Bodhi's translation, except I changed *vedanā* from "feeling" to "sensation" and translated *bhikkhus* to "monks" to match the rest of this book.

37. Majjhima Nikāya 28.

38. The reason I gave both the Sanskrit and Pali words here is because the teachings of early Buddhism, which constitute most of this book, were mostly preserved in Pali, while the teachings of later Buddhism, such as the *MMK*, were mostly preserved in Sanskrit.

39. Dhammapada 279.

40. Majjhima Nikāya 43.

41. This sentence is the summary of Chapter 2 of Mūlamadhyamakakārikā, but please do read the whole thing yourself.

42. Mūlamadhyamakakārikā 3.

43. Mūlamadhyamakakārikā 10.

44. Mūlamadhyamakakārikā 18, Jay Garfield's translation, with minor edits by me.

45. Mūlamadhyamakakārikā 18.

46. Leigh Brasington, "Emptiness and Freedom," *Insight Journal*, winter 2010, https://www.buddhistinquiry.org/article/emptiness-and-freedom/.

47. Saṃyutta Nikāya 20.7, among other places.

48. Mūlamadhyamakakārikā 24, Jay Garfield's translation.

49. Aṅguttara Nikāya 2.24.

50. Saṃyutta Nikāya 12.15.

51. Dīgha Nikāya 9.

52. Mūlamadhyamakakārikā 18. Soryu half-jokingly responds, "I disagree with every line of this verse. But that doesn't mean that I disagree with Nāgārjuna, because if Nāgārjuna agreed with any of it, he wouldn't have been in a position to write it."

53. "无老死, 亦无老死尽." Quoted from *The Heart of the Perfection of Wisdom* (Chinese: 般若波罗蜜多心经, Sanskrit: *Prajñāpāramitāhṛdaya*), more commonly known as the Heart Sutra.

Chapter Eleven

1. Saṃyutta Nikāya 55.5 states that the stream-enterer enters the stream of the Noble Eightfold path (i.e., the practice). Saṃyutta Nikāya 55.38 compares the enlightenment process to rainwater flowing from creek to pool to stream to river and to ocean. Saṃyutta Nikāya 46.1 compares the enlightenment process to a mythical *nāga* going from pond to stream to river to ocean as it gets bigger and stronger.

2. Saṃyutta Nikāya 56.51.

3. This list comes from the commentary on Majjhima Nikāya 7 in the medieval text Majjhima Nikāya Aṭṭhakathā.

4. Dhammapada 178.

5. In Pali: *sakkāya-diṭṭhi*. It literally means "view of existing in or owning the body" (*sa* means "own," *kāya* means "body," and *diṭṭhi* means "view"), which is why it is sometimes translated as "embodiment view." Despite its literal meaning, identity view goes beyond the body. See Bhikkhu Ñāṇamoli: *The Life of the Buddha: According to the Pali Canon* (Onalaska, Washington: Pariyatti Publishing, 2003).

6. Saṃyutta Nikāya 22.82, Majjhima Nikāya 44, and Majjhima Nikāya 109.

7. In Pali: *vicikicchā*.

8. Nyanatiloka Mahāthera, *Buddhist Dictionary* (Kandy, Sri Lanka: Buddhist Publication Society, 1980).

9. Bhikkhu Bodhi's translation. In Pali: *sīlabbata-parāmāsa*.

10. Majjhima Nikāya 7.

11. Nyanatiloka Mahāthera, *Fundamentals of Buddhism*, Wheel

Publication no. 394/396 (Kandy, Sri Lanka: Buddhist Publication Society, 1994). This quote is very likely based on Sutta Nipāta 2.2.11.

12. Majjhima Nikāya 57.

13. Saṃyutta Nikāya 12.68.

14. Visuddhimagga 22.126–27.

15. It is found in the Papancasudani, the commentary to the Majjhima Nikāya, commentary to sutta number 47.

16. Majjhima Nikāya 56.

17. Udāna 1.10.

Chapter Twelve

1. See Chapter 9.

2. Aṅguttara Nikāya 3.13. This is my favorite of all the Buddha's analogies.

3. Also known as the Dunning-Kruger effect.

4. Majjhima Nikāya 19.

5. See Chapter 4.

6. See Chapter 11.

7. See Chapter 10.

8. Saṃyutta Nikāya 22.95. Also see Chapter 10.

9. For example, see Majjhima Nikāya 43 and Saṃyutta Nikāya 41.7.

10. See Chapter 8.

Chapter Thirteen

1. Known as the *pārājikas*, which literally means "defeats." If a monastic breaks any of these rules, he or she is considered "defeated" and is immediately expelled.

2. Theravadin Vinaya Khandhaka 15.

3. Fascinatingly, according to popular lore passed down in Chinese Buddhism, before the Buddha passed, he asked a small group of arahants to stay in samsara for the benefit of all sentient beings, and Piṇḍola was first on that list.

4. His story is in Theravadin Vinaya Khandhaka 7.

5. Kevaddha Sutta (Dīgha Nikāya 11).

6. Theravada Vinaya on the Second Training Rule (Vin iii 41).

7. Saṃyutta Nikāya 1.52.

8. Saṃyutta Nikāya 2.9.

9. Aṅguttara Nikāya 6.10.

10. The story is in Dīgha Nikāya 11.

11. Maurice Walshe's translation, with Soryu's minor edits.

12. Most translators translate *āvuso* as "friend" while Bhikkhu Sujato translates it to "reverend" because *āvuso* comes from *ayu*, meaning "age," which means it is a reverential term. You can think of *āvuso* as addressing a friend in a respectful way, perhaps the same way a Chinese person like me might address a friend as "Old Chen" (老陈) or "Old Wang" (老王).

13. Dīgha Nikāya 1.

14. Majjhima Nikāya 101. Specifically, the Buddha joked, "If beings experience pleasure and pain based on the creative act of a supreme God, then obviously [those ascetics] have been created by a bad God . . . While the Tathāgata obviously has been created by an excellent supreme God, which is why he now feels such pleasure free from defilement."

15. Majjhima Nikāya 32.

16. Saṃyutta Nikāya 56.31.

17. As defined in the Merriam-Webster Dictionary, and others.

18. Amitāyurdhyāna Sūtra (佛说观无量寿佛经). The specific phrase, instructed to one on the eve of death: "With your full heart, with a voice uninterrupted, complete ten recitations of Namo Amitābha Buddha" (如是至心，令声不绝，具足十念，称南无阿弥陀佛).

19. Dīgha Nikāya 16.

20. Taken largely from Nyanaponika and Hellmuth Hecker, *Great Disciples of the Buddha* (Somersville, Massachusetts: Wisdom Publications, 2003).

21. Aṅguttara Nikāya 2.33.

22. The words in the source text are "she stood leaning by the door of her own room."

Chapter Fourteen

1. "First There Is a Mountain (Then There Is No Mountain)." *Tricycle*, fall 2008, https://tricycle.org/magazine/first-there-mountain-then-there -no-mountain/.

2. *The Dalai Lama: Scientist* (Arvada, Colorado: PeaceJam Foundation, 2019).

3. Aṅguttara Nikāya 3.65.

4. Fascinatingly, in the parallel of this discourse in the Chinese Āgamas (see Chapter 15), the Buddha actually said that the Kālāmas should just accept what he said. It is one of very few instances where the Āgamas disagreed meaningfully with the Nikāyas. Which one is correct? Fortunately, in the even more important Vīmaṁsaka Sutta, where the Buddha said his disciples should closely investigate him, both the Āgamas and Nikāyas versions agree. This, and the overriding importance the Buddha placed repeatedly on investigation everywhere else, gives me confidence that the version in the Nikāyas is correct.

5. Śrīmahābālatantrarāja tantra.

6. Majjhima Nikāya 47.

7. Yuval Noah Harari, *Sapiens: A Brief History of Humankind* (New York: Random House, 2015), Chapter 15.

8. Majjhima Nikāya 63.

9. Aṅguttara Nikāya 4.257.

10. Majjhima Nikāya 22.

11. Suddhaṭṭhaka Sutta (Sutta Nipāta 4.4, verse 8).

12. Paramaṭṭhaka Sutta (Sutta Nipāta 4.5, verse 7).

13. Mahābyūha Sutta (Sutta Nipāta 4.13, verse 17).

Chapter Fifteen

1. Dīgha Nikāya 16.

2. Edited from Dīgha Nikāya 16, not an exact quote.

3. Sujato's translation, https://suttacentral.net/dn16/en/sujato.

4. Maurice Walshe's translation. Soryu has a translation that is less literal, but also more readable: "Everything that comes together falls apart—urgently and sincerely realize your goal."

5. The stories of Ānanda and Mahā Kassapa are taken largely from Nyanaponika and Hecker's *Great Disciples of the Buddha* (Somersville, Massachusetts: Wisdom Publications, 2003).

6. Dīgha Nikāya 16.

7. Aṅguttara Nikāya 3.78.

8. Aṅguttara Nikāya 1.191.

9. Saṃyutta Nikāya 16.5.

10. Aṅguttara Nikāya 1.244.

11. Recorded in the fifth-century CE publication the Mahāvaṃsa.

12. The story of Upāli can be found in Khandhaka 17 of the Theravada Vinaya, and part of it is retold in Nyanaponika and Hecker, *Great Disciples of the Buddha*.

13. *The Pali Text Society's Pali-English Dictionary* (Chipstead, Surrey, United Kingdom: Pali Text Society, 1921–1925).

14. Aṅguttara Nikāya 1.24.

15. Theravada Vinaya Khandhaka 21.

16. According to Bhikkhu Bodhi, if we go by dates more widely accepted by scholars, the Buddha may have passed away around 420 BCE, and the texts were written in the first century BCE.

17. Richard Gombrich, *What the Buddha Thought* (Sheffield, England: Oxford Centre for Buddhist Studies Monographs: Equinox, 2009).

18. Fun fact: the 1985 edition of the *Guinness Book of World Records* lists a Burmese monk as having "recited 16,000 pages of Buddhist canonical texts [from memory] in Rangoon, Burma, in May 1974."

19. Nārada Mahāthera, *A Manual of Buddhism* (Kuala Lumpur, Malaysia: The Buddhist Missionary Society, 1992).

20. The Pali collections were also called Āgamas, so the word is not really distinctive to the Chinese collections, but colloquially, people find it convenient to shorthand the Pali collections as the Nikāyas and the Chinese ones as the Āgamas.

21. Bhikkhu Sujato and Bhikkhu Brahmali, *The Authenticity of the Early Buddhist Texts* (Kandy, Sri Lanka: Buddhist Publication Society, 2014), p. 90.

22. Madhyama Āgama 81.

23. Aṅguttara Nikāya 7.61.

24. Sujato and Brahmali, *The Authenticity of the Early Buddhist Texts*.

25. Sujato and Brahmali, *The Authenticity of the Early Buddhist Texts*, p. 4.

26. Aṅguttara Nikāya 9.3.

27. Majjhima Nikāya 128.

28. Majjhima Nikāya 1.

29. Dīgha Nikāya 3, Saṃyutta Nikāya 7.3, and Saṃyutta Nikāya 7.9.

30. Majjhima Nikāya 65.

31. Majjhima Nikāya 53.

32. Aṅguttara Nikāya 8.86.

33. Saṃyutta Nikāya 3.13.

34. Theravada Vinaya ii 289–90.

Chapter Sixteen

1. The transcript is available as a book titled *Meeting of Minds: A Dialogue on Tibetan and Chinese Buddhism* (Taipei, Taiwan: Dharma Drum Publications, 1999). Sadly, they edited out all the joking and friendly bantering between the two masters. An edited video recording with Chinese subtitles can be found on YouTube at https://www.youtube .com/watch?v=_l-qqCT38q4.

2. Written as "Theravada, Mahayana, and Vajrayana" instead of "Theravāda, Mahāyāna, and Vajrayāna" because we try our best to use English words, and all three (without diacritics) are listed in the Merriam-Webster Dictionary, making them English words (i.e., it's not a bug, it's a feature).

3. Charles S. Prebish, *Buddhism: A Modern Perspective* (State College: Pennsylvania State University, 1975).

4. Chinese title: 阿毘達磨大毘婆沙論.

5. Janos Harmatta, et al., *History of Civilizations of Central Asia: Volume II* (Paris, France: Unesco Publishing, 1994).

6. K.L. Dhammajoti, "Sarvāstivāda Abhidharma," *Oxford Research Encyclopedias* (2020), https://doi.org/10.1093/ acrefore/9780199340378.013.682.

7. Andrew Buncombe, "Oldest University on Earth Is Reborn after 800 Years," *The Independent*, October 23, 2011.

8. "Tibetan Buddhism Tradition Is True Nalanda Tradition: Dalai Lama," *Hindustan Times*, February 18, 2021.

9. Bhikkhu Sujato, *Sects and Sectarianism* (Bundanoon, NSW, Australia: Santipada, 2012).

10. This list is based on one compiled by Walpola Rahula, in the article titled "Theravada–Mahayana Buddhism," in *Gems of Buddhist Wisdom* (Kuala Lumpur, Malaysia: Buddhist Missionary Society, 1983).

11. Udāna 5.5. Also, Aṅguttara Nikāya 8.19.

12. Diamond Sūtra (Chinese: 金刚经), more formally known as *The Diamond Cutter of the Perfection of Wisdom Sūtra* (Sanskrit: *Vajracchedikā Prajñāpāramitā*; Chinese: 金刚般若波罗蜜经).

13. Yes, friends, I am aware that Baskin-Robbins really had more than thirty-one flavors of ice cream.

Chapter Seventeen

1. Majjhima Nikāya 56.

2. Soryu and I being among the worst offenders, I know.

3. See Chapter 9.

4. Paul F. Knitter, *Without Buddha I Could Not Be a Christian* (London, England: Oneworld Academic, 2013).

5. Dalai Lama, *Kindness, Clarity, and Insight* (Ithaca, New York: Snow Lion Publications, 1984).

6. Majjhima Nikāya 26.

7. Joseph Goldstein and Jack Kornfield, *Seeking the Heart of Wisdom* (Boulder, Colorado: Shambhala, 2001). This story appears to be based on one in Aṅguttara Nikāya 4.36.

8. If I were a god of that high a level, instead of "Oh my God," I would have said, "Oh my Self!"

9. Saṃyutta Nikāya 6.1, also Majjhima Nikāya 26.

Epilogues

1. Aṅguttara Nikāya 1.27–30.

Printed in Great Britain
by Amazon